Jump Start Devotions: A Year of Devotional Starts to Help Us Come Closer to Christ

Ginger Chapman

Published by Embrace Imperfection Press, 2024.

While every precaution has been taken in the preparation of this book, the publisher assumes no responsibility for errors or omissions, or for damages resulting from the use of the information contained herein.

JUMP START DEVOTIONS: A YEAR OF DEVOTIONAL STARTS TO HELP US COME CLOSER TO CHRIST

First edition. January 29, 2024.

Copyright © 2024 Ginger Chapman.

ISBN: 979-8224733019

Written by Ginger Chapman.

Table of Contents

Forward

How to Use this Book

These devotions are meant to be a jump start for your own devotional time. They are to help you decide what scripture to use for the day. Because of space, usually, only one verse of scripture is recorded. It is important to get your favorite translation of the Holy Bible out and read the surrounding verses of the quoted scripture to gain a better understanding. There are no dates for these devotions so you can choose according to the scripture used or title given. The titles might seem a little strange for some of the devotions. I've written over 5,000 devotions and producing different titles has been a challenge. I pray you find these devotions helpful in enriching your own devotional time. May God bless and guide you on your spiritual journey.

Luke 24:45 Scriptures

Then he opened their minds so they could understand the Scriptures. (NIV)

Scriptures

After several decades of meditating and studying the scriptures, I needed a fresh outlook. One time I rewrote the Book of John making it written to me personally by putting in the appropriate pronouns or my name to fit the sentences. It made it come alive. Now I am in the process of rewriting the book of Psalms, making those prayers personal prayers from me to God. Sometimes I must change more than pronouns to make them my prayers. I've even been able to include the elections in this country in some of the psalms and many personal subjects. Below is an example I encourage you to give it a try but in your way.

Psalm 3

Lord, how many are the foes of this nation

Even many in this nation are against Your children

Many are saying

Christians cannot pray

or say the name of God or Jesus in public

You are a shield around us

You lift our heads high

We call out to You, Lord

Answer us from Your holy mountain.

We lie down and sleep

When we wake, You sustain us.

We will not fear

though our nation appears against us.

And assails our very freedom

Arise Lord

Deliver us from our enemies

Strike them in their mouths

Break their bit against our freedom

From You comes deliverance

May Your blessing be on us, Your children

Psalms 113:3 Sunrise

From the rising of the sun to the place where it sets, the name of the Lord is to be praised. (NIV)

Sunrise

I enjoy doing my prayer walk at sunrise. It is such a joy to praise God while looking at His beautiful artwork. Today it was foggy. No sunrise was visible. That didn't mean there was no sunrise. The sun never rises; the earth turns making it appear the sun is rising. Even when we can't see the sun "rise" it still becomes daylight, evidence of the sun "rising." God is Spirit. We cannot see His Spirit. But, like the evidence of daylight showing that the sun did indeed "rise," there is evidence all around us that God's Spirit is here. We cannot deny God created all. The variety in our creation, so many kinds of insects in their intricate and unique forms, so many kinds of vegetation with different forms of beauty, and so on and on. As we look over our lives, we can see evidence of God's protection. Many times, we're in the fog and the evidence is harder to see but that doesn't mean God isn't here. As I walked in the fog seeing only the step right in front of me, so we are to walk through life even when we only see the step right in front of us that God reveals. I trust there will be mornings without fog, and I can once again enjoy the "sunrise," and I trust when I only see one step in front of me, God will show me each step to take in my (and your) life.

Acts 12:14 Voice

When she recognized Peter's voice, she was so overjoyed she ran back without opening it and exclaimed, "Peter is at the door!" (NIV)

Voice

We live in a day where we text, message, twitter, and e-mail people. It seems that using our cell phones to make a call is a burden to us. We would rather just send a text. We might think it's more convenient for all involved or maybe we think we're saving time. There is something about the human voice. We can identify people by their voices. Yes, our cell phones also identify who is texting or calling but, when we hear a voice, we hear more than just mere words. We hear the emotions behind it whether it be pain, anger, love, or any other emotion. The girl at the door didn't need Peter to identify himself; she knew his voice. Neither did Mary at the empty tomb of Jesus. She didn't recognize Him by sight but as soon as He said her name, she knew it was Jesus who spoke. The voice and the expression in the voice give meaning to the words. When we speak vocally to one another we are communicating more than just words. We are putting real meaning behind the words. There are times when just sending the words electronically is the right thing to do. We need to have discernment. Let us slow down a little and ask God how he wants us to communicate from time to time.

Matthew 6:34 Tomorrow

Therefore, do not worry about tomorrow, for tomorrow will worry about itself. Each day has enough trouble of its own. (NIV)

Tomorrow

Several nights ago, I didn't sleep. I was stressed and worried about something I was going to have to do in a few days. I was full of "what ifs." I tried to tell myself it would be covered in prayer and God would be with me but that didn't help the stress and worry. I had already done the same thing a week before and it was very costly and difficult. Granted, it could have been even worse, but God did protect me. A few days before this event was to take place, I was told I didn't need to do it. What relief. But what peace was wasted by my stressing out over what might be but turned out not to be? Jesus gave such wonderful advice. We don't know what tomorrow will bring. We don't know what the next hour or minute will bring. Stressing and worrying about what isn't yet right in front of us is a waste of time, energy, and emotion. How wonderful that we need not do that. We can choose to be in total peace because we have a loving and powerful Father Who has promised to meet all our needs and give us a full and abundant life. Our Father always keeps His promises. He holds all our tomorrows in His loving, powerful hands.

Acts 13:22 After God's Own Heart

After removing Saul, he made David their king. God testified concerning him: 'I have found David son of Jesse, a man after my own heart; he will do everything I want him to do.' (NIV)

After God's Own Heart

What a wonderful statement God made about David. David was a man after God's own heart. This was because David, though not always obedient to God by doing everything God wanted him to do, continually looked to God. Our question for us is, do we want to be a child of God after His own heart? If yes, do we want it enough to be obedient in everything God asks of us and always look to Him? We may think that is impossible for us. We may think there are too many commands in God's written word for us to follow all of them all the time. We must read about David's life. There are times when David didn't obey the commands of God. Look them up for yourself. The difference is as soon as David was aware he was disobedient he not only confessed with much sorrow of his disobedience, but he also repented and decided to turn from that wrong and go the way of obedience. So often we just say, "That's the way it is" or "I just can't help it" or "So and so made me do it." We like to accuse anyone or anything else as the reason for our choices. Obedience is a choice. Are we willing to put our own self-centered, fleshly desires behind us, desiring first to be obedient to the One Who loves us more than anyone has, does, or will ever love us? The choice is ours to make.

Acts 13:40-41 Scoffers

Take care that what the prophets have said does not happen to you: 'Look, you scoffers, wonder and perish, for I am going to do something in your days that you would never believe, even if someone told you. (NIV)

Scoffers

This prophecy is still alive today. Our nation is full of scoffers. They are scoffing at God. They scoff at those of us who worship God. We already see some things occurring that are hard to believe. If we Christians don't intercede, if we remain quiet in the presence of scoffers, if we turn our eyes away from sin we are being as the scoffers for we are being disobedient to God. It is time for us to spend much time in prayer rather than complaining. We must make sure our own lives (actions, inactions, speech, and thoughts) are following the Word of God. If we are not praying for our country, our government, and our leaders we have no business complaining. God promised if we would humble ourselves and pray, He would forgive our sins and heal our land. If we love God, if we love the freedom to worship Him, we had better get busy and do what He has said.

1 Corinthians 6:11 Sanctified

And that is what some of you were. But you were washed, you were sanctified, you were justified in the name of the Lord Jesus Christ and by the Spirit of our God. (NIV)

Sanctified

The word "sanctified" means to be set apart. When we accept Jesus as our Lord and Savior, God sets us apart. He expects us to be different from those who are not sanctified. He has a specific purpose for us. Our question is, can people say that we are different from the unbelievers? Do we have to wear a cross around our neck or have a Christian symbol on our car for people to know we are different? They should be able to tell by our speech, what we do, what we don't do, and even how we drive. Think about what you did yesterday, what you said, what you didn't do, and how you drove. Were you a reflection of Jesus? Let us practice being true to our sanctification. Let us demonstrate to the world how a sanctified person acts, speaks, and the things we don't do. Let us consistently honor our calling to follow our Lord Jesus, God's Son, by reflecting Him in all we are.

Psalms 89:16 Psalms 89

They rejoice in Your name all day long; they celebrate Your righteousness. (NIV)

Psalms 89

Watching the rejoicing over the Chicago Cubs winning the World Series I can't help but wonder why we don't rejoice like that over our salvation and over all the wonderful blessings God freely gives us. The Cubs fans are so extremely excited. Where is our excitement? We may show some excitement for a moment, but the Cubs fans went on throughout the night with their excitement and they're still excited today and rejoicing, letting the whole world know they are the winners. When was the last time we stayed up all night praising our God? We are the winners of a full, abundant life throughout all eternity. What are we doing, as individuals, to let all around us know of the joy, salvation, and blessing that can be there as well? Enough words were written. Just think about it. Are we doing what Psalms 89:16 says?

Ephesians 2:8-10 God's Grace

For it is by grace you have been saved, through faith—and this is not from yourselves, it is the gift of God— not by works, so that no one can boast. (NIV)

God's Grace

We can memorize the entire Bible and not be saved for eternal life and forgiven for our sins. We can go to church every time the doors are open, be a leader or pastor in church, and still not be saved. We can do all manner of what is good and not be saved. The only way to be saved is by the grace of God. The way to receive that grace is to ask God for forgiveness and accept His Son, Jesus, into our hearts, minds, and lives as the Lord, the ruler of our entire being. When we accept Him and choose to follow Jesus in obedience to what is recorded in His written word, The Holy Bible, God gives us His grace of forgiveness and adopts us as His children. He fills us with His love and His Holy Spirit Who enables us to love God. When we love someone, we want to please them. To please God, we walk in obedience to His statutes. When we fall, we ask forgiveness and choose to move on from that falling and walk on. We bear the consequences of our actions or inactions in our physical bodies, but we also enjoy the forgiveness of God and the knowledge that nothing can separate us from His love once we receive it through His Son, Jesus. Let us praise and thank God today for the gift of His grace we choose to show Him our love through obedience by allowing His Holy Spirit to love and help others through us.

Ecclesiastes 3:1 Extra Hour

There is a time for everything, and a season for every activity under the heavens: (NIV)

Extra Hour

I enjoyed having an extra hour yesterday, especially on a Sunday. It gave me extra time to prepare my heart to join other believers in the worship of our God. But by the time 11 PM came, I wasn't so delighted to have a day that was 25 hours rather than 24. When God designed the day into 24 hours, He knew the endurance of the fleshly body. We may think we need extra time each day, but God, in His wisdom, knows we would abuse the time by abusing our bodies even more than we do now. There is a time appointed for everything we need to do. Our problem is we don't consult God on how to use the time He provides for us what to do and when to do it. We all have the same amount of time in a day. Some may think the days are too long and some may think the days are too short. Some of us vacillate between the two thoughts depending on the day. To start our day out talking to God and asking Him to order our day is the best use of our time and, when we do this, we will find the time we have in that day is just the exact right amount of time. Let us let the Creator of the day, the Creator of time, guide us in the best use of it.

2 Chronicles 7:14 Heal the Land

If my people, who are called by my name, will humble themselves and pray and seek my face and turn from their wicked ways, then I will hear from heaven, and I will forgive their sin and will heal their land. (NIV)

Heal the Land

We cannot think and act on this subject enough. We need to do more than think or complain about our government. We need to be among the many who have been praying and continue to pray for our nation, its leaders, and the elections. There is a very important condition in the above scripture for our prayers or our nation to be heard and answered. We must first humble ourselves. To humble ourselves means we must confess our sins, repent (decide to turn away from them), receive forgiveness from God, and then pray for the nation, leaders, and elections. Sin separates us from God. Confessing it is the second thing we do when we pray. First, we address God, glorify Him, and thank Him. Then we address our sins and ask for forgiveness. After that, we place our needs, intercessions, and desires before His throne of grace. Let's all take time today and every day to keep our confessions and repentance up to date so God can hear our prayers and answer them. Then be sure to pray for Him to heal our land.

2 Timothy 3:16 Instruction

All Scripture is God-breathed and is useful for teaching, rebuking, correcting, and training in righteousness, (NIV)

Instruction

I just learned something about my laptop. There is a button on it which mutes the sound. I've been going to another place and decreasing the sound to the mute. This button is so much faster. I can leave the volume where I like it and just turn it on and off. I would have known about this if I had read the instructions that came with the laptop. I'm one of those who doesn't read the instructions until all else fails. The same is true with our Christian walk. We have a book of instructions for life given to us called "The Holy Bible". It does nothing when just sitting on a table or a bookshelf. It must be read and studied to have a stress-free productive, enjoyable, and abundant life. We must study it before all else fails.

Psalms 32:8 Be Specific

I will instruct you and teach you in the way you should go;
I will counsel you with my loving eye on you. (NIV)

Be Specific

They lost the only car key they had. They searched high and low. Stress and panic were building. I came to look help look for them. I asked if they had asked God where it was. She said she asked Him to help her find it. We kept looking. She asked Him for help but wasn't specific in asking Him where it was. She did keep sensing to look in the garbage, but she didn't want to go through household garbage. Finally, no place was left to look, and she went through the household garbage. There, in the bottom of the can was the key. It is that way with our lives. We get in trouble and ask God to bail us out, but we quite often don't want to go the way He tells us. We try all sorts of other ways. We think we know best where to go when and what to do when. We end up taking a lot of rabbit trails. If we would just learn to pray in specifics, listen, and go immediately to what we sense God is telling us, we would save ourselves so very much stress and time. We are a stubborn lot.

I learned to pray very specifically when we were building a house. We were in our rental house and gathered around the table for breakfast, holding hands and praying for God to give us an abundance of good water. I was meeting the well-digger after breakfast. Sure enough, he reached a good source of water at only 53 feet. I returned to the rental house and, as I opened the door, I heard what sounded like our aquarium pump. I thought that was strange for our aquarium is storage. As I stepped through the door, I found myself ankle-deep in water. The bottom of the water heater in the kitchen had succumbed to rust while no one was in the house. We prayed for an abundance of water, but we didn't specify where we wanted the water. God does have a sense of humor as He patiently teaches us the lessons we must learn. I have always been specific in my prayers ever since.

Acts 4:29 Boldness

Now, Lord, consider their threats and enable your servants to speak your word with great boldness. (NIV)

Boldness

My college chorus director said, "Sing loud enough so if you make a mistake, you can hear it's a mistake and you can correct it." So many of us are afraid to witness or share what we hear the Lord say to us because we are afraid, we might be wrong. We are afraid to hurt the witness or misquote. God is bigger than any of our mistakes. He has promised His word would not come back void. We are to share God, His love, and His word with boldness. It is better to make a mistake by action than the mistake of inaction. Let us speak with the boldness of God's Holy Spirit and have the faith to know God is bigger than any mistake we might and will make. When we find we are wrong, confess it, learn from it, and try again. If our motives are correct, God will see to it that what we speak will be heard through the filtering of His Holy Spirit.

Luke 6:38 Giving

Give, and it will be given to you. A good measure, pressed down, shaken together, and running over, will be poured into your lap. For with the measure you use, it will be measured to you." (NIV)

Giving

My car was in the shop for three weeks due to a deer hitting it. When I went to pay, I expected to pay all my deductible plus the part my insurance declined. I was so surprised when the shop said my deductible was $100 less and they would take care of the insurance difference. This is a perfect example of God using people to give to those who are faithful in giving. Our tithe always came first before any bills or other expenses. Then there were the love offerings as God would lead us to give to others. It is a joy to be a giver. It is even nice when you unexpectedly receive. But whether you are the giver or the receiver, it is all through God's loving hand. However, we must be careful not to use the above verse in a self-centered way; giving to receive. That is a prosperity message believed and tooted by many misguided people. The reason we give is not to get back but for the real joy of God using us to bless someone else. Let's always be open to receiving that joy and be open to being the recipient for others receiving the joy of giving.

John 14:12 Conditional

Very truly I tell you, whoever believes in me will do the works I have been doing, and they will do even greater things than these because I am going to the Father. (NIV)

Conditional

Are we doing the works Jesus did and even greater things? He said we could. Did you realize every promise or blessing in the Bible has a condition attached to it? This is one of them. We can and should be doing the same works or greater works than Jesus did but only if we believe in Him and in all He said. This writing is short because I want to challenge you to look through the Bible and notice how every promise and every blessing has a condition with it. I could mention many more but when we look for things ourselves, we will remember them better. Just as we can't digest food without chewing and then swallowing it, we can't digest God's Word without chewing on it ourselves and then swallowing it into the very fiber of our being making it a part of ourselves. Happy eating.

John 17:20-23 One

"My prayer is not for them alone. I pray also for those who will believe in me through their message, that all of them may be one, Father, just as you are in me, and I am in you. May they also be in us so that the world may believe that you have sent me. Then the world will know that you sent me and have loved them even as you have loved me. (NIV)

One

My favorite prayer in the Bible is the prayer Jesus prayed just before He was crucified. In His prayer, He prayed for me (and for you). Our question is what did He mean when He prayed for us to all be one just as He and the Father are one? We are all individual people. Look around at how we act toward one another. Even in our churches, there are signs of animosity and bitterness. I believe a major part of being one is to be of one purpose. Jesus and the Father had the purpose of showing us the love of God and how God created us to live our lives. We have a common purpose that should unite us as one. We are to love and glorify God and share Him with others. We each are unique and have a unique way of doing this. How God leads me to share His love with others is different from the way He leads you to share. This doesn't mean my way is right and yours is wrong. We should remember we are unified in our purpose even though our way of showing and fulfilling that purpose might be different. Let us not be so quick to judge or criticize another but look at each other recognizing our oneness of purpose and relationship to Jesus and our Father through the one and same Holy Spirit living in each of us. Through His Holy Spirit, we are one.

Proverbs 20:24 Steps

A person's steps are directed by the Lord. How then can anyone understand their way? (NIV)

Steps

I have a crushed vertebra. It is my fault. I was determined I could do something by myself which I have always done before. I was wrong. My body is older than it was before. We tend to not acknowledge changes in our bodies. The same is true of our ministry. Just because God has us doing a particular ministry at one time doesn't mean we are always to be doing that ministry. As we grow in the Lord our ability to hear and to flow with His Holy Spirit changes with our growth. We must learn to be open to change. God has ordered our steps throughout our lives. If we get too comfortable in one place, we might miss the new blessings God has for us in new places. Let us always be listening for a change in the direction of our steps. I know from experience God is using me in ways I would have never thought possible several years ago. Remember, the Holy Spirit is in each of us with all the gifts that belong to the Holy Spirit. We don't own any one gift. They are the Holy Spirit's gifts. All the gifts are available for our use at the time we need to use them. One day God may use you to flow in the gift of healing, another day it may be giving or a prophecy. Let us be always open and available for whatever God wants to do through us.

Proverbs 24:17 Gloating

Do not gloat when your enemy falls; when they stumble,
do not let your heart rejoice,

Gloating

Do you drive by a car that's been pulled over for speeding and think, "Aha, he got what he deserved?" Do you judge someone who isn't obeying a certain scripture verse that you have no trouble obeying? This is gloating. We are putting ourselves in the place of judging others. There is only one judge. His name is Jesus. We have no right to judge others when we, ourselves, are far from perfect. We each have our areas of temptation, failure, and success. We are each different. Jesus said for us to love one another and encourage one another. Let's put our efforts into our relationship with Jesus and through growing in Him others will see our actions hear our words and be encouraged to work on their relationship with Jesus. Gloating is nothing more than pride and we have nothing in and by ourselves to be prideful. Let us thank and praise God that He loves us just the way we yet love us so much that He desires the best for us.

1 Corinthians 15:41 Super Moon

The sun has one kind of splendor, the moon another and the stars another; and star differs from star in splendor. (NIV)

Super Moon

Last night was the "super moon." My son-in-law set up the telescope. It was a beautiful, clear night, perfect for viewing. We could see the craters on the moon. We could also see lots of planets and stars. We were looking at the awesomeness of God's creation. It also brought back memories of sitting by the television waiting for man's first step on the moon. That God has given us the ability to explore some of His creation outside of the earth is amazing. The more we learn through exploration and science of His creation, the more we are awed by His power. His creation obeys Him. It doesn't argue but simply does as He created it to do. That is all but mankind that He created. We fight Him. We fight to do what He created us to do. He created us to let His glory shine through us even brighter and bigger than this supermoon shined. Yet He continues to love us. Let us choose to be the supermoon and let His glory shine through us through our obedience to His word. Let us choose to let His love shine through us to all His creation, including all mankind regardless of their beliefs. Let us love.

Romans 8:28-29 Good or Best

And we know that in all things God works for the good of those who love Him, who have been called according to His purpose. (NIV)

Romans 19:21 Many are the plans in a person's heart, but it is the Lord's purpose that prevails. (NIV)

Good or Best

One of my children is applying for a new position in their job. It looks like a particularly good opportunity. Often, we see something good and go after it. But God wants more than the good for us. He wants the best. When we push hard to gain what we see as good, when we force doors open to gain it, sometimes we are settling for only the good when God has the best lined up for us at the right time. It is hard to wait. I've learned by experience not to force open doors for something I think is good. I've learned to wait on God's timing and find delightful surprises of things so much better than the good I was after. We have a tough time waiting. We live in a world of instant access. God knows when we are ready to move on to something new. We need to learn to be content where we are, yet, at the same time, always be ready to move on with God to something new. When He moves us in His time, we can be assured that He has also equipped us for success in the new.

Philippians 4:4 Every Day

Rejoice in the Lord always. I will say it again: Rejoice! (NIV)

Every Day

We've been practicing Christmas music for the past few months. One of the songs has the words, "I'm going to live Christmas every day." That is so very right on. Christmas is a day we rejoice in the birth of our Savior, God's Son, Jesus Christ. Every day as we wake up, we should feel our new birth in Him and rejoice. We do this by asking His Holy Spirit to refill us every day. There's no way I could ever make it through any part of a day without His Holy Spirit to guide me and give me the wisdom I need to get through each day. We may think decorations are going up too early, but they are there to remind us of the great joy that God, the Father, sent down to us. Let us rejoice like it is Christmas morning every day.

2 Timothy 3:16 Translations

All Scripture is God-breathed and is useful for teaching, rebuking, correcting, and training in righteousness, (NIV)

Translations

There are many different translations of God's Holy Word. Most of us latch on to one. It is good to read various translations because the different ways of wording the same thoughts can open us up to new understanding. I recently watched a video version of the Gospel of John. It stayed right with the written text but also included action. It was very refreshing. It also instilled in me a strong desire to re-read this gospel in several versions again. As we come closer to the season of Advent, or any other time of the year, let's open ourselves up to rereading and meditation on scripture in a version we haven't read, or at least not read in a while. This helps to heighten our excitement and refresh His Word in our minds while enabling us to put new zest in our actions for His glory.

John 5:30 Sending

By myself I can do nothing; I judge only as I hear, and my judgment is just, for I seek not to please myself but him who sent me. (NIV)

Sending

Jesus said many times that it was God Who sent Him to continue God the Father's work. He is also sending each of us to continue His work here on Earth. Our question is, are we listening to where He wants to send us? Are we too distracted to hear or unwilling to respond and go? We don't need to look for some big change like going to a foreign land. God can send us to the grocery store to speak to someone about Him and His love and saving grace. So often we miss what God is saying to us or wanting to do through us because we are looking for something big. Let us open our minds and hearts to go wherever and do whatever and say whatever God wants us to do. It might be something as simple as a smile for someone who needs it or holding a hand. God is just as much in the small as He is in the big. Let us just do and speak.

Philippians 4:7 Peace

And the peace of God, which transcends all understanding, will guard your hearts and your minds in Christ Jesus. (NIV)

Peace

I can't imagine living without the Holy Spirit living in me. Life would be extremely depressing and lonely. He is always with me to comfort me. He is always with me to give me wisdom and direction. Any time I want to talk, He listens. Any time I want to listen, He talks to me. He doesn't use audible words, but the inner voice is so very real, that it might as well be audible. If you haven't learned to hear His voice, ask Him to teach you to listen. Immersing yourself in the scriptures, the Holy Bible is a good beginning. As we become more familiar with the recorded words, we become more familiar with the sound of His voice and what He says to us. He is always there. He never leaves us alone. Be it in quiet or a din of noise around us, He is there to speak with us. Notice I said "with" us not "to" us. He wants to fellowship with us. He wants to hear us, but He also wants us to hear Him. I pray you do hear Him. If not, I pray you will allow Him to speak to you. He is already speaking to you. You only need to listen. Let's be sure to start each day listening and then continue to listen throughout the day, always taking time to respond to what He says to us. This is the way to the greatest, deepest peace beyond all understanding. The peace that is with us in all circumstances. God's peace which truly transcends all understanding.

Genesis 2:17 Tree of Life

but you must not eat from the tree of the knowledge of good and evil, for when you eat from it you will certainly die." (NIV)

Genesis 3:22 And the Lord God said, "The man has now become like one of us, knowing good and evil. He must not be allowed to reach out his hand and take also from the tree of life and eat and live forever." (NIV)

Tree of Life

Have you noticed there is only one tree God told Adam he couldn't eat from its fruit? The Tree of Life was also in the garden, but Adam wasn't told not to eat of it. If he was obedient and abstained from the knowledge of good and evil, therefore, only being good as God created him, he was free to eat from the Tree of Life for he was in the image of God and had God's life in him. When Adam became disobedient, the knowledge of evil entered him, and therefore sin which separated him from the life in and of God. God separated Adam, and all mankind, from the Tree of Life. In time, God sent the Tree of Life, Jesus, His only Son, to this planet to give mankind the opportunity to eat the Tree of Life. We eat of it every time we partake of the elements of bread and wine which we call "the Lord's Supper." But these elements only become the tree of life when we take them in the humility of a forgiven sinner desiring to walk in obedience to the Word, Jesus. How wonderful God restored us to be able to eat from that Tree of Life and live eternally with Him.

John 8:15 Praises

You judge by human standards; I pass judgment on no one. (NIV)

Praises

As a retired professional musician, it is very hard not to sit in judgment when music is presented at church. I learned a long time ago that God hears our music very differently from the way we hear it. We were all enjoying singing our praises to God. The man next to me was clapping way off the beat and singing notes I didn't know even existed in our musical scales. He was only aware of His love for God and not aware of anyone else around him. I heard God ask me who was singing the most beautiful praises to Him. I felt very smug until I heard Him say it was the man next to me. God said He listens to the heart doing the praise, not the voice. Now I try to tune in to the person's heart rather than their notes, rhythm, or pronunciation. I must admit many times I must remind myself of what I learned to be able to relax and join inwardly with the person presenting their praise to God. All praises to God are beautiful and perfect.

James 4:17 Omission

If anyone, then, knows the good they ought to do and doesn't do it, it is sin for them. (NIV)

Omission

When we ask God to reveal sins we need to confess, be forgiven, and repent by choosing not to repeat them we fail to remember that there are also sins of omission. Sins of omission are opportunities we have missed where God was going to do or say something through us. God is bigger than our omission and will bless someone else who is willing to listen and act. But we, through our omission, are the ones who have missed a blessing. Asking God to reveal to us the things we have missed during our day is a way to sharpen our hearing. Let us practice listening, confessing the omissions He reveals to us, and putting more action in our lives for God to bless others through us.

Matthew 6:6 Distractions

But when you pray, go into your room, close the door and pray to your Father, who is unseen. Then your Father, who sees what is done in secret, will reward you. (NIV)

Distractions

I put the water into the coffee maker and the grounds in the holder. There was a commotion outside and I went to investigate. When I got back, I discovered I hadn't put the mug under the maker and coffee was everywhere. At least it was a one-cup coffee maker. Distractions are dangerous things. That is why we are told to go into our room, close the door, and pray. We need a place, at least once a day, where we can talk with our father without any distractions. Distractions keep us from listening fully. We pray throughout the day, but we pray amid distractions and hearing is filtered by those distractions. We need a time every day when we can hear clearly what God tells us. Try to set one place in your home that is free from any distractions (people, electronics, needed attention to cleaning, etc.) and spend some time every day without any distractions talking and listening to the One who knows you best and loves you the most.

Luke 24:45 Understand

Then he opened their minds so they could understand the Scriptures. (NIV)

Understand

In the art museum in Rome, Italy there are boxes next to each painting. If coins aren't fed into the box, the lights on the paintings go off. It is the same with our understanding of God's written Word, the Holy Bible. If we neglect feeding our spirits with prayer, communication with God, and giving Him the time to open our minds, His Light that gives us the understanding of the written Word goes off. Let us be sure that Light never fades.

Matthew 6:20 Black Friday

But store up for yourselves treasures in heaven, where moths and vermin do not destroy, and where thieves do not break in and steal. (NIV)

Black Friday

There is a day called "Black Friday." I believe that is correctly named. It is a day we are encouraged to buy "treasures" on this earth that we don't necessarily need and that might put us in debt. Some people wait for hours to buy their "treasures." Some people get into fights over "treasures." We listen to our sinful nature saying, "I want, I need, It's mine. etc." Black is a color standing for mourning. I guess we are to mourn the loss of our hard-earned money being replaced by "treasures" that will break, wear out, and maybe even be stolen or sit in a storage shed. The "Black Friday" I'm most familiar with celebrating is three days before Easter. It is the day Jesus died a horrible death on the Roman cross and put into a borrowed grave. He did this just for me and me to restore our relationship with God and rebirth us into the way God created us. On that "Black Friday" I mourn my sinful nature and what God had to do to such an extreme as to send His only Son to this earth of sinful people to die for us and take on our sins. Strangely, Thanksgiving Day precedes "Black Friday." I think it should be reversed because I am so very thankful for God's grace and willingness to sacrifice His Son for me. I like to quickly turn my mourning into joy of the resurrection of God's Son and my rebirth.

Proverbs 15:1 Misspoken

A gentle answer turns away wrath, but a harsh word stirs up anger. (NIV)

Misspoken

Many of us try to put too much into our weekends; especially when it's a three- or four-day weekend due to a holiday. We are trying to do everything we've put on hold in just those few days. People are getting tired. Tempers tend to flare, and words are spoken without thought. Quite often harsh words are spoken before thought is given to why we are angry. We just erupt. In this day of so many things being instantaneous, we think we should speak instantaneously. So many misspoken words would never be spoken if we would take just a quick moment and check out what we think we want to say with what God wants us to say. It's in the scripture. We are to use words that build one another up, not words to tear others down. Harsh and angry words never mend; they always tear down. When we are tired, we tend to think less and react more. Let us commit our day and time to God before we arise from our beds. God has our day planned and it will never be more than we can withstand. When we start with praise it is harder for anger to enter. Keep our celebrations during every weekend and every holiday season full of love, peace, and encouragement.

Proverbs 16:3 Plans

Commit to the Lord whatever you do, and He will establish your plans. (NIV)

Plans

So many people misinterpret this proverb. They think they can make their plans and then ask God to bless them. What this proverb says is to listen to the established plans He has made for us, then commit to do them in His timing and His way. My husband always wanted a flow chart. He wanted to see all the steps between point A and point Z. It took him a while to learn God wants us to trust Him to the point that we can place the heel of our foot down before we know which direction the toe of our foot will point. If our ears are tuned to His quiet voice within us, we will always hear, "This is the way, walk in it." I find it easier because I don't enjoy the planning stage of anything. This doesn't mean we should never plan. Our plans should always be open for review and adjustment. We can and should make plans but only as we listen to God and, when we find they need adjustment or changing, be very flexible and adjust or change as needed to always be in His perfect will and timing. It is only by the grace of God that we draw our next breath. Let us rejoice that He, who knows the future, will always lead us on the right path.

Proverbs 18:16 Gifts

A gift opens the way and ushers the giver into the presence of the great. (NIV)

Gifts

Giving gifts at Christmas started with the Magi who came with gifts for Jesus. Then the tradition became of giving to show a desire and appreciation for a relationship. Now they seem to be obligatory. We are in a rush to open them, say a quick thank you then move on to open the next gift. A gift should be something from the heart that says I appreciate our relationship. It doesn't need to be material. The best gifts are those of service and time. Our question this season and any time of year is what gift will we bring to the Christ Child? Will we offer Him our best? How about a gift of time? Why not pray and ask Him where He wants us to donate a gift of time? Let us be more prayerful as we think about what gifts to give to whom and give our best to exemplify the relationships we appreciate.

Genesis 2:2 Creation

By the seventh day God had finished the work he had been doing; so, on the seventh day he rested from all his work. (NIV)

John 19:30 When he had received the drink, Jesus said, "It is finished." With that, He bowed His head and gave up His spirit. (NIV)

Creation

When God finished creation after six God days (with God a day is as a thousand years or more and a thousand years or more is as a day), all things that exist or ever will exist were created and finished except for the atoning of the sins of mankind. Jesus finished that on the cross. I learned that all was finished sitting on my porch swing one day and having a vision of songs and words and other things floating around in the air. God spoke to my heart and said all that is or will be in our time and space are already created by Him and waiting for us to see, hear, latch on, and bring into our time and space. We sometimes think we're so smart and clever with what "we" create. All creation comes from God and is just there waiting for us to unite with His creation. The question we must answer is what is it that we, as individuals, are to see, hear, and bring into being in our time and space. Each of us has a unique calling in this process. Many things are delayed by our distraction from other things. Let us learn to ask God each day what He is waiting for us to hear, see, and bring forth.

Matthew 3:3 Advent

This is He who was spoken of through the prophet Isaiah: "A voice of one calling in the wilderness, 'Prepare the way for the Lord, make straight paths for him.'" (NIV)

Advent

Advent is a time of preparation for celebrating the birth of our Savior. So many churches and believers no longer acknowledge the Advent season. Preparing for a celebration is a good thing to do. We prepare in many ways in our homes by decorating, baking, sending Christmas cards, etc. We must also prepare our hearts. We are inundated by so much commercialism that sometimes it's hard to remember what Christmas is about. Taking time to prepare our hearts keeps the "Christ" in Christmas. This is a suitable time to discipline our meditation, scripture, and prayer time. This is also a good time to review how we are doing in giving our time and our finances to spreading the good news of the coming of Jesus into our world and our lives. John, the Baptizer, gave his time, and eventually, his life, calling all to prepare to receive Jesus as their Lord and Savior. During the four weeks of Advent, let us join the baptizer in preparing not only ourselves but preparing others to receive Jesus into our lives, minds, and hearts. Let us always keep Advent every day in preparation for the return of Jesus when He comes to bring His Bride (the universal church of believers) home to the wedding feast prepared for us.

Luke 1:38 Mary

"I am the Lord's servant," Mary answered. "May your word to me be fulfilled." Then the angel left her. (NIV)

Mary

As we continue through the Advent season along with other times of the year, let's take time to think about what we call the Christmas Story. We'll start with Mary. In our day and time, she would be a teenager in high school. Imagine what she felt hearing that, not married (only engaged), and being a virgin, she was to become pregnant. Most girls her age would be full of fear. What would everyone think? In her day she would be stoned to death for being pregnant without already being married. How would anyone believe she was still a virgin? Then we look at her response. What faith she had. What willingness to submit to the will of God regardless of how it may affect her. Then we must consider the things God tells us to do. What is our response? Let's take time to ask God to reveal to us the times we have turned away from what He asks of us through His written Word and sometimes by the quiet nudging of His Holy Spirit. Let us repent and become as willing as Mary.

Hebrews 5:8 Suffering

Son though He was, He learned obedience from what he suffered (NIV)

Suffering

We are creatures of comfort. We want everything to be nice and easy. When things get hard, we get upset. We expect God to keep all manner of hardness, difficulty, or pain away from us. Jesus, the Son of God, was already perfect yet he still had to learn obedience to the Father in His fleshly nature through suffering. How much more do we have to learn? We tend not to pay attention when things are pleasant and easy. It takes discomfort and sometimes suffering, for God to get our attention. Sometimes we suffer not for ourselves but for someone else to turn their attention to God. Jesus didn't need to suffer for the Father to get His attention. He always had it. Jesus suffered as an example for us of how we can walk through suffering times. So often, when we're suffering, we look at those who are having an easy time and we complain to God, "Why me?" "Why not them?" Let us remember how the Book of James begins. If you've forgotten, get your Bible out and read it for yourself. Suffering has a purpose. Our reaction should be to find the purpose each time we suffer. This can shorten the time we are walking through that event. I praise God for the things I have suffered because they brought me into the relationship, I have with Him. I know there will be other times ahead, but I know I will never walk them alone because God has promised never to leave or forsake me and that goes for you also.

2 Corinthians 3:18 Reflection

And we all, who with unveiled faces contemplate the Lord's glory, are being transformed into His image with ever-increasing glory, which comes from the Lord, who is the Spirit. (NIV)

Reflection

Watching nature shows of beautiful scenery on television I think they are only a reflection of the real beauty I would see if I was there in person. It makes me want to make the effort to be there. The same should be true when people look at us, as God's children. When others look at us, they should see a reflection of our Lord and Savior, Jesus Christ. The reflection they see should make them want to see Jesus for themselves. It should give them a hunger and desire to know Him and experience Him in person. We must ask what our reflection reveals about Jesus. Is our reflection consistent? Can they see a reflection of Him in us when we're shopping, at work, at school, driving in traffic, or anything else we might be doing? How do we clear the shadows off our reflection so Jesus shines through us more brilliantly? We must be in the Word, the Holy Bible, putting it deep into our minds and hearts and have one time in prayer getting to know Him better. As we get to know Him, more and more of our Lord will shine out through us and give others a thirst to know Him more. During Advent let's take time to polish His reflection through us.

Matthew 1:19 Joseph

Because Joseph her husband was faithful to the law, and yet did not want to expose her to public disgrace, he had in mind to divorce her quietly. (NIV)

Joseph

Imagine being Joseph. He knew he hadn't had relations with Mary. How could he believe she was telling the truth and was a pregnant virgin? This seemed like a physical impossibility. Yet, he loved Mary and didn't wish her harm though he didn't want to be with her anymore. It took a very real dream to change Joseph into a believer. But this also required a lot of courage and faith. People would talk and pass judgment on both. Yet he was obedient to the word given to him in his dream. He did take Mary to be his wife and became the stepfather of Jesus, helping Him to grow. Sometimes God might ask us to accept something we have a hard time believing or maybe ask us to do something that will bring criticism from others. Will we have the courage of Joseph to walk in obedience to anything God asks of us, even if it means others will criticize us for it?

2 Thessalonians 3:2 News

And pray that we may be delivered from wicked and evil people, for not everyone has faith. (NIV)

News

I had a desire to quit watching the news. I decided to pray about not watching anymore. Then, as I read this verse, I realized we must pray against the evil we see so much on the news. Not only should we be praying against the evil we witness, but we also need to pray for the ones who are hurting. You never know, you might be the only person who has ever prayed for the one you hear about on the news. When we stand before God's throne, I don't want Him to say to me that I heard about the situation, and I failed to pray about it connecting the power of God with the event or person in our time and space. Let us be less quick to judge and very quick to pray.

Luke 1:31 Mary's Parents

You will conceive and give birth to a son, and you are to call him Jesus. (NIV)

Mary's Parents

Let us think about Mary's parents. As parents, we know the shock we would feel if our teenage daughter told us she was pregnant. We would be filled with a mixture of emotions. We would feel shame, embarrassment, anger, and concern yet still love her. Even though the angel told Mary of her cousin, Elizabeth's, pregnancy, I'm sure her parents encouraged her to leave and go to Elizabeth. They needed time to think about what to do. They knew the penalty was to stone their daughter to death, but they loved their daughter. Imagine their anguish. It was hard to believe what Mary was telling them about the angelic visit. It was hard to believe she was still a virgin. They were probably very concerned about Joseph's reaction when he found out. With all those emotions, they helped their daughter prepare for the trip to her cousin's. We don't know what the outcome was with Mary's relationship with her parents. We do know how we respond to the various problems and situations our teens bring to us. Let us learn to pray and not jump to judgment. Let us support our teens the way God does, with love yet also with correction in that love and encouragement to turn to God's way.

Luke 1:41 Elizabeth

When Elizabeth heard Mary's greeting, the baby leaped in her womb, and Elizabeth was filled with the Holy Spirit. (NIV)

Elizabeth

Mary went to see her cousin Elizabeth. I imagine Mary was still feeling a little confused, insecure, and fearful. When Elizabeth heard Mary, Elizabeth was filled with the Holy Spirit. Before the resurrection and then the Pentecost (the releasing of God's Holy Spirit), the Holy Spirit only came on certain people at certain times for a specific purpose. This time it was to confirm through Elizabeth to Mary all the angels had said to her. Not only did God use Elizabeth to prepare Mary for the birth of Jesus, but He also used her son, John, as the voice in the wilderness preparing the way for Mary's child, Jesus. God uses many people, coordinating them, for His purpose. We are all like a choir or orchestra. No one part is more or less important than another. All parts must blend and flow together for a singular purpose. No ministry is more important than another. All ministries, all gifts, and each one of God's children must blend and flow together for the sole purpose of glorifying God while on this earth. Let's encourage one another to do our parts in the "orchestra or choir" of God's family and shine forth His praises and love to the world around us.

Luke 2:1-2 Cesar Augustus

In those days Caesar Augustus issued a decree that a census should be taken of the entire Roman world. (NIV)

Caesar Augustus

God uses anyone He desires to move people where they must be for His purpose. He even used a harsh ruler, Caesar Augustus. Without the requirement that each family go to the point of their origin, a prophecy wouldn't have been fulfilled. There was no way Joseph would take Mary on such a long and uncomfortable trip while pregnant without the government forcing such a trip. Many times, we look at our governments and question how God can accomplish His will. God is bigger than any government. He says (Romans 13:1 NIV) Let everyone be subject to the governing authorities, for there is no authority except that which God has established. The authorities that exist have been established by God for His ultimate purpose. We have an important part in this. We are to pray for the authorities over our lands. We are to obey the laws of the lands if they don't conflict with God's law. God says we are to love and pray for our enemies. Are we praying as we should?

Luke 2:7 Stable Owner

and she gave birth to her firstborn, a son. She wrapped him in cloths and placed him in a manger, because there was no guest room available for them. (NIV)

Stable Owner

Imagine the stress on Joseph as he sought a room for Mary. The city was overcrowded, and no rooms were available. But someone had mercy for their situation. Someone owned the stable. It was not like today's barns. It was just a shelter for the horses and donkeys that the people used for transportation. But whoever owned this stable cleared a place for Joseph and Mary to have shelter. This person had no idea that what he did would be the birthplace of the Son of God. God uses us many times without our knowledge of what is taking place. It might be just a smile we give someone who needs to see a smile or a friendly face that keeps someone from harming themselves. It could be just as simple as giving a lonely person a call or visit. We need to keep ourselves available for God to use us in ways we see as small. We tend to want to be used in a big way thinking that's what is important. What the owner of the stable did was particularly important. Just as in an orchestra or choir it takes every member to make beautiful music, it takes each believer using the gifts God gives in their unique way to let God's glory shine on this earth. Let's keep His light shining through us in any way He chooses.

Luke 2:8 Shepherds

And there were shepherds living out in the fields nearby, keeping watch over their flocks at night. (NIV)

Shepherds

Shepherds were uneducated people. They were brave in protecting their sheep from predatory animals. But imagine their fear when the night sky suddenly burst into light. They had never seen or heard of such a thing. Then there was the voice that suddenly told them of an event they never heard of happening. Then the explosion of music praising God. They must have been in shock at so much happening. But these shepherds heard the invitation to see this newborn baby. It had to take more than curiosity to leave their sheep behind and go into a town bursting with strangers to find one stable amongst so many. They not only heard the invitation, but they also went, sought, and found this baby. We have an invitation also. We are invited to come to this baby, who has now grown into a man, the very Son of Man and Son of God. This baby grew, walked this Earth showing us how to live, died on the cross showing us the immeasurable love of God and taking on our sins, and then rose from death to give us eternal life in the very presence of God. Have you said yes to the invitation? After saying yes, you must seek Him to be involved in your everyday life. I pray you have said yes and have found Him and are walking in His Presence in your life.

Luke 2:13-14 Angel

Suddenly a great company of the heavenly host appeared with the angel, praising God and saying, "Glory to God in the highest heaven, and on earth peace to those on whom His favor rests." (NIV)

Angel

It's hard for us to imagine how the angel felt. I know two things about angels. They enjoy being God's messengers and they love to sing God's praises. The angel probably knew about God's plan to send His Word, His Son, to earth to show mankind His love and to take the place of mankind for their sins. It must have been exciting to see this come about. Sometimes I like to close my eyes and, in my mind, try to hear the beautiful praising music of the angels. We must ask ourselves what we enjoy doing. Do we enjoy telling others about the coming of God, in Jesus, and why He came? Do we enjoy praising Him? What are we doing during Advent and all the year? Let's make sure a day doesn't go by without telling someone about Jesus and giving Him praise.

Luke 2:17 Others

When they had seen Him, they spread the word concerning what had been told them about this child, (NIV)

Others

The shepherds could not keep such good news quiet. They had to spread it to all they met. We have extremely good, life-changing, and saving news. Our question is, are we spreading this news? Are we telling our families, our friends, our neighbors, and the strangers we meet about the One who has come, walked this earth, died, and risen again for our salvation and our eternal life in the Presence of God? If not, why? Do we not believe it for ourselves? Are we more afraid of the judgment of others than their lives and the desire of God who wants no one to be lost? Take time and reflect on who you have shared this news with. How long has it been? Are you quiet now or are you still excited like when you first received Jesus for yourself and couldn't keep it quiet? Let us be bold. Let us ask God to refresh us and excite us to share the news.

Luke 2:25 Simeon

Now there was a man in Jerusalem called Simeon, who was righteous and devout. He was waiting for the consolation of Israel, and the Holy Spirit was on him. (NIV)

Simeon

Simeon was an old man. He was a man of prayer and worship of God. He received a word from God that he would see the Messiah before he died. He went to the temple daily for years, waiting in faith and patience that God would be true to His word. Then the day came. The Spirit within him witnessed that the baby he saw was the promised Messiah. He blessed Mary and Joseph but then prophesied to Mary that this baby would cause the fall and the rising of many in Israel and would reveal the thoughts of hearts of many. He also said her own heart would be pierced. We are waiting for the return of the Messiah, Jesus. He promised He would come back for His Bride, the believers. How are we waiting? Are we being faithful every day in our prayers and worship and trusting in faith? Are we living each day in expectation?

Luke 2:36 Anna

There was also a prophet, Anna, the daughter of Penuel, of the tribe of Asher. She was very old; she had lived with her husband for seven years after her marriage, (NIV)

Anna

Anna was expecting to see the Messiah in her lifetime. She was so sure, she refused to leave the temple. I'm not sure if she might have thought she could miss Him if she continued with her normal life. God doesn't expect us to quit living where He put us by staying in a church and never leaving. He expects us to be out amongst the people with our prayers and sharing how to worship Him while we wait for His second coming. There are times to devote exclusively to prayer and worship, but we are also to incorporate prayers and worship in our public lives to introduce others to the love and forgiveness of God through His Son, Jesus, the Messiah. Anna and Simeon recognized Jesus because they were looking for Him and expecting to see Him. Are we looking with expectation to see Him at work within our lives and the lives of others? I pray we are all looking with expectation and don't miss the marvelous ways God is at work within our lives and those around us.

Matthew 2:1 Wise Men

After Jesus was born in Bethlehem in Judea, during the time of King Herod, Magi from the east came to Jerusalem (NIV)

Wise Men

The first visitors to come and worship God's Son were lowly, uneducated shepherds. Now we see well-to-do, highly educated men come from great distances to worship Him. The worship of Jesus is for all people regardless of intellect, education, wealth, or any other circumstance. We don't know how many were in that group. Tradition says three because three types of gifts were mentioned. What we do know is they traveled from afar for the sole purpose of worshiping a king. They didn't understand what the kingdom was to be, but they knew He was an important king as His birth was announced by a bright, new star that directed the wise men to where He lay. At this time, they had moved from the stable to a house, not wanting to risk traveling back to their hometown, a five-day hard journey, with a young baby. We will be discussing the gifts for the next three devotionals. Right now, let's fill our minds with the fact that all mankind, regardless of race, culture, education, or any other characteristic, are called to come and worship the Son of God. Our question is, are we willing to be the star and guide others to the King?

Matthew 2:11 Gold

On coming to the house, they saw the child with his mother Mary, and they bowed down and worshiped Him. Then they opened their treasures and presented Him with gifts of gold, frankincense, and myrrh. (NIV)

Gold

Gold has been an international measure of wealth practically since the dawn of history, with each culture and era expressing gold weights and value according to their custom. It has never mattered what country or time you are in; gold is always accepted as a medium of exchange. The gold the visitors brought would cover expenses that Joseph and Mary had until after they were able to return home, and Joseph could return to his carpentry. We don't know how much of their wealth they were giving to the family, but we do know they went to a lot of trouble to bring them their gift. How much trouble are we willing to go to bring our gifts to our Lord?

Matthew 2:11 Frankincense

On coming to the house, they saw the child with His mother Mary, and they bowed down and worshiped Him. Then they opened their treasures and presented Him with gifts of gold, frankincense, and myrrh. (NIV)

Frankincense

Frankincense is a milky white resin extracted from species of the genus Boswellia, which thrive in arid, cool areas of the Arabian Peninsula, East Africa, and India. It's a small tree that grows to a height of 16 feet. It has papery bark, sparse bunches of paired leaves, and flowers with white petals and a yellow or red center. It had religious, medicinal, and personal uses and was highly treasured. When burned, the smoke was prayers rising to heaven. Our prayers are as the smoke of frankincense. As we pray, are we aware that our words are as the smoke of frankincense rising to heaven to the very ears of our God? As frankincense was treasured, so does God treasure our prayers.

Matthew 2:11 Myrrh

On coming to the house, they saw the child with His mother Mary, and they bowed down and worshiped Him. Then they opened their treasures and presented Him with gifts of gold, frankincense, and myrrh. (NIV)

Myrrh

Myrrh comes from a small bushy tree. It is an expensive spice, used for making perfume, incense, medicine, and for anointing the dead. It is a spice for a king. The Bible cites myrrh three times in the life and death of Jesus Christ. The above verse in Matthew states that the kings visited the child Jesus, bringing gifts of gold, frankincense, and myrrh. Mark notes that when Jesus was dying on the cross, someone offered him wine mixed with myrrh to stop the pain, but he did not take it. Nicodemus brought a mixture of 75 pounds of myrrh and aloes to anoint Jesus' body when it was laid in the tomb. It was a much-treasured spice for kings. Our question is, what do we highly treasure that we can bring to our King, Jesus? What is most valuable to us? Is it our money, our time, our talents, or whatever we highly treasure? Let us give our treasure to our King, Jesus, to be used in glorifying Him and bringing others to glorify Him.

Matthew 2:7 Herod

Then Herod called the Magi secretly and found out from them the exact time the star had appeared.

Matthew 2:12 And having been warned in a dream not to go back to Herod, they returned to their country by another route.

Matthew 2:16 When Herod realized that he had been outwitted by the Magi, he was furious, and he gave orders to kill all the boys in Bethlehem and its vicinity who were two years old and under, in accordance with the time he had learned from the Magi. (NIV)

Herod

Herod played a significant role in fulfilling the prophecies about Jesus.

In Jeremiah 31:15: This is what the Lord says: "A voice is heard in Ramah, mourning and great weeping, Rachel weeping for her children and refusing to be comforted because they are no more."

We also read in Hosea 11:1: "When Israel was a child, I loved him, and out of Egypt I called my son."

It's doubtful Joseph and Mary would have fled to Egypt if the angel hadn't told him to go there in a dream. We can't understand why God allowed all boy babies to be slaughtered, but we can't see the entire picture. We must choose to continue to trust God has only good for His children but sometimes we must wade through the bad and hurtful to get to God's good because until Jesus God's Son comes for God's children on this earth, Satan still is at large. It is up to us to stand up to the evil deeds of Satan to bring God's peace and joy into our time and space. Our question today is what are we doing to communicate God's love and peace to those around us?

Matthew 2:22 Nazareth

But when he heard that Archelaus was reigning in Judea in place of his father Herod, he was afraid to go there. Having been warned in a dream, he withdrew to the district of Galilee,

Matthew 2:23 and he went and lived in a town called Nazareth. So was fulfilled what was said through the prophets, that he would be called a Nazarene. (NIV)

Nazareth

Even more prophecies are fulfilled. We often question the circumstances we find we must walk through. Here is another example of a circumstance that changed Joseph's direction and caused a prophecy to be fulfilled. When we find a circumstance has changed our direction, we need to take time to pray and ask God what we are to do. God speaks to us in unusual ways. The primary way is through His written word, the Holy Bible. He also speaks to us through that still, inner voice of His Holy Spirit within us. He also speaks to us through others who are mature in their faith. He also speaks to us through our circumstances. Instead of complaining, we need to embrace the circumstance and ask God for wisdom in walking through the new circumstance. When we are determined to evade a new circumstance by walking around it or resisting it and staying the course we were on, we miss God's blessing for us on the other side. As we continue to celebrate the first coming of our Savior to this earth let us also be open to any circumstance God chooses to allow to come to us, trusting His wisdom to guide us through and into His blessing for us.

Matthew 2:9 Star

After they had heard the king, they went on their way, and the star they had seen when it rose went ahead of them until it stopped over the place where the child was. (NIV)

Star

Many people put a star on top of their Christmas tree. They put it on top because it was a star that guided the wise men to Bethlehem to worship and present their gifts to the Christ child, Jesus. As far as what the star was, there are interesting opinions on the internet. I recommend you search for the Bethlehem Star, but I caution you to check out the source before reading. The point is there was a star or something that appeared to be a star that guided the wise men to the right place. As Jesus walked this earth and after His death and resurrection, we no longer need a star or light in the heavens. Jesus is the light and when we follow Him and the precepts, He has given us in His written Word, the Holy Bible, we can be assured of being guided in the right direction for our lives. Jesus is the Light of the world. Our question for today is do we continually choose to follow the Light or do we choose to follow our way?

Nehemiah 9:6 Angel Servants

You alone are the Lord. You made the heavens, even the highest heavens, and all their starry host, the earth and all that is on it, the seas and all that is in them. You give life to everything, and the multitudes of heaven worship You.

Angel Servants

Before creating man, God created angels. They serve God in many ways: messenger, protector, servant of God, and worshiper of God. A good study is to do a word search in the Bible and see all the things angels do. Many people put an angel on the top of their Christmas tree. The angel on the tree serves to remind us of the role of angels in the announcing of the coming of God's Son to this earth. The first one spoke to Mary. Then, one appeared in a dream to Joseph. An angel appeared to the shepherds to tell them where to find the Messiah. Joseph saw an angel in another dream telling him to take his family and flee to Egypt before Herod could kill Jesus along with all the boy children in Bethlehem. Angels are not to be worshiped. They worship God and do His bidding to help God's children on this earth. Angels are still at work today. They work in ways some of us see and they work behind the scenes in ways we aren't aware. There are also fallen angels but during the Advent season, I choose not to think about the evil but only about the love God sent to us. Let us thank God for His serving angels.

Luke 2:12 Manger

This will be a sign to you: You will find a baby wrapped in cloths and lying in a manger

Manger

A manger is a wooden trough used to hold food for animals. The baby Jesus was put in a manger that had hay in it. In scripture, we read, (John 6:35 NIV) Then Jesus declared, "I am the bread of life. Whoever comes to me will never go hungry, and whoever believes in me will never be thirsty." Our bread of life was laid in a manger. Several years ago, I wrote a song with the following words.

When I walked into the barn

Early one cold morn,

My eyes fell on the manger bed

Looking old and worn

Then I heard You softly say,

"Twas in a place like this,

snuggled in some old dry hay

I first laid to rest."

As my Savior grew to serve

He wandered all around.

Never did He have a place

He could call His own.

When He died upon the cross

On that dismal day

They laid Him in a borrowed tomb

To wait for that third day.

Now that You have conquered death

Make Your home in me

Fill me with your warmth and peace,

Free Your love through me.

Keep my mind full of Your thoughts

Set my spirit free

To be united with Your own

Then One we'll ever be.

As we continue to celebrate the coming of our Lord and Savior, Jesus Christ, let us remember He is the very bread of life, and we are to eat and digest His words making them part of our being.

Genesis 38:26 Tamar

Judah recognized them and said, "She is more righteous than I, since I wouldn't give her to my son Shelah." And he did not sleep with her again.

Tamar

Tamar was a fighter. She was mistreated by her father-in-law, Judah. She was also very smart and was able to make plans to cause Judah to honor her according to Jewish law. Her story is very worth the time to read in Genesis 38, and I encourage you to do so. Reading it straight from scripture is much better than my rewriting it in my own words. By including Tamar in the genealogy of Jesus, God was showing that He welcomes sinners into His family. Tamar was mistreated but used deception to gain what was being denied to her. We can learn from Tamar to persevere when mistreated, not through deception but according to the precepts set down for us in God's written word, the Holy Bible.

2 Samuel 12:24 Bethsheba

Then David comforted his wife Bathsheba, and he went to her and made love to her. She gave birth to a son, and they named him Solomon. The Lord loved him;(NIV)

Bethsheba

Once again, we find a woman who was a sinner in the lineage of Jesus. By now we should all be assured that even though we are sinners that doesn't stop God from working His will and purpose through us. During these last few days of Advent or any other time, let's ask the Holy Spirit to reveal to us any sin that is holding us back from being free to allow God's Holy Spirit to flow through us. Confess what He reveals to us and receive His forgiveness. Then be sure to forgive ourselves. Stand on the fact that this sin no longer separates us from God and is considered gone forever. If it's a sin of repetition, make up our minds to no longer be chained to that sinful habit and turn our backs and our minds away from it. If it is an action, let's be sure to replace it with an action pleasing to God.

Matthew 1:5 5 Rahab

Salmon the father of Boaz, whose mother was Rahab, (NIV)

Rahab

Rahab was a harlot. But she took mercy on the Israelite spies and hid them for their protection. She had heard how the Hebrews were defeating all who stood in their way and wanted to find a way to protect herself and her family. She promised the spies safety if they would protect her when they defeated the city. You can read her story in Joshua 2 and 6. Though Rahab wasn't a believer in the one, true God, she had heard of His power. Protecting the spies turned her life around. She, though a harlot in her past, was honored and included in the lineage of Jesus. Our past is under the cross of Jesus and our lives, when we come to the cross, are redeemed and we are honored as children of the Most High God. Rahab put her past behind and we can too.

Matthew 20:18-19 Christmas Day

"We are going up to Jerusalem, and the Son of Man will be delivered over to the chief priests and the teachers of the law. They will condemn Him to death and will hand him over to the Gentiles to be mocked, flogged, and crucified. On the third day, He will be raised to life!" (NIV)

Christmas Day

We celebrate today as the day Jesus was born of the Virgin, Mary, as flesh and blood. As the very Word of God, he left God the Father for the sole purpose of dying on the cross for our sins so we can once again be in the image of God. His entire walk on earth He knew what His purpose was and what He would be facing. Christmas day, as is any and every day, is of no consequence without the death and resurrection of Jesus. As we celebrate His first coming, let's be sure to thank Him for His sacrifice for us and continue to prepare for His second coming for us, His Bride by sharing this glorious news with all we meet.

Happy Birthday, Jesus. Thank You for coming, dying, resurrecting, and the promise of coming back for us.

Matthew 3:16-17 After Advent

As soon as Jesus was baptized, He went up out of the water. At that moment heaven was opened, and He saw the Spirit of God descending like a dove and alighting on Him. And a voice from heaven said, "This is my Son, whom I love; with Him I am well pleased." (NIV)

After Advent

Advent is over. We've celebrated the first coming of the Son of God, Jesus. Now we continue to grow in Him. These verses are an example of when all three persons of the Trinity were present. We start with Jesus, God's only Son, the Word of God in flesh humbly submitting to John for baptism. John was right in saying he should be baptized by Jesus, but Jesus was giving us a living example of humility and love. The next thing was the Holy Spirit descending in the form of a dove and landing on Jesus. When we come to Jesus, we also receive the Holy Spirit within us. There is no way to minister God's love to others without the Holy Spirit within us. Jesus left the Holy Spirit when He became man and reunited with the Spirit when He was baptized. Then we hear God, the Father speak from heaven. Though His audible voice is seldom heard, we, being filled with the Holy Spirit, can also hear God the Father speak to us through His Spirit. We learn to recognize His voice through reading studying and meditating on His written Word, the Holy Bible. As we become more familiar with what is recorded, we become able to recognize the Holy Spirit speaking within us. As we prepare to move into a new year, let us commit to growing in the Word of God.

Matthew 4:1 Led to Temptation

Then Jesus was led by the Spirit into the wilderness to be tempted by the devil. (NIV)

Led to Temptation

After Jesus was baptized and reunited with the Holy Spirit He was led into the wilderness. Notice the Spirit led Him. Jesus did not decide on His own to go into the wilderness. Many times, we choose to take the wilderness route on our own. When we choose to do this, God leaves us to our own devices until we repent. When God leads us into the wilderness through His Holy Spirit, He does so for our own growth and spiritual strength. He goes with us into the wilderness to teach us how to stand up to the temptations of the wilderness. When we find ourselves in the wilderness, we must ask ourselves how we got there. Did we choose to follow a temptation that we knew was against God's will for us? Are we choosing to go into places where we know sin abounds? Are we reading or looking at things we know are strong temptations for us? Let us be honest with ourselves, recognize why we are where we are, repent when it is our choosing, and allow God's Holy Spirit to give us wisdom to walk on through and out of it.

Matthew 4:2 Fasting

After fasting forty days and forty nights, He was hungry. (NIV)

Fasting

When Jesus was led into the wilderness He began to fast. Fasting is a means of humbling the soul. It shows man's dependence on God and on needing to eat from the Bread of Life. Fasting not just from food but from all normal activity, helps the mind to concentrate more on God and less on the material things of this world. There are many types of fasting. Jesus did a total fast, eating nothing. He probably did drink water, but we don't know. He was miraculously sustained to be able to fast for 40 days. We can do a shorter fast when led by God's Holy Spirit. We can also do a partial fast. John Wesley did a daily fast of no food or drink until after 3 P.M. We can fast one meal or we can fast a certain type of food. We can fast certain activities. Fasting is a giving up of something for a period. What counts is the reason we fast and what we do with the time we are fasting. Fasting is to get our mind more fully on God and what He wants to say to us. It is not meant for us to lose weight to look better. It is not meant for us to have more time to work on other things. When we fast, we take that time to pray, read the Bible, and meditate. Notice I said, "When we fast." Fasting is part of our discipline in growing spiritually and more intimate with God.

In Matthew 6:17 (NIV) Jesus said,

> "But when you fast, put oil on your head and wash your face,"

He fully expects us to spend some time fasting. But fasting is a private thing. We are to fast unto God, not unto the praises of other people. As we approach this new year, let us ask God about when and how we are to fast. There may be medical reasons why we cannot do a complete fast. The type of fast we do is not as important as what we do when we do fast. The important thing is to humble ourselves before our God and show Him we are dependent on Him in all we think and do.

Matthew 4:4 Quoting Scripture

Jesus answered, "It is written: 'Man shall not live on bread alone, but on every word that comes from the mouth of God. (NIV)

Quoting Scripture

Every time Jesus was faced with a temptation, He quoted Scripture from the Torah. Now we have both the Old and the New Testaments to quote. God's word is stronger than any temptation. Therefore, it is so important for us not only to read the Bible and study and meditate on it. We also need to memorize scripture to be armed and ready when temptation suddenly appears. There is scripture for every temptation that can ever come. It is up to us to be familiar enough with the written word that the Holy Spirit will be able to bring the right scripture which we've already learned up to our conscious mind. I print out single verses and put them on my refrigerator door. I read them every time I go to the refrigerator. I must admit it now takes me longer than it used to memorize the verses. Most of my memory verses are set to music so when I quote them, I tend to speak to them in the rhythm I use to sing them. The method of memorizing isn't important. What is important is that we commit them to memory.

Matthew 4:3 Bread

The tempter came to Him and said, "If you are the Son of God, tell these stones to become bread." (NIV)

Bread

The first temptation Jesus faced was to focus on the here and now rather than eternity. Jesus knew He was here to serve God and not just live for the moment. Living in the moment is different than living in the present. Living for the moment means we are not concerned about what our choices now will mean in the future, especially in the light of all eternity. Jesus showed He was trusting in God's provision for the future. So often we are looking for the quick fix or quick answer to a trial. We need to learn to take time to pray, seeking God's answer and wisdom rather than taking the first "fix" we see to get out of a problem, trial, or temptation. When we decide, we must ask God to show us what it will mean for His path for us or His purpose for another. We live in the present, not the past or the future, but we live in the present with our eyes on God and eternity. The way we look at eternity affects how we choose to walk through the present. Those who don't believe they will have everlasting life with God will choose quick-term convenience and comfort rather than the consequences of the future. Refusing to take the "quick fix" confirms we know there is a tomorrow, whether it's on this earth or in the very presence of God.

Matthew 4:6 Child of God

"If you are the Son of God," he said, "throw yourself down. For it is written: "'He will command his angels concerning you, and they will lift you up in their hands, so that you will not strike your foot against a stone.'" (NIV)

Child of God

In this temptation, Jesus was asked to justify His existence. Jesus did not need to prove who He is. God the Father had already declared Him to be His Son. God had already declared His love. (More on this later.) Jesus had total confidence in His relationship with the Father. Our question is, do we feel confident in who we are in Christ Jesus? If not, we are not into the scripture enough. Immersing ourselves in the recorded words of God in the Holy Bible will increase our confidence. In it, we read we were created for fellowship with the Father. When we come to Him through Jesus, His Son, we become joint heirs with Jesus. Joint heirs mean all that Jesus has we also have. We do not need to test God. He has spoken. He never lies. We can choose to believe and trust. God's love for us is unshakeable. He proved it by sending Jesus down, letting Him go on the cross for our sins, and giving Him life again so we may live.

Matthew 4:9 Joint Heirs

"All this I will give you," he said, "if you will bow down and worship me."

Joint Heirs

Jesus knew His purpose was to worship God. He also knew all in existence was already His. We were created to fellowship with and worship God. Because we are joint heirs with Jesus, we already own all that is in existence. We are here to be good stewards of all that is. When God created us in His image, He put a space in us that needs to worship. When we choose to put anything else ahead of God, we are worshiping whatever we put ahead of God. Because that space God put in us is for Him and Him alone, nothing else will satisfy that space. We can keep changing what we worship, and what we put before God, but nothing will ever satisfy. When we find ourselves not satisfied, we need to see what it is we are putting before God. A full, abundant life can only be found as we worship God, putting Him first in all things.

Matthew 3:17 Relationship

And a voice from heaven said, "This is my Son, whom I love; with him I am well pleased." (NIV)

Relationship

Before we follow Jesus' ministry let's take a moment to reflect on what God, the Father said before Jesus began His ministry. This is before He turned water into wine, healed anyone, fed multitudes with a meal for one, walked on water, calmed a storm, and went to the cross; before He performed a single miracle. God said Jesus is His Son. He was stating the relationship between Jesus and Himself. Then God said He loved Jesus. This is before Jesus did anything for God the Father. Then He tops it all off by saying He is well pleased with Jesus. Jesus hadn't done anything yet and despite that, God is well pleased with Him.

We are so very task oriented. We think we must be busy doing to be appreciated, loved, accepted, or valued. God loves us for who we are, His children, not for what we do. Our doing is not for being more approved or loved or valued by God, but it flows out of our relationship with Him and His love for us and our love for Him. God sent His son while we were out of relationship with Him and before we ever thought of doing anything to honor or obey Him. As we continue to walk through this year, let's take time to relax and enjoy being in a child/father relationship with God. It is time for us to enjoy fellowshipping with Him. It is time for us to chat with Him as children chat with their fathers. Let's take time to reflect on a loving, child/father relationship; let us immerse ourselves in it and all else will follow naturally.

Matthew 4:13-14 Moving Forward

Leaving Nazareth, he went and lived in Capernaum, which was by the lake in the area of Zebulun and Naphtali— to fulfill what was said through the prophet Isaiah: (NIV)

Moving Forward

It is hard to fully understand the movements and ministry of Jesus without knowing the Old Testament prophecies. Jesus left Nazareth because of their unbelief and refusal to accept His teaching. So often those closest to you are the ones who are most against your success. Quite often it is because of jealousy. After Jesus' baptism and wilderness experience, He started teaching. His teaching was the same as his cousin, John. All must repent to draw near to God. So many don't want to admit they have anything to repent. Though we might be harsh judges of ourselves, we don't want to admit we are wrong because we are insecure already and don't want to risk more insecurity. Every day is a new day. Hopefully, we have allowed the Holy Spirit to give us a good and honest look at ourselves. We know we are children of God and greatly loved by Him so we should be able to look honestly at our thoughts and actions or inactions and be able to see them for what they are or aren't and repent where necessary so we can walk on in the Presence of our God.

Matthew 4:17 Kingdom of Heaven

From that time on Jesus began to preach, "Repent, for the kingdom of heaven has come near." (NIV)

Kingdom of Heaven

Jesus began His ministry of preaching. He called people to repent as John had been doing. But John talked about One Who would follow him Who is greater than he is. Jesus said the kingdom of heaven is near. They didn't realize how very near it was. Jesus contained the kingdom of heaven and seeing how He lived on this earth gives us a glimpse of how the kingdom of heaven is. We are blessed to have His Holy Spirit dwelling in us. As we learn more about Jesus and experience more of the Holy Spirit, we are given glimpses of the Kingdom of Heaven for, since the Holy Spirit is in us, the kingdom of heaven is also in us. We can start experiencing it to some degree right now. Take time to meditate on Jesus and His words allow yourself to feel His presence and the presence of the Holy Spirit within you and realize a little of the kingdom of heaven.

Matthew 4:18-20 Fish for People

As Jesus was walking beside the Sea of Galilee, He saw two brothers, Simon called Peter and his brother Andrew. They were casting a net into the lake, for they were fishermen. "Come, follow me," Jesus said, "and I will send you out to fish for people." At once they left their nets and followed Him. (NIV)

Fish for People

Jesus starts to select His disciples. The first two, Simon (Peter) and his brother Andrew are fishermen. Have you ever wondered why they left immediately? Jesus wasn't new to them. They had heard John the Baptizer preaching and they heard Jesus's preaching. They might have even been there when Jesus was baptized for John the Baptizer was the major attraction in the area. They were probably also intrigued by Jesus saying they would be fishing for people. I'm sure they didn't understand what He meant by that.

When we fish, we use bait to catch the fish. The bait Jesus used was God's love through teaching, healing, forgiveness, and miracles. We must ask ourselves if we are fishing for people, when they look or listen to us what do they see and hear? God's love or our judgment? Are our words in line with God's? Does what we say promote healing? Do we have a spirit of forgiveness? Do we have the faith to pray for miracles? Let us be true disciples and fish for people.

Matthew 4:23 Good News

Jesus went throughout Galilee, teaching in their synagogues, proclaiming the good news of the kingdom, and healing every disease and sickness among the people (NIV)

Good News

Jesus called two more brothers, James, son of Zebedee, and his brother John, then continued (Matthew 4:23 NIV) teaching in their synagogues, proclaiming the good news of the kingdom and healing every disease and sickness among the people. He does this walking throughout Galilee. News of His teaching and healing travels fast. Sometimes it seems bad news travels faster than good news. It seems today bad news gets more press than good news does. The news programs start with the bad news. Sometimes they end with a small, good news item. Gossip is usually about bad news and negative things about other people. The world would be so much better if we were more eager to spread good news quickly and pray over the bad, we hear rather than being the ones to pass it on.

Wouldn't be wonderful if we were as excited over good news rather than acting excited over the bad? We must consider what kind of news we pass on to others. What do we do with the bad news we hear? Do we just pass it on showing we're "in the know" or do we take this bad news to the throne of God for His intercession? Let's do as Jesus and proclaim the good news throughout the kingdom where we find ourselves.

Matthew 4:25 Show and Tell

Large crowds from Galilee, the Decapolis, Jerusalem, Judea and the region across the Jordan followed Him (NIV)

Show and Tell

Large crowds from all over started following Jesus. They were drawn to Him because so many people were being healed of so many things. As they were healed, they would go home and tell others what Jesus had done for them. That brought others to see Him. As believers, we have all experienced various things Jesus has done for us. Our question is, who have we told, and who have we shown? Yes, Jesus touches us for our benefit but not for that alone. He expects us to share what He does. After Jesus was resurrected and went back home to heaven we became His mouth, His hands, and His feet. Are we functioning or are we just acting as babies saying give me and do for me? Let us go out into our neighborhoods, our schools, our places of work, and even our churches and show and tell. Every one of us has something to tell.

Matthew 5:1-2 Beatitudes

Now when Jesus saw the crowds, he went up on a mountainside and sat down. His disciples came to him, and he began to teach them (NIV)

Beatitudes

This is the first recorded teaching of Jesus. In it, He gives us eight characteristics of thought and behavior we need to be blessed by God. This is the beginning of His teaching us how to seek good and hate evil by following His word. We call this "the Sermon on the Mount" or the "Beatitudes." We will be looking at one each devotional. But to prepare ourselves, we must open our hearts and minds to a fresh look at each one. We've read and heard them so much that we tend to pass them off as something we already know. This attitude blocks us from learning deeper meaning from God as we grow in Him. We need this attitude of not knowing already with all the scripture we read so we can meditate afresh with an open and eager mind and heart. All scripture is like an onion. It has multiple layers. As we peel an onion it gets smaller and smaller with each layer removed. Scripture has multiple layers. As we perceive each layer our self-righteousness gets less and less and our understanding and intimacy with God becomes bigger and bigger. It is a daily renewing of our minds through our opening them to the wisdom and knowledge of the Holy Spirit.

Matthew 5:3 Poor in Spirit

"Blessed are the poor in spirit, for theirs is the kingdom of heaven. (NIV)

Poor in Spirit

To be "poor in spirit" means to be humble, not to think very highly of yourself. It means to know you are needy. Without being poor in spirit or humble one can see no need to depend on or look to God. Those not humble are prideful and think they are all sufficient in themselves. They either ignore the vacuum God placed inside them for His Holy Spirit or they try to fill it with themselves, other people, or other things. God blesses those who are humble and seek Him for His love, wisdom, and direction. We must ask ourselves are we "poor in spirit?" Do we recognize apart from God we are nothing? Do we look to Him for all our needs and all our directions in this life? Let's take time to reflect on what areas in our own lives where we are not humble and ask God's Holy Spirit to come into those areas.

Matthew 5:4 Mourning

Blessed are those who mourn, for they will be comforted. (NIV)

Mourning

When Jesus talked about mourning, He was not talking about the grief that's experienced when a loved one dies. He was talking about mourning our sinful nature. It is only as we realize how much our sinful nature separates us from experiencing the love of God that we can mourn sin's effects on us and our relationship with Him. We tend to find excuses for sin. We tend to put God on a shelf to keep Him there until something massive occurs and we've exhausted any other source. It is only in really mourning, really hating our sin that we can truly receive the comfort of God. He comforts us with the assurance of His love and His total forgiveness. To have regret means we have not recognized the act, words spoken, or lack of act or words spoken that can be confessed to God and forgiven. If we choose to wallow in regret, we are not believing God when He says He loves us and forgives, yes even forgets, any confessed sin. Mourning brings confession which brings forgiveness which restores intimate, loving relationships. Our question is do we mourn the things that separate us from the oneness with God which Jesus prayed for us just before He faced the cross?

Matthew 5:5 Meek

Blessed are the meek, for they will inherit the earth (NIV)

Meek

Meek is the opposite of proud. When you are meek you quietly submit to God and do not feel you must work to impress others. When you are insulted, you follow the example of Jesus and keep silent allowing God to be your defense. Your speech is kind, and you are patient. All this makes you a happy person living in the presence of God and full of His Holy Spirit. You enjoy your intimate fellowship with Him throughout each day. You are quick to confess sin to God and quick to receive His forgiveness. You are also quick to forgive others. Our question is, does this describe us? Let's take time to reflect on each of these characteristics and ask God to show us in what areas we need more help.

Matthew 5:6 Righteousness

Blessed are those who hunger and thirst for righteousness, for they will be filled. (NIV)

Righteousness

No one is righteous but Jesus Christ. When we hunger and thirst for righteousness we are hungering and thirsting for Christ. We want to be filled with the righteousness of Christ; therefore, we want to be filled with Him. This takes place by the daily filling of the Holy Spirit. It is the Holy Spirit who enables us to be filled with the character of Jesus Christ. We can't know His character without really getting into the written Word, the Holy Bible. To be filled we must read the Word, meditate on the Word, ingest, and digest the Word, and practice the Word. The question we must ask ourselves is, do we hunger and thirst after the word? We are promised we will be filled if we do. Do we want to be filled? The filling is up to us. It is there for our filling. Let's get some filling today.

Matthew 5:8 Pure Heart

Blessed are the pure in heart, for they will see God (NIV)

Pure Heart

Only the pure in heart will see God and spend eternity in His presence. In Psalms, we read, "Create in me a clean heart and renew a right spirit within me." We are asking God for a pure heart. To have a pure heart doesn't mean we are without sin. It means we have given our heart to God through His Son, Jesus Christ, as our Lord and Savior. It means we have chosen to obey His word as given to us in the Holy Bible. It means we confess our sins and repent, choosing to turn away from sin and walk in His light and His righteousness. It is only by following Jesus that our hearts can be pure. We cannot do enough "good works" to purify our hearts. Only through Jesus and the infilling of His Holy Spirit can our hearts be purified. They are purified by God's mercy and grace through His Son. With a pure heart, we confess our love for God. With a pure heart, we repent and walk anew in the forgiveness God gives us. Let's keep our hearts pure through Jesus by meditating on His word and fellowshipping with Him every day.

Matthew 5:9 Peacemakers

Blessed are the peacemakers, for they will be called children of God (NIV)

Peacemakers

Peacemakers are children of God because to be full of peace we must be full of God's Holy Spirit. To be full of God's Holy Spirit we must be forgiven and forgiving. Without forgiveness, there can't be peace.

When peace is within us, we carry it with us and show it to others by our words and actions. Quite often a peacemaker is an arbitrator helping others come to terms with issues and come into God's peace.

We all seek peace. It is our nature to seek peace. God is peace so when we seek peace, we are seeking God. As we allow more of God into our lives, our families, our neighborhoods, our cities, our states, our nation, and the world, we will find peace. We can't just pray for peace. We must embody it in us, our words, and our actions through the Holy Spirit. Our question is are we at peace with God, with ourselves, and with others? Let us ask God to show us any area within us where we haven't allowed His peace to enter.

Matthew 5:7 Mercy

Blessed are the merciful, for they will be shown mercy (NIV)

Mercy

We've all heard the expression, "What goes around comes around." The Bible puts it another way, "Give and it will be given unto you." We've also heard "There but for the grace of God go I." Jesus gave us the example of showing mercy. The blind man called out, "Jesus, Son of God, have mercy on me." We don't know where someone else has walked so we can't judge them, but we can show them mercy. We are told to mourn with those who mourn and rejoice with those who rejoice. We are also told to forgive as we are forgiven. We are so quick to judge and criticize. God wants us to be quick to show mercy. We are to be His hands, feet, and mouth and reach out to others with mercy that comes from God's love flowing through us. The next time we see a homeless person or someone hurting, let's reach out to them in whatever way God provides for us to do so. Mercy can be given in a listening ear, a smile, a hand on a shoulder, a few dollars, or a multitude of ways. We only need to be open to listening to the Holy Spirit who will lead us in the way mercy is needed to be expressed.

Matthew 5:10 Persecuted

Blessed are those who are persecuted because of righteousness, for theirs is the kingdom of heaven (NIV)

Persecuted

This is hard for our finite minds to understand. That's because we don't have a concept of eternity. We are locked into a 24-hour day, a 7-day a week, and on and on according to our clocks and calendars. Eternity is hard to grasp. We do grasp persecution and we don't like it. Some like to be on the persecuting end of it but no one likes to be on the receiving end. Persecution takes many forms. We can be persecuted verbally, socially, financially, or physically. We don't feel blessed when we are persecuted Many times we respond in anger. Sometimes persecution is not because of our righteousness in Jesus. But, when we are persecuted because we stand with Jesus and we won't back down, we are blessed because we are assured by Jesus that we will be in the kingdom of heaven. Stephen is a good example. As he was being persecuted by stoning, he saw heaven open to receive him. This doesn't mean we don't pray for the Christians around the world who are being persecuted. We pray for them for protection, for strong faith, for release, and for the strength of God. We also pray that their faithfulness will have an impact on those persecuting them and will turn their persecutors to God through His Son, Jesus.

Matthew 5:13 Salt

"You are the salt of the earth. But if the salt loses its saltiness, how can it be made salty again? It is no longer good for anything, except to be thrown out and trampled underfoot. (NIV)

Salt

Salt has several uses. It is used as a preservative for meat and fish. It is also used to enhance the flavor of food. I have used it to clean pots and pans and, diluted slightly in water to ease a sore throat. We are to be salt to those around us. We are to bring preservation to others by introducing them to Jesus. We are to demonstrate a full abundant life enhanced through Jesus. We are to tell them about being cleansed from sin through the blood of Jesus. We are to pray for the healing of those who are sick because of the stripes from the lashes Jesus took on our behalf. We must ask ourselves if we are salty and allow the Holy Spirit through us to function in all the areas salt functions.

Matthew 5:14-16 Light

"You are the light of the world. A town built on a hill cannot be hidden. Neither do people light a lamp and put it under a bowl. Instead, they put it on its stand, and it gives light to everyone in the house. In the same way, let your light shine before others, so that they may see your good deeds and glorify your Father in heaven. (NIV)

Light

There is a song I sang as a child. "This little light of mine, I'm gonna let it shine. Hide it under a bush, no, no. I'm gonna let it shine. Won't let Satan blow it out. Let it shine til Jesus comes." Those are some of the words of the song. It is based on the above verses. Our light is the love of Jesus within us through His Holy Spirit. God's love shines through all who love Him and serve Him, following His precepts. Many things can keep our God's light in us from shining on others. We can be too busy and too involved in our own little world, we can be too distracted, we can be disobeying His Word, we can be out of fellowship with God, and many other reasons. We must remember our purpose on this earth. We are to love God with all our heart, mind, and strength and our neighbor as ourselves. When we do this His light shines through us. Our question is where are our hearts, our minds, and our eyes? Are we loving, fellowshipping, and looking to God and others or are we looking to ourselves? Let's be sure we allow God's light to shine in and through us.

Matthew 5:17-20 The Law

"Do not think that I have come to abolish the Law or the Prophets; I have not come to abolish them but to fulfill them. For truly I tell you, until heaven and earth disappear, not the smallest letter, not the least stroke of a pen, will by any means disappear from the Law until everything is accomplished. Therefore, anyone who sets aside one of the least of these commands and teaches others accordingly will be called least in the kingdom of heaven, but whoever practices and teaches these commands will be called great in the kingdom of heaven. For I tell you that unless your righteousness surpasses that of the Pharisees and the teachers of the law, you will certainly not enter the kingdom of heaven. (NIV)

The Law

No man can obey all the laws in the Old Testament that God gave through the prophets. Even if someone could, they are still unrighteous because only Jesus is righteous. It is only through the cross and through Jesus and God's grace that forgiveness can be given and eternal life in heaven with God be given. When Jesus was on the cross, He said, "It is finished." We are no longer under the law to be forgiven. No longer do we have to sacrifice an animal for the blood offering for our sin. The blood of Jesus is the final sacrifice for sin. We do live by the law because of our love for God. The law and the words of Jesus show us how God designed us to live but it is His grace and the acceptance of Jesus as our Lord and Savior and the shedding of His blood that gives us forgiveness and eternal life. We must ask if we are striving to be good to get into heaven or if are we striving to be good because we love God. Let us study all the words of Jesus and put the first two commandments (love the Lord God with all our heart, mind, and strength and our neighbor as ourselves) deep into our minds and hearts and all else will follow.

Matthew 5:21-24 Anger

"You have heard that it was said to the people long ago, 'You shall not murder, and anyone who murders will be subject to judgment.' But I tell you that anyone who is angry with a brother or sister will be subject to judgment. Again, anyone who says to a brother or sister, 'Raca,' is answerable to the court. And anyone who says, 'You fool!' will be in danger of the fire of hell. "Therefore, if you are offering your gift at the altar and there remember that your brother or sister has something against you, leave your gift there in front of the altar. First go and be reconciled to them; then come and offer your gift. (NIV)

Anger

Jesus equated anger and murder together. When we display anger towards someone, we are murdering their spirit. This anger is not the righteous anger Jesus had when He turned over the money tables in the temple. His anger was directed against the tables and what they represented, not the people. When we are angry with someone, we tend to say derogatory things to them. These things can penetrate their spirit. If we are harboring anger against someone our gift of praise or tithe is unacceptable to God for while we carry anger, we are out of fellowship with Him. We are to make peace before we can get back into fellowship with God. Anger usually comes from our pride. We don't like to be wrong. We want what we want when we want it. Let us be sure we recognize anger quickly, deal with it immediately, and stay in fellowship with God and with those around us.

Matthew 5:27-30 Lust

"You have heard that it was said, 'You shall not commit adultery.' But I tell you that anyone who looks at a woman lustfully has already committed adultery with her in his heart. If your right eye causes you to stumble, gouge it out and throw it away. It is better for you to lose one part of your body than for your whole body to be thrown into hell. And if your right hand causes you to stumble, cut it off and throw it away. It is better for you to lose one part of your body than for your whole body to go into hell. (NIV)

Lust

Jesus didn't mean literally to cut off our hands or gouge out our eyes. What He was telling us is, that in any area we are tempted, stay away from that area. If we are tempted to adultery, we avoid being in any situation where that would be possible. If we are tempted to get drunk, we avoid drinking alcohol. If we are tempted to steal someone else's money, we don't touch anybody's money. We know our desires. We know what God's word says about these desires. If our desire would separate our fellowship with God, we stay away from that desire and fill it with something else. Gouging out our eye means not letting our eye wander where it shouldn't. Cutting off our hands means only putting our hands where they will glorify God. No, that doesn't mean our hands can't do menial chores. We still must do dishes and take out the garbage. We don't use our hands to hurt others or take things from others. We do use them to give to others. The essence of what Jesus said is in all we see and do, let it be to glorify God.

Matthew 5:33-37 Oaths

"Again, you have heard that it was said to the people long ago, 'Do not break your oath, but fulfill to the Lord the vows you have made.' But I tell you, do not swear an oath at all: either by heaven, for it is God's throne; or by the earth, for it is his footstool; or by Jerusalem, for it is the city of the Great King. And do not swear by your head, for you cannot make even one hair white or black. All you need to say is simply 'Yes' or 'No'; anything beyond this comes from the evil one (NIV)

Oaths

How many times has someone asked us to pray for them and we said yes then we forgot? Saying yes is the same as a promise and Jesus says we are not to break our promises. I've learned, that when someone asks me to pray for them, I do it with them right away. Then, when or if I remember later, I pray for them again. We are to be true to our yeses. We are also to be true to our nos. How many times have we told God we would not do a certain thing anymore and then we do it? We need to be careful with our nos as well as our yeses. It comes down to asking God before we say either yes or no.

Matthew 5:39-40 Turn the Other Cheek

But I tell you, do not resist an evil person. If anyone slaps you on the right cheek, turn to them the other cheek also (NIV)

Turn the Other Cheek

We've all been hearing our politicians in a name-calling contest. It seems when one calls another a derogatory name the other will try to call a more derogatory name and they go back and forth. Jesus set the example for us when He kept His mouth shut in front of Pilot. Trying to pay tit for tat doesn't get us anywhere but deeper in the mire. How do we keep from doing this to each other? We must remember we are not perfect nor are we the only ones with the right answer. We must remember that all of us are loved by God, and we should choose to love one another. But the attitude of wanting to get even with someone who's hurt or offended us doesn't start with the mouth. It starts with our thoughts. As soon as a negative thought enters our mind, we are to ask God's forgiveness and ask the Holy Spirit to help us replace that negative thought with one that will build up the other person rather than tear him down. Saying something good and positive to someone angry or hurtful is like putting water in a hot coal. Let us learn to water hot tempers with the love of Jesus.

Matthew 5:43-47 Love Enemies

"You have heard that it was said, 'Love your neighbor and hate your enemy.' But I tell you, love your enemies and pray for those who persecute you, that you may be children of your Father in heaven. He causes his sun to rise on the evil and the good and sends rain on the righteous and the unrighteous. If you love those who love you, what reward will you get? Are not even the tax collectors doing that? And if you greet only your own people, what are you doing more than others? Do not even pagans do that? (NIV)

Love Enemies

I spent several months visiting almost all the churches in my area. I was looking to see what God was being allowed to do and not allowed to do in the various churches. I found out a lot. The big churches had their official greeters, so I was greeted at the door. Yet, even when the congregation was asked to shake the hands of those around them, I found their backs turned to me as they were shaking and talking to their friends. The little churches had no official greater and, sad to say, most of them had no interest in welcoming a stranger except for the minister. There was one church, a small church where I was the only one of my race. Every person in that church came and welcomed me before the service then every person spoke to me and invited me back after the service. I'm sure none of the churches considered me to be an enemy. If they had a hard time welcoming a stranger coming into their church on a Sunday for the worship service, how would they obey the above verses? The word love in these verses comes from the word "agape." This is not an emotional love but a love that wants God's best for others. But we are God's hands, feet, and mouth on this earth, and it is up to us to communicate God's love to ALL we meet. Their race, gender, age, social status, profession, or even religion doesn't change our responsibility. God's desire is for all mankind to know and accept His love. We must ask ourselves if we are being a good channel for His love.

Matthew 5:48 Perfect

Be perfect, therefore, as your heavenly Father is perfect (NIV)

Perfect

Another translation for the word perfect comes from purpose. We are to live our lives with purpose. Our purpose should prevail in all parts of our life. Our purpose is to fellowship with God and through that fellowship shine His love and demonstrate His love to those around us. Being perfect, or singleness of purpose, doesn't mean we won't sin. It means our eyes and minds and hearts are focused on God and our purpose. It means when we slip up, we immediately confess and move on following our purpose with God. Our question is, do we desire to follow our purpose? Let's take some time checking the different areas of our lives and seeing when we are following our purpose or when our minds and hearts are elsewhere.

Matthew 6:1 Show-Off

"Be careful not to practice your righteousness in front of others to be seen by them. If you do, you will have no reward from your Father in heaven (NIV)

Show-Off

There was a time, early in my walk with Christ, when I put money in the collection plate, I put it in a way that the amount would show. I was proud of how much I was giving. That wasn't a gift to God. It was a prideful boast of how much better I was than those around me. That attitude by itself was enough to make everyone else around me much better than me. Shakespeare said, "Life is a stage." Our problem is we are playing to the wrong audience. It is God Who is always watching us. He even knows our unspoken thoughts and actions. Knowing this and comparing us with Jesus must lead us to the decision there is no righteousness in us except where we allow God's Holy Spirit to rule. Yes, God's light in us is to be seen by others but not so they see how good or righteous we are but that they see how much God loves them through us and how forgiving He is. Why, when we follow the precepts of God, are we doing so? Is it because it makes us feel more righteous than others or is it because we love God and want to be pleasing to Him? We must answer this question in all areas of our life.

Matthew 6:6 Closet

But when you pray, go into your room, close the door and pray to your Father, who is unseen. Then your Father, who sees what is done in secret, will reward you (NIV)

Closet

Prayer. One of my favorite subjects and favorite things to do. I enjoy talking to God throughout my day, but I also take special time to go into my prayer place and, leaving all possible interruptions away, pray to God. It is important to have a special place where we won't be distracted to talk to our Father. If we are around electronics or see jobs that must be done, we can easily be distracted. Distraction is one of Satan's weapons. He doesn't want us to talk to God, let alone listen to Him. I live in a small park model so don't have a room. I do have a loft that is free of distractions. John Wesley's mother didn't even have that so she would sit in her kitchen chair and pull her apron over her head. This blocked her eyes from distraction and gave a strong message to the children to be quiet and leave her alone while she had her time with her Father. Let us be sure we have a place, free from distractions, where all we do there is pray. It becomes a special place (or small area) and can even be called a "war room" when we do intercession for others.

Matthew 6:8 Needs

Do not be like them, for your Father knows what you need before you ask him. (NIV)

Needs

Wow. God knows everything we need. So, why should we ask for our needs? We ask because we need to give voice to what we consider to be a need. Many things we think we need are not needed. They are wishing and wants. That doesn't mean they're bad or frivolous or something we shouldn't have. It just means we need to consider what we need versus what we just would like to have. When we ask God for our needs we ask, acknowledging that He knows, and He is our provider. We ask in a spirit of thanks that He hears, and He provides. When we ask for our desires, we ask in an attitude of submission to God and His knowledge of timing or even providing such desires. We should never be afraid of asking if we ask in an attitude of submission. Let's continue with our asking, but never omit our thanksgiving.

Matthew 6:7-8 Babbling

And when you pray, do not keep on babbling like pagans, for they think they will be heard because of their many words. (NIV)

Babbling

We've all heard them. People on TV and in churches pray aloud but, instead of talking with God, they are trying to give a message to those around who can hear them. When we pray, we are talking to God. We are not talking to others though we might be praying aloud, and they might be joining us in agreement with our prayer. We are addressing God and not trying to prove a point or give a message to others in the guise of prayer. We talk to God in the same voice we speak to others. We don't need to yell at Him. He can even hear our thoughts so His hearing must be awesome. We don't need to keep repeating His name. He knows His name and knows we are talking to Him. We don't make demands but do speak with faith on His promises recorded in His written word. We don't need to change our language to some formal, old-fashioned words. We just need to talk with Him. Prayer is a two-way conversation. Even in public prayer, we should give Him time to respond to all those who joined their hearts and minds in that prayer. In private prayer, we should give Him even more time to respond to us. Prayer is not just a "give me quick, God" time. Prayer is a conversation between two who love each other. There are times we might speak a quick, "Help me or Help them" prayer but we need special time every day to confirm our love for each other. I have a praise, worship, and prayer group at my house every other week. Whoever has a song in their heart starts it and whoever knows it joins in. Whoever has a word of praise or thanks to God or worship speaks it out. Whoever has a prayer in their heart for our nation or community speaks it out. They only pray a few sentences, and we don't repeat what they pray in our own words because we are all in agreement with their prayer. The one thing we must learn is to pray loud enough for everyone in the group to hear or we can't be unified in agreement. I encourage all of you to think about starting a small group to worship God and pray for our nation. It only takes an hour every so often and, if more of us would do this, God said, "If my people who are called by my name would humble themselves and pray, I will heal their land." Let us do our part and God will heal our land.

Matthew 6:9 Adoration

"This, then, is how you should pray (NIV)

Adoration

Please notice one three-letter word. How. Jesus gave us this prayer as an example of "how" to pray. Though there is nothing wrong with reciting this prayer word for word, the intention was for it to be an example of what we should include in our prayers. As we read verses 9 through 13, we notice it begins with an address. "Our Father." This tells us we are to pray to God, the Father. It also reminds us that we aren't God's only child. We have siblings. Next is "in heaven." Reminding us of where our Father is and where our home is since our home is with our Father. "Hallowed be your name" means His name is Holy. Here, after the address, is the praise and worship. We are acknowledging God our Father is Holy. We adore Him. We will continue with the remaining verses tomorrow. Right now, we must ask ourselves if we start our prayers with addressing God, our Father, and if we go into adoration or if we just start with our wants and needs.

Matthew 6:10 Kingdom

your kingdom come, your will be done, on earth as it is in heaven (NIV)

Kingdom

God's kingdom is righteousness, peace, and joy. When we ask God's Son, Jesus, into our hearts, minds and lives to be our Savior and the Lord of our lives, God's kingdom comes into us in the form of the righteousness of Jesus and the peace and joy given us through God's Holy Spirit. When we have His kingdom in us, we want His will done. His will is always done in heaven without question. We want it done the same way on earth. We must ask ourselves if we really want His will done His way on earth or are we trying to bargain with Him to have things go our way. Let's take some time to ask Him to show us areas where we are blocking His will from being done in us just as perfectly as His will is done in heaven.

Matthew 6:11 Daily Bread

Give us today our daily bread. (NIV)

Daily Bread

Give us. We must remember all we have is a gift from God. That includes the air we breathe. It is only because of the grace of God we can take our next breath. We are asking Him for "daily" bread. We are asking for the day. He has told us not to worry about tomorrow and to leave the past behind. It is for this day that we are to pray, and it is for this day that He provides. "Bread." This is more than the physical food we need to eat to nourish our fleshly bodies. Jesus said He is the "Bread of Life." We are to eat from Him every day. We do this through His written word, The Holy Bible, and His Holy Spirit by listening and responding to His voice. We are asking God to give us the ability to hear, receive, and consume Him and all He has for us on this day. We must ask ourselves do we know what we are asking, and do we want to do our part in the receiving of our request.

Matthew 6:12 Debts

And forgive us our debts, as we also have forgiven our debtors (NIV)

Debts

Debts are not limited to financial debts. Many translations use the word "trespasses." In God's eyes, they are called "sins." We are asking God to forgive our sins. This is a daily task as I doubt any of us ever go a day without sin whether it be in thought or action or non-action. The biggest word in this verse is "as." Yes, it's only two letters but on this word, hangs our forgiveness from God. There are three things necessary for His forgiveness. We can only receive it through God's Son, Jesus. Without going through Him as God's only Son and our Lord and Savior there is no forgiveness.

Next, we must acknowledge and confess our sins to God. This isn't for God's benefit. He knows our sins. This is for our benefit in knowing what it is we did, thought, or didn't do so we can repent, that is turn away from and not redo it again.

The third is probably the hardest for many of us. We must forgive the sins, the hurts and things done to or not done to us by others in the same way God forgives us. This means we don't hold it over their heads anymore. We don't bring it up again. We want God's best for them. We must remember that forgiveness is a choice, not an emotion. We choose to forgive and with time and prayer, emotions might follow later. Someone asked me if that means we must trust the person. Trust is something that must be earned. Forgiveness is given freely. We are told when we partake in communion (eating of the bread and drinking of the cup in remembrance of the death of Jesus for our sins.) we are not to do it if there is unforgiveness in our hearts. Let's get into the practice of what I call spiritual breathing. Exhale sin and unforgiveness and inhale forgiveness every day.

Matthew 6:13 Temptation

And lead us not into temptation but deliver us from the evil one. (NIV)

James 1:13: "Let no one say when he is tempted, I'm being tempted by God, for God cannot be tempted by evil and He Himself doesn't tempt anyone."

Temptation

I added James 1:13 to assure everyone that it is not God Who leads us into temptation. We live in a world surrounded by temptation. It assaults us from every direction by sight and by sound. We are acknowledging our weakness to withstand temptation and asking God to be sure to lead us away from giving in to temptation. It is only through the power of God that we can be delivered from evil. But, when we pray this, we must understand our part. It is our responsibility to avoid what we know would be a great temptation for us. When we are on a diet of no sugar, we don't buy sugar products in a grocery store and bring them into our house. If we are an alcoholic, we don't go into a bar. We are asking God to reveal the weak areas in us and protect us from giving in to those temptations. We ask Him to deliver us from those temptations. Let us remember every promise God has made has a condition we must meet. To be forgiven we must confess and forgive, to be delivered from temptation, we must be willing to submit to the precepts of God.

Matthew 6:16 When We Fast

"When you fast, do not look somber as the hypocrites do, for they disfigure their faces to show others they are fasting. Truly I tell you, they have received their reward in full. (NIV)

When We Fast

Fasting is a spiritual practice. It is a time between the one fasting and God. It is to separate us from whatever we are fasting to concentrate more on God. There are several types of fasting. It is not always food. We can fast from an activity and replace the time on that activity with more Bible study or prayer. When we fast from food there are many ways of doing this. It can be for a particular meal or all day or several days. It can include all food or certain types of food. However, we fast, it must be to use that time to put our minds and hearts more attuned to God. It is not something to boast about. It is a private time encouraging discipline, humility, and a desire to draw closer to God. The most important word in this verse is "When." It doesn't say "If." Fasting should be a part of our meditation with God at whatever interval He leads us. When we find ourselves going through a dry period it is a good indication that we need a time of fasting. We must be sure that we replace whatever we are giving up with worship, praise, Bible study prayer and/or meditation.

Matthew 6:19-21 Treasures

"Do not store up for yourselves treasures on earth, where moths and vermin destroy, and where thieves break in and steal. But store up for yourselves treasures in heaven, where moths and vermin do not destroy, and where thieves do not break in and steal. For where your treasure is, there your heart will be also (NIV)

Treasures

Many confess Jesus as Lord and Savior, but their actions tell the truth. What is it we hang on to? For many, it's money. If we don't tithe, we are stealing God's money because the tithe (10% of our money) belongs to Him for His use. Then we are to give offerings. How many times do we see someone in need, and we just walk by as if we don't see? Our closets also tell a story. My rule is if I haven't worn it in a year, I don't need it but someone else does. Many conduct garage sales because they want as much money as they can get for the items they no longer want or need. Then they keep the money for themselves, not even tithing a portion of it. All those items we no longer need are needed by people who can't pay anything for them. Another treasure many store up is their time. We tend to forget all our time is a gift from God. He wants us to share our time with those around us. It might be a visit to a nursing home or taking food to a sick friend. Our treasures are what come first into our hearts and minds. Scripture tells us to let all we do be done as to God. Let's ask ourselves if what we are doing today will put a smile on our God's face today.

Matthew 6:24 Which Master

"No one can serve two masters. Either you will hate the one and love the other, or you will be devoted to the one and despise the other. You cannot serve both God and money (NIV)

Which Master

When we think about what or who is number one in our lives, we must look at how we spend our time. What or who is our priority? We must work at a job 40 hours a week and we have family needs to attend which takes time. But our attitude in doing it tells a lot.

In Colossians 3:23 we read "And whatsoever ye do, do it heartily, as to the Lord, and not unto men." We can go to work because we want power or money, or we can go to work as a vessel for God's provision for those around us. We can care for our family's needs from obligation, or we can care for them because God has entrusted them to us. We can spend our free time pursuing our fleshly desires or we can spend our free time worshiping, serving, and learning more about God. Let us reflect on where God is in our life.

Matthew 6:25-27 Worry

"Therefore, I tell you, do not worry about your life, what you will eat or drink; or about your body, what you will wear. Is not life more than food, and the body more than clothes? Look at the birds of the air; they do not sow or reap or store away in barns, and yet your heavenly Father feeds them. Are you not much more valuable than they? Can any one of you by worrying add a single hour to your life? (NIV)

Worry

Worry. My mother-in-law said if there wasn't something to worry about, she would make something up. She equated worrying about someone meant you were showing them you loved them. Worry shows a lack of trust that God is in control of our lives. God says nothing can touch us without first passing through His hand. He also says for us to rejoice in Him through all situations and to be content in all things. When we worry, we are negating God's love. Worry and concern are different. Worrying produces anxiety. Concern produces prayer. When we find ourselves starting to worry, we need to turn immediately to prayer. We need to confess our lack of trust in God over the situation and ask God to increase our faith and trust in Him. God is faithful. God holds us in the palm of His hand. In God's love, there is nothing to fear. Thank Him today for His faithfulness.

Matthew 6:33 Seeking

But seek first his kingdom and his righteousness, and all these things will be given to you as well (NIV)

Seeking

This has been one of my major guiding verses. It's among the first few verses I memorized. Jesus said the kingdom of God is within us when we accept Him into our hearts, minds, and lives as our Lord and Savior. Since His kingdom is within us, we must make every endeavor to seek it, nurture it, and let it grow more and more within us. We do this through worship, prayer, meditation, and studying the Holy Bible. We are also to seek the righteousness of Jesus. Jesus is righteousness. We seek His righteousness the same way we seek the kingdom of God. These are first in our hearts, minds, and lives. Everything else will fall into order if we keep God as our priority. Our question is, what are we most seeking? Let's take some time out today to check our priorities.

Matthew 7:1-2 Judgements

"Do not judge, or you too will be judged. For in the same way, you judge others, you will be judged, and with the measure you use, it will be measured to you. (NIV)

Judgments

This is a hard one. We are raised to judge our actions and the actions of others. That leads us to judge others by what we perceive are their actions. Over the years of practicing judging others, we tend to become even more judgmental. We may not meet the standards we hold for ourselves, but we don't like when others don't meet our standards. Not only do they need to meet our standards, but we also expect them to do it in the same way we would. This verse tells us our attitude of judgment will be mirrored back to us. Now, if we look at it from another standpoint, if our measure is replacing love for judgment, it is that same love that comes back to us. I have long quoted to myself that when I find myself becoming judgmental, I say, "There but for the grace of God go I." We seldom know what is behind a person's behavior. We are to judge by the scriptures on right or wrong, but it is the act we are to judge, not the person doing the act. We are to pray for the person doing the wrong act. The only way we can do this is through the power of God's Holy Spirit. Let's try to make a habit of asking God to love others through us and keep our judgments to the actions, not the people.

Matthew 7:7-8 Knocking

"Ask and it will be given to you; seek and you will find; knock and the door will be opened to you. For everyone who asks receives; the one who seeks finds; and to the one who knocks, the door will be opened (NIV)

Knocking

What is it we are to ask? We went over that in the Lord's Prayer. But after we ask, we must seek it. To seek means to look for the answer. So many times, the answer is looking for us in the face, but we don't see it because we are looking for a preconceived answer. When we think we've found what we are seeking we must knock on the door to see if it is an open door. That means we don't force our way into the answer.

My husband and I learned this the hard way. We were determined that a particular house was the one we were to buy and did some very creative financing to get it. We forced the sale through. When we had to sell, it took 4 years and set us back financially for quite a while. When we ask, we are to ask in a way that accepts the answer that God is providing for us in His way and His time. We must check to see what we have been asking, what our attitude is in asking, and what our preconceived answer is and give it all to God.

Matthew 7:12 Golden Rule

So, in everything, do to others what you would have them do to you, for this sums up the Law and the Prophets. (NIV)

Golden Rule

This verse is known as the "Golden Rule." We must notice it says, "what you would have them do to you." It doesn't say what they have done to you. So often we want to retaliate. We see this in the political scene with the name-calling. It seems to be a contest on who can call the worst name last. We also see this at Christmas in a competition of outgiving the other. We forget the reason for all our words and actions is love. This love is God's love. It is a love that wants God's best for others. We do not know what anyone else wants. They may not like what we want or how we want to be treated. But, as followers of Jesus and having God's Holy Spirit inside us to guide us, we can pray before we speak or act and ask Him what it is we are to say or do. We must notice this verse starts with "So in everything." There are no exceptions to our words or actions. All must be in line with God's love, not only for us but for others. We must ask God to show us the areas and/or the people where we have not been doing this, ask for forgiveness and repent and make the correct changes in our words and/or actions with the ones He reveals to us.

Matthew 7:13-14 Narrow Gate

"Enter through the narrow gate. For wide is the gate and broad is the road that leads to destruction, and many enter through it. But small is the gate and narrow the road that leads to life, and only a few find it. (NIV)

Narrow Gate

So many people think they can approach God and go to heaven by being good. They think there are many different roads to the same place. They are partly right. There are many different roads to eternal hell but there is only one road to heaven. That road must go through the cross of Jesus Christ, God's only begotten Son, who was and is the Word through Whom God created all that is or will ever be. People think because God is love that He will welcome all good people into His home in heaven. God is love. Because He loves us, He did provide a way into His home in heaven. He sent His Word, His Son, Jesus Christ, to take our place and die for the penalty of our sins so we can become righteous through the righteousness of Jesus and be able to stand in the presence of God. Sin cannot stand before God for God is without sin. This is the purest form of love. A love that wants the best for us in our lives on this earth and throughout eternity in His home. All are invited to walk through that one gate. Unfortunately, not all will want to walk that gate. It is up to us to help as many as possible find this one gate and help them enter and be with God throughout eternity. Our question is, are we living up to our responsibility?

Matthew 7:16 Fruits

By their fruit you will recognize them (NIV)

Galatians 5:22-23 But the fruit of the Spirit is love, joy, peace, forbearance, kindness, goodness, faithfulness, gentleness, and self-control. (NIV)

Fruits

Though this verse in Matthew is referring to recognizing false prophets by their fruit, it means their fruit is not the fruit of the Spirit quoted in Galatians. We must consider ourselves. What fruit do people see in us? We need to look at each one of these fruits with a nakedly honest attitude and see what fruit we have not permitted to grow in us. We are given the bud of each of these fruits when we receive God's Holy Spirit. All buds must be nourished to grow. We nourish through the studying and meditation on the Word of God (The Holy Bible) and through our conversational prayer with God. Then we must practice the fruit which is the digesting process. We don't like being that honest with ourselves but to grow the fruit God's Spirit has given us, we must look honestly. This does not mean hyper-critically. Putting ourselves down doesn't help. We must view this as a learning and growing process. We can't work on all the fruits at once so let's ask God to show us which one we need to work on first. It helps to memorize these two verses in Galatians so we can use it as a guide as we walk out our days. Just remember the first fruit is love and we must love ourselves as we look honestly at our weaknesses. After all, God loves us so who are we not to love the one God loves.

Matthew 7:21 Lord

"Not everyone who says to me, 'Lord, Lord,' will enter the kingdom of heaven, but only the one who does the will of my Father who is in heaven (NIV)

Lord

Many today call themselves Christians but, as we read yesterday, their fruits don't confirm it. They have had to take many verses out of the Bible for they choose not to obey them. We can't choose which of God's commands for living we will follow and which ones we will claim are not for today. God doesn't change, nor do His commands. They think, because God is love, it is okay for them to continue to walk in sin because it is no longer sin today and if it were, God would forgive them anyway. There is no need for repentance (turning away from the sin) as God's forgiveness doesn't require it from them because of His love. It is so sad that they are so deceived by the desires of the flesh and the changes in culture. Those who do their best to obey the will of the Father must pray for and set an example for and speak in love to those who have changed the rules of daily living as recorded in the Holy Bible. We must ask ourselves if there are rules of God we have chosen not to follow. If so, we must confess, repent, and ask the Holy Spirit to lead us away from that path and stand strong in obedience.

Matthew 7:24 Practice

"Therefore, everyone who hears these words of mine and puts them into practice is like a wise man who built his house on the rock (NIV)

Practice

Do we hear the words of Jesus as we read the Bible? When we read, do we read to really hear and understand and let the words really sink into our mind and heart? Are we as eager to hear His words as we were when we first realized we were in love with someone? If so, are we putting those words we are hearing into practice? Practice means to keep going over and over until it becomes natural. When I first started piano lessons, I had to learn my scales. I had to play them over and over until I could play them without even thinking about them. Have we made the words spoken by Jesus so much a part of ourselves that we can and do follow them as a natural part of who we are? This is our goal. This should be our hearts desire. Jesus prayed for us to become one in Him as He is One with the Father. I pray you want this as much as I do.

Help us Holy Spirit to desire, to hear, to practice and to become One.

Matthew 8:2-3 Reach Out

A man with leprosy came and knelt before him and said, "Lord, if you are willing, you can make me clean." Jesus reached out his hand and touched the man. "I am willing," he said. "Be clean!" (NIV)

Reach Out

Jesus is still willing. Not only to heal our physical ailments but to clean us from sin. All we need do is ask Him. But when we ask, we must be willing to receive. He also wants to heal others through our touch. He is not physically on this earth and has given us His Holy Spirit and the power within for us to reach our hands out and touch others. Our touch is to connect them with His Spirit and bring healing, both physical, emotional, and spiritual. Our question must be, are we reaching out to others? What are we communicating to them with our touch? Jesus communicated love and wholeness. Let us do likewise.

Matthew 8:13 Believe It

Then Jesus said to the centurion, "Go! Let it be done just as you believed it would." (NIV)

Believe It

Jesus still says that to us today. Go and it will happen just as we believe it will. Our question is, what do we believe? When we pray and ask for something, what is really in our hearts and minds about the answer? When we lived in Florida near the beach, we had a group of college students who wanted to be baptized. It was the boys who wanted this. We took them to the beach, and it was a storm surge, which means very big and frequent waves. They were baptized several times before they waded out far enough to be officially baptized. There were several older men on the beach who, individually and quietly were praying for the waves to be still as Jesus commanded on the lake. That did not happen. On the way to our house, the girls in the group decided they wanted to be baptized also. I always kept several swimsuits of various sizes in the house for such an occasion. While the girls were getting dressed, the older men said what they were each praying and wondering why it didn't happen. They were asked, "Did you speak out loud in faith?" The answer was no. They were afraid it wouldn't happen and didn't want to be embarrassed. That is why it didn't happen. When we took the girls to the beach the men spoke in unison out loud, "Ocean, be still." There was a half-circle surrounding the girls that followed them out that was like glass. The girls were baptized in the stillness with the storm surge surrounding the half circle. As they walked back to the beach the storm surge followed behind them. We must learn to speak the commands of God in the same boldness and faith Jesus spoke.

Matthew 8:8 Humility

The centurion replied, "Lord, I do not deserve to have you come under my roof. But just say the word, and my servant will be healed (NIV)

Humility

The prayer of faith is a wonderful thing. It can travel miles and miles to any location without the person praying to travel with it. The fuel it uses to travel is the assurance of faith. But the one with the faith must recognize it is not themselves, their righteousness, their power, or anything about them that fulfills the prayer of faith. It is only the righteousness of Jesus and the power grace and mercy of God that fulfills the prayer. We do not deserve such grace and mercy. It is given to us by the pure love of God through His Son, Jesus. Our faith must be based on true humility of the recognition of our sinfulness and God's righteousness. There is a big difference between a prayer being spoken in the boldness of a humble faith and one being spoken in the boldness of pride. We must continually examine ourselves and be sure we remain truly humble.

Matthew 8:14-15 Touching

When Jesus came into Peter's house, he saw Peter's mother-in-law lying in bed with a fever. He touched her hand, and the fever left her, and she got up and began to wait on him (NIV)

Touching

There are many truths in these two verses. One is that it is fine to be married and in ministry. Peter was married and Jesus healed Peter's mother-in-law. The next is touching. There is a lot of communication in the simple touch of a hand. Touch can communicate love, caring, acceptance and through healing, and comfort. I am a volunteer chaplain at our regional hospital. When I pray for the sick, I hold their hand. This communicates peace and comfort. Another truth in these verses is after healing comes serving Jesus. We are not healed for our comfort but to continue in the service of our God, praising, worshiping, and thanking Him as we communicate His love, peace, and healing to others. This is how we serve our God, through serving others. As we walk through this day, we must ask God to show us who we are to serve in serving Him this day.

Matthew 8:22 Follow Me

But Jesus told him, "Follow me, and let the dead bury their own dead." (NIV)

Follow Me

Jesus wasn't being harsh or insensitive. He was giving a lesson in priorities of the heart. In this case and the one in the verses just before, this is where the scribe says he wants to follow Jesus but is told there is no permanent housing and the scribe turns away, Jesus is telling us God comes before everything else. If we are faithful in our obedience and devotion to God, if we put Him first place in our hearts and minds, all else will fall into place. These men wanted to do it backward. They wanted to see everything in the place they desired before they followed Jesus in devotion and obedience.

We must ask ourselves daily if we are truly putting God first or our fleshly desires first. Some want into public ministry and boast of their service to God because they want to appear great and knowledgeable about God. We can spot them easily. Our desire for service to God, whether it be publicly displayed to thousands or privately centered on a few is only as real as our heart desiring it purely for the pleasure of God Himself. It is not my concern if any read these devotions. I write them daily because God gives them to me daily and it is good for my growth and obedience. It is up to God if others are blessed through them. This is our attitude in ministry and all we do. Scripture tells us in everything we do, do it as unto the Lord. We must continually remind ourselves of this and remain humble and obedient to our Lord God.

Matthew 8:26 Faith

He replied, "You of little faith, why are you so afraid?"
Then he got up and rebuked the winds and the waves, and
it was completely calm (NIV)

Faith

God does not give us a spirit of fear but a spirit of peace and a
sound mind. When the storms of life hit us, when we are about to
stress, what is it we do? Do we go to God in prayer and ask Him
for direction or do we allow fear or stress to consume us? Do we
believe God will work all things out for good or are we short-sighted
and only seeing the storm without seeing God's hand? Fear is only
present when we allow faith to falter. There is an old hymn that goes,
"Be not dismayed what ere betide, God will take care of you." No
matter what we must face in life on this earth, God has promised
never to leave or forsake us. He is true to His promise. Our problem
is, we must look with the spiritual eyes He gives us and stand firm
on the faith. Faith grows with exercise. Times of storms are a good
time for exercising that faith. We must ask ourselves how our exercise
routine is doing.

Matthew 8:34 Demons

Then the whole town went out to meet Jesus. And when they saw him, they pleaded with him to leave their region (NIV)

Demons

Many people think there is no such thing as a demon. Look at all the mass shootings. There are many demons in this world: demons of alcohol, demons of drugs, demons of hate, and on and on. As children of God, we are given the power to resist these demons. When they put a thought of temptation in us, we need to boldly speak the word, "Go" just as Jesus did. But these demons become comfortable if we allow them into us. The town had comfortable demons and didn't like being broken from them. We must stand our ground against all demons. If we stay in the Word of God and keep our communication with God through His Holy Spirit, our hearts and minds will be full without room for demons to enter. Let us continually guard our minds with God's Word deeply rooted.

Matthew 9:6 Take Up Your Mat

But I want you to know that the Son of Man has authority on earth to forgive sins." So he said to the paralyzed man, "Get up, take your mat, and go home." (NIV)

Take Up Your Mat

Being in a state of unforgiveness can paralyze us. If we are feeling unforgiven or if we are unforgiving of others, it has the same effect on us. Jesus spoke forgiveness and told the paralyzed man to pick up his mat and go home. He was telling the man to get on with his life and fulfill the responsibilities God had given him. We are to confess our sins, accept the forgiveness of God, and forgive others so we can pick up and move on with God giving Him the freedom to work through us. When we feel paralyzed, that is unable to follow through on something God has asked us to do, we must confess both our sins and be sure we aren't harboring unforgiveness to someone else. Sin paralyzes and unforgiveness is a sin. Let us learn to keep short accounts with God and to be quick in forgiving others. Clean slates serve better.

Matthew 9:13 Mercy and Judgement

But go and learn what this means: 'I desire mercy, not sacrifice.' (NIV)

Mercy and Judgment

When we are trying to live a life of obedience to God's precepts, we tend to become judgmental of those who don't appear to be trying to live that way. Instead of just not condoning their actions, we judge the person. Jesus didn't judge the person and He had every right to do so. Instead, He showed mercy, led them to turn away from their actions, and encouraged them to follow His way. How much more peaceful this world would be if, instead of sitting, thinking, and speaking in judgment we showed mercy to the person we have been judging. Showing mercy is not the same thing as agreeing with the action. Showing mercy is accepting the person as one who is loved by God and setting an example both of God's love and acceptance of the individual while showing the joy of following the precepts of God. Let us quit pointing our fingers and saying harsh and judgmental words and encourage others by accepting them as people of value and showing them the love and joy that is available when following the precepts of God.

Matthew 9:15-16 Smile

Jesus answered, "How can the guests of the bridegroom mourn while he is with them? The time will come when the bridegroom will be taken from them; then they will fast (NIV)

Smile

I've written several devotions on fasting. Fasting is an important part of our spiritual exercise. Many people think they must be gloomy to show how spiritual they are. We have the gift of Jesus with us in the Holy Spirit and that is more than enough to be rejoicing. There are times too fast. There are many ways to fast. We must not neglect them. But we must be sure to let others see the joy of our Lord in us. I was won to Jesus by a lady's smile. It's amazing what a smile can do for someone. Let us be sure we aren't walking around with a glum expression or a frown. When we must wait in a long line what are we displaying? Displaying displeasure or impatience doesn't communicate the joy of Jesus Who is with and in us. Let us show His joy so much to make others ask why we are so happy, and we can share God's love with others.

Matthew 9:24 Sleeping or Awake

He said, "Go away. The girl is not dead but asleep." But they laughed at him. (NIV)

Sleeping or Awake

There are several types of death. Yes, there is a physical death. There is also an emotional and a spiritual death. Though I was raised in a church, worked in a church, and claimed to be a Christian, I was spiritually dead. I didn't understand the difference between believing Jesus is the Son of God (Satan knows that.) and believing IN Jesus, the Son of God, as my Savior and my Lord. The day I realized that (another story too long for this) I felt Jesus touch me. It only takes one touch from Him to heal and bring someone back to life. My emotions were healed, and my spirit was brought back from death to life. To me, this is more important than my physical death because as a child of God through His Son, Jesus, my body will die but I will live in His very real presence for all eternity. So many people are spiritually dead. So many people in churches who call themselves Christians are spiritually asleep. We must ask ourselves if we've allowed Jesus to touch us and if we are fully awake.

Matthew 9:29 Belief

Then he touched their eyes and said, "According to your faith let it be done to you" (NIV)

Belief

Wow. What's done to us is according to our faith. If we believe we're a failure, we will fail. If we believe we cannot do something, we won't be able to. If we believe we can do anything through Christ, we will be able to do anything. What we believe we think and what we think about becomes part of us. We are told to think about whatever is lovely or of good repute. We are told this for a very good reason. We are what we think. Likewise, God does for and in us what we allow Him to do if we believe He'll do it. Believing is a choice, not an emotion. We can choose to believe or choose to doubt. We must ask ourselves what it is we have chosen to believe. If we find our belief vacillates, we must pray for help to stand firm. Let us be careful in our choice of what to believe and make sure our beliefs are founded on the written Word of God.

Matthew 9:37-38 Harvest

Then he said to his disciples, "The harvest is plentiful, but the workers are few. Ask the Lord of the harvest, therefore, to send out workers into his harvest field."

Harvest

Time is getting shorter every day. We don't know what day Jesus will come for His Bride (those who believe in Him and follow Him). We do know it is not God's will that one soul should be lost. We who do believe and claim to follow are the ones God calls to work. There are so very many lost souls around us, even in our churches. They need harvesting. That means they need to hear about Jesus from our mouths and see Jesus in our faces and through our actions. We must ask ourselves if we are working. How has our harvest been? We are called, but are we answering with action?

Matthew 10:6-7 Go Out

Go rather to the lost sheep of Israel. (NIV)

Go Out

After Jesus appointed His twelve disciples, he told them to go. Not to stay within their group but to go out to those who didn't believe. Early in our walk with God, we realized all our friends and neighbors were believers. We did not know any outside our church family. We decided to take square dancing lessons to meet other people. The first couple we met were from our church. We politely told them it was good to see them but our purpose in coming was to meet people who didn't go to church. As the lessons continued, we were blessed to make relationships with several non-believers and were able to watch as God's Spirit worked through us drawing them into questions and eventually into personal relationships with God through Jesus. We must ask ourselves if we are in church or our church family so much that we aren't out witnessing to those who need to hear God's message.

Matthew 10:32 Acknowledge

"Whoever acknowledges me before others, I will also acknowledge before my Father in heaven. (NIV)

Acknowledge

Acknowledging Jesus before others is not limited to vocal confession. Many people claim to be followers of Jesus. Acknowledging must also be confirmed through our actions. When we are at work, do others see Jesus in our attitude? When we're driving in traffic are we respectful of other drivers? We must acknowledge Jesus in every area of our lives and in every way, we speak, express our feelings, and act. We are quick to judge others for their words or actions that don't give glory to Jesus but what about our actions? It's not only our vocal words or our actions, but our thoughts also as well need to be thoughts that confirm our acknowledgment of Jesus as our Lord and Savior. Lent is one of many good times to check this out. I am giving up judging and critiquing others in my thoughts. I've learned not to do this out loud but it's still in my thought pattern. I'm replacing it with thoughts of others being so loved by God and my wanting His best for them. We must be honest with ourselves and open to hearing God.

Matthew 10:38 Take Up the Cross

Whoever does not take up their cross and follow me is not worthy of me. (NIV)

Take Up the Cross

Jesus is not referring to the cross of the crucifixion. He is referring to self-sacrifice. We are to sacrifice pride. We are to accept whatever He allows to come our way and walk through it in faith and trust. There is an adage, "God didn't promise you a rose garden." I find that adage a little strange. Roses are beautiful and have a beautiful aroma, but they also have thorns that can scratch, pierce, draw blood, and even leave scars. Life is very much like that. When walking with Jesus, life is beautiful. Our praises produce a sweet aroma for God. But as we walk the things that come our way we get scraped, pierced, and scared. However, our scars heal when given to God. Lent is one of many good times for us to remember to "take up our cross" no matter what that is currently. As we take it up let it be in an attitude of worship, praise, and thanksgiving to God that no matter what the cross might be, He will guide and sustain us and through it, we will reflect His beauty and the sweet aroma as our praises unite with Him.

Matthew 10:40-42 Giving Cycle

"Anyone who welcomes you welcomes me, and anyone who welcomes me welcomes the one who sent me. Whoever welcomes a prophet as a prophet will receive a prophet's reward, and whoever welcomes a righteous person as a righteous person will receive a righteous person's reward. And if anyone gives even a cup of cold water to one of these little ones who is my disciple, truly I tell you, that person will certainly not lose their reward. (NIV)

Giving Cycle

These are aspects of hospitality. We are to be welcoming to people and giving and helpful. We do these things not because we will be rewarded, though we will be. We do these things because we love God and His love is in us and needs to pass through us to others. The only way we can get more of God's love in us is to let it pass through us to make more room for more love. It is a circle of through and out and in through and out through all eternity. We can never do enough or give enough because God is all giving and all doing. What is amazing is that He trusts and loves us enough to work through us. This is more than enough reward. It is a joy to experience God blessing someone through us. Let us practice increasing this cycle not only during Lent but every day until it becomes a natural part of our being as we become more and more one in our Lord, Jesus.

Matthew 11:4-6 Hear and See

Jesus replied, "Go back and report to John what you hear and see: The blind receive sight, the lame walk, those who have leprosy are cleansed, the deaf hear, the dead are raised, and the good news is proclaimed to the poor. (NIV)

Hear and See

We are to report to others what we see and hear from God. Miracles through touches from God happen all around us every day. Unfortunately, we are so consumed with things of this world we miss many of them. We even miss things He does in our own lives. We need to ask the help of the Holy Spirit to make us more sensitive to see and hear His workings in, around, and through us and speak of them to others that they will hear and see. God is at work every day. He works in many ways. Some have no explanation, some through others, and some through us. Let us learn to look, see, and hear that we may share.

Matthew 11:19b Wisdom and Deeds

But wisdom is proved right by her deeds." (NIV)

Wisdom and Deeds

Just one question for us to meditate on today. Do our deeds show we have the wisdom of God? It takes stark honesty to look at ourselves and accept the bad with the good. We are to acknowledge where we have gone wrong but love ourselves and trust God enough to forgive us, forgive ourselves, and turn away from the wrong moving on with the wisdom of God to the good. Where are we today and where does God want us?

Matthew 11:24 Day of Judgment

But I tell you that it will be more bearable for Sodom on the day of judgment than for you." (NIV)

Day of Judgment

We've talked about opening our eyes, minds, and hearts to see the miracles surrounding us. Sodom didn't believe in miracles. They only believed in the physical and emotional satisfaction of their lusts and desires. They were judged because of their beliefs. We will face a day of judgment before the throne of God. We will be judged by our beliefs. The only belief that will pass judgment is the belief in Jesus Christ as the Son of God and the Lord of our life in our minds and our hearts. We must ask ourselves if we are truly ready for that judgment. Do we know Jesus intimately, believe all He says, and follow in obedience the life He demonstrated for us? We have an advantage over Sodom. We have the help, comfort, and assurance of His Holy Spirit. Let us not turn away from the Helper Jesus sent to us.

Matthew 11:27-28 Revealed

"All things have been committed to me by my Father. No one knows the Son except the Father, and no one knows the Father except the Son and those to whom the Son chooses to reveal Him. (NIV)

Revealed

It's hard to believe that there are some to whom God doesn't choose to reveal Himself. If you are reading this, you are not one of those. You are one He has chosen to reveal Himself to. Our problem is not looking and listening for that revelation. God wants us to know Him intimately. He created us for intimacy. He reveals Himself to us through His written word (the Bible), through His Son, Jesus, through His Holy Spirit, and through others who know Him intimately. It takes time and communication to know someone intimately. Communication must be two-way. We must talk and we must listen. We must ask ourselves if we want Him to reveal Himself to us. If we do, are we doing our part to get to know Him? Do we talk to Him the first thing when we wake up and the last thing before we sleep? Let's check our hearts and minds to be sure we are open and eager to do all we can to receive all the revelations God wants us to have.

Matthew 11:29-30 Yoked

Take my yoke upon you and learn from me, for I am gentle and humble in heart, and you will find rest for your souls. (NIV)

Yoked

A yoke is a device put on oxen. It holds two oxen together so they can share the load of pulling a wagon. The load is shared equally so as they work together, they have no trouble in pulling the load. Jesus said we can be yoked to Him. If we are yoked to Him, we are pulling our load of life with Him, going in the same direction at the same speed. Yokes don't allow one member of the team to work separately. Yoked with Jesus means we are gentle and humble in heart because He is. It means we are in a state of rest, not stressed or worried about anything because He is right with us keeping us right with Him. As wonderful as being yoked with Jesus is, it amazes me that, along with many others, I sometimes try to free myself from the yoke. I sometimes decide to run ahead, lag, or do it my way. When I do this stress comes into my soul instead of rest. I no longer act gently or humbly. Certain triggers often contribute to our taking ourselves out of the yoke. Lent is only one of many good times to ask the Holy Spirit to reveal to us what contributes to our unyoking, accept, and confess what He reveals to us, and choose to repent, turn the other way, and stay yoked.

Matthew 12:7 Mercy

If you had known what these words mean, 'I desire mercy, not sacrifice,' you would not have condemned the innocent. (NIV)

Mercy

It seems people who consider themselves "religious" are people who would rather judge and condemn rather than show mercy. A wise person once said, "There but for the grace of God go I." I quote that to myself a lot when I find I'm getting impatient with someone. It is so easy to sit in judgment or point fingers at someone who does or says something we consider to be wrong. We tend to forget our sins and the amount of grace God shows us every day. God shows us mercy through forgiveness and showing us and encouraging us to a better way. His grace is a wonderful love gift of underserved mercy. As much as we don't deserve God's mercy, we should give it to others. How can we not show mercy to someone whom God shows mercy? Instead of looking judgmentally or critically let's ask God's Holy Spirit to help us look at others with the mercy He looks at us. Let us show and encourage others to a better way in God's way.

Matthew 12:18 Proclaim

"Here is my servant whom I have chosen, the one I love, in whom I delight; I will put my Spirit on him, and he will proclaim justice to the nations. (NIV)

Proclaim

Many prophecies are for more than one thing. This is about Jesus, but it is also about us, God's children through the blood of Jesus who have been filled with the Holy Spirit. It's hard for us to accept that God delights in us, but He says that many times in His written Word. As His children, we are also His servants, not by demand but by love. We must ask ourselves are we proclaiming justice to all we meet? In proclaiming justice, we proclaim God, for God is just. When we proclaim God, we proclaim His mercy, grace, and love for us. We should never let a day pass without proclaiming justice (God) to someone. Are we doing this?

Matthew 12:25 Division

Jesus knew their thoughts and said to them, "Every kingdom divided against itself will be ruined, and every city or household divided against itself will not stand. (NIV)

Division

Our country is divided against itself. Our churches have division within them. Families have division within them. This is seen in the divorce rate. There is only one thing that can unite any of them. That one thing is the love of God. That love is connected to us through prayer. Love is only realized through communication. We tend to try to solve divisions in our finite wisdom. Divisions can only be solved through God's wisdom and love. Our part is to pray and to ask His Holy Spirit to enable us to show and share God's love. We don't have to agree with each other on the interpretation of various aspects of scripture. Scripture is a living word and says different things to each of us at different times according to our circumstances, relationship with God, and openness to understanding. We only need to agree that Jesus is the Son of God came in the flesh of man to demonstrate God's love and take our sins away; to reunite us with God, the Father through His death and resurrection. Let us demonstrate His love and share His love.

Matthew 12:30 Gather

"Whoever is not with me is against me, and whoever does not gather with me scatters. (NIV)

Gather

Jesus said in Romans 8:17 Now if we are children, then we are heirs—heirs of God and co-heirs with Christ, if indeed we share in his sufferings so that we may also share in his glory. Since we are co-heirs, we must also be co-workers. We have a responsibility to work with Jesus. When He speaks of gathering or scattering, He is talking about the lost sheep, those who don't know Him. We scatter by not showing them the love, grace, and mercy of God. We gather by loving and showing them the grace and mercy of God through our words and our actions. We get so consumed in our own lives that we forget our purpose. We must continually check on ourselves and see if we are a gatherer or a scatterer. Who are you going to talk to about Jesus today?

Matthew 12:33 By Our Fruits

"Make a tree good and its fruit will be good or make a tree bad and its fruit will be bad, for a tree is recognized by its fruit.

But the fruit of the Spirit is love, joy, peace, forbearance, kindness, goodness, faithfulness, gentleness, and self-control. Galatians 5:22-23 (NIV)

By Our Fruits

These are the fruits every child of God should bear. The seeds of these fruits are implanted in us when we accept Jesus as our Lord and Savior and receive His Holy Spirit. The seeds need to be nourished and watered by the Holy Spirit as we read, study, and meditate on the Holy Scriptures and learn to put the fruit into practice in our lives. We must ask ourselves very honestly how we are doing with the growth and use of these fruits. Are we nurturing everyone? If not, which ones are we lacking? Take each one of these fruits in prayer and listen to God as He directs us in how we are doing and encourages us to continue to allow the fruits to grow and flourish in and through us.

Matthew 12:36 Give Account

But I tell you that everyone will have to give account on the day of judgment for every empty word they have spoken. (NIV)

Give Account

This should sober us up. Every word spoken also includes every word thought. It should make us more careful not only about what we say out loud but careful about what thoughts we allow to form and remain in our minds. But along with this verse, we are promised if we confess our sins, He is faithful and just to forgive our sins. Therefore, as we talk to God every night and confess our sins of the day, so we start anew in the morning. We also have an advocate with the Father Judge in His Son, Jesus, who will attest to our confession and His forgiveness. Hopefully, as we grow in the Spirit, we will find we have less to confess, and our words spoken, and thought will be words pleasing to our God.

Matthew 12:43-45 Keep Immersed

"When an impure spirit comes out of a person, it goes through arid places seeking rest and does not find it. Then it says, 'I will return to the house I left.' When it arrives, it finds the house unoccupied, swept clean and put in order. Then it goes and takes with it seven other spirits more wicked than itself, and they go in and live there. And the final condition of that person is worse than the first. That is how it will be with this wicked generation." (NIV)

Keep Immersed

When we've confessed our sins, we must be sure we ask the Holy Spirit to fill us anew. As we live in this sinful world and see all the temptations around us, we become accustomed to these temptations. Eventually, we begin to accept them as not so bad and eventually participate in them. This is happening more and more in our world. What was considered evil is now taken as good. This is how generations become wicked. We must immerse ourselves in the written word of God and keep His precepts in our minds and hearts. We, as believers and followers of Jesus, are no longer of this world. Let us keep His word in our minds and hearts and not give in to the idea that God's precepts no longer belong in this modern age. God is the same yesterday, today, and forever. Pray Holy Spirit, keep us full of You so there is no room for the evil one.

Matthew 12:50 Family

For whoever does the will of my Father in heaven is my brother and sister and mother." (NIV)

Family

Not only are all believers part of God's family, but we are also all part of each other's family. Families do things together, both working and playing. Families look out for each other. Families want only the best for each other. Families share equally not only in the responsibilities but in the pleasures. We must ask ourselves how we treat other believers. In many churches, there are feelings of competition. Some think they own a certain seat or should have a certain job regardless of how the Spirit is moving. We are so often stuck with the words "my or mine." What we need to be doing is the will of God. He said we are to love one another. He said we are to be giving more than getting. He said we are only to speak of the good. He said we are to pray for one another not to gossip. So often our prayer requests resemble gossip more than pure prayer. Families are forgiving. We must make sure we don't harbor resentment against any believer. The older of us are to be mothers or fathers of the younger believers and encourage them through teaching and example. We must ask, what kind of example are we setting for the younger believers?

Matthew 13:3 Soil

Then he told them many things in parables, saying: "A farmer went out to sow his seed. (NIV)

Soil

Open your own Bible and re-read this parable of the Sower. Read it slowly and carefully. Even if you have it memorized. Read about where the different seeds land and what happens to them. Then ask the Holy Spirit to match the areas of the seeds thrown with the different areas in your own life. We all have areas in us that are like rocky places as well as those that are good soil. It is time for us to get serious about all aspects of our lives and be sure we develop good soil in every area. God wants all our hearts and minds, not just a few areas.

Matthew 13:29 Weeds

"'No,' he answered, 'because while you are pulling the weeds, you may uproot the wheat with them. (NIV)

Weeds

I enjoy the parables Jesus gave. This one is the parable of the weeds. When we accept Jesus as our Lord and Savior, He doesn't remove us from the culture or society where we live. He expects us to grow in Him amid where we are. We are to remain where we are and be His light amid the darkness. If all we do is stay in church or with the people in our churches, we have no impact on the world around us. A healthy plant survives amid the weeds and is not choked out. We must ask ourselves if we are being choked out or if are we being the Light of God amid our dark and weed-infested garden of life.

Matthew 13:44

"The kingdom of heaven is like treasure hidden in a field. When a man found it, he hid it again, and then in his joy went and sold all he had and bought that field. (NIV)

All For Treasure

The kingdom of heaven is described as a hidden treasure. But God has provided us a generous taste of that treasure in the written word, the Holy Bible. It is full of treasures that can be gleaned every day. These treasures are hidden from those who don't know Jesus and are without the gift of His Holy Spirit. It is only as the Holy Spirit reveals what is hidden in the treasure that understanding can come. It is wonderful we don't have to wait until the day we leave this earth for our home in heaven to have that treasure. Our question is, do we value the treasure available to us enough to seek it with all our hearts and mind? The man in the parable sold all he had for that treasure. Jesus gave His life for us to have the treasure. All we need do is believe Him and seek Him through His written word with the Holy Spirit to have joy abundantly.

Matthew 13:49 Separation of wicked from Righteous

This is how it will be at the end of the age. The angels will come and separate the wicked from the righteous (NIV)

Separation of Wicked from Righteous

Separate the wicked from the righteous. We are all sinners. That means we are all wicked even though we don't like to use that word. The only way we can be righteous is through the blood of Jesus Christ by believing in Him and accepting Him as the Lord of our lives, minds, and hearts. Why? Because only Jesus is righteous. He is God and He is without sin. He loves us so much that God, who is in three persons, separated Himself and sent His Word down to us in the form of a human baby to grow as we must grow and to demonstrate how we are to live and how much He loves us. When He returned to Himself in Heaven as Father and Son (the Word), He sent His Holy Spirit down to dwell in every believer so we can share in the righteousness of Jesus. Our question we each must answer is whether we are sharing in that righteousness.

Matthew 13:57 Honor Now

And they took offense at him. But Jesus said to them, "A prophet is not without honor except in his own town and in his own home." (NIV)

Honor Now

Sometimes it seems the people closest to us are the most critical of us. Of course, we can turn that backward and say sometimes we are the most critical of those closest to us. We need to make sure we build our loved ones up and let them know how much we love, honor, respect, and appreciate them. At memorial services, we say all sorts of good and loving things about the one who has died. It is a shame we don't say those things to the one who is with us while they are with us. In our mind, we can write an obituary about someone we have been criticizing and then pray and ask God for forgiveness for our critical thoughts and words. Then let's be sure we verbally give love and honor to that person in the here and now. Let us be sure we honor the ones closest to us even more than we honor others we hold in esteem.

Matthew 14:13a Grieving

When Jesus heard what had happened, he withdrew by boat privately to a solitary place. (NIV)

Grieving

Jesus withdrew to a private place to be alone. He had just been told His cousin, John the Baptizer, had been beheaded. Jesus wanted some time alone to grieve. He knew John was with His Father in heaven, but He still grieved. It's okay to grieve when we lose someone we love. It doesn't mean we don't have faith, or we don't trust God. It just means we miss the one we love. We seem to think we must show a brave face to the world, or they will think we don't have faith. Jesus had more than faith. He had absolute knowledge, yet He still grieved at John's departure from this world. We must not criticize or condemn those who are mourning. Jesus even said those who mourn will be blessed. So, if you've lost someone you love it's okay to grieve. Just do it with Jesus, telling the Father thanks for the time you've had with that person even though a certain amount of sadness remains. His joy in you can partner with the sadness of the loss.

Matthew 14:18-19 Giving Multiplied

"Bring them here to me," he said. And He directed the people to sit down on the grass. Taking the five loaves and the two fish and looking up to heaven, He gave thanks and broke the loaves. Then He gave them to the disciples, and the disciples gave them to the people. (NIV)

Giving Multiplied

What we give to God with a thankful heart will be multiplied. We don't give out of obligation or just because we are supposed to be giving. We give out of thanks and love for God, who He is, and what He has and does do. The giving involves our hearts, minds, and possessions. We don't give up expecting to get something back. We give because we want to give. The little boy wanted to give his two fish and five loaves to Jesus. Jesus gave them to God. God blessed them more times over than we can count. We must ask what we are holding back from God. It may be money or possessions or time or a past hurt or anything else. We need to ask God to show us what it is and choose to give it to Him. Then watch and see how He blesses us.

Matthew 14:27 Don't Be Afraid

But Jesus immediately said to them: "Take courage! It is I. Don't be afraid." (NIV)

Don't Be Afraid

The disciples weren't sure what they were seeing was real. They were afraid. Jesus' response to fear is to trust Him. Quite often we see things that bring fear into us. Fear isn't bad if it directs us to Jesus. He is our guide and our protector. When we need wisdom to get out of a bad situation all we need to do is ask. He has promised to give wisdom to those who ask. If we are in danger, we can trust Him to be with us. He has promised never to leave us alone. Even a past president said there is nothing to fear but fear itself. Fear is only there to get our attention. It's what we do with the fear that can bring trouble. When fear comes, we must choose to look to God immediately and trust Him. He is never changing and is always faithful. Right now, I am under a tornado watch. Several people called to see if I was okay and if would I like to come over with them. There is no need. I know Who oversees my life and I rest comfortably and confidently in His hands. Let us always take courage. It is God the Father, the Son, and the Holy Spirit. There is nothing to fear.

Matthew 14:31 Why Doubt

Immediately Jesus reached out his hand and caught him. "You of little faith," he said, "why did you doubt?" (NIV)

Why Doubt

Jesus asked this of Peter as Peter was walking out to Him on the water. Peter's problem was he took his eyes away from Jesus and turned them on the stormy situation. We must ask ourselves how often in a day Jesus says that to us. How often do we focus on our circumstances instead of Jesus? What is our first thought when we see we're in a stormy situation? Do we keep focused on the situation or do we turn our eyes to Jesus? When we do turn our eyes on Jesus, do we look at Him with the eyes of faith? It comes down to a choice. Either we believe what God tells us in the Scriptures or we don't. The Scriptures come in an entire package. We can't pick and choose what we will believe or what we will obey. When we give our hearts, minds, and lives to Jesus it is all or nothing. His hand is reaching down to us. Do we choose to reach our hand up to Him so He can hold it and lead us? Let us think and pray honestly and openly and ask the Holy Spirit to reveal to us areas where we are not focused on God.

Matthew 15:4 Honor Parents

For God said, 'Honor your father and mother' and 'Anyone who curses their father or mother is to be put to death.' (NIV)

Honor Parents

We live in an age where adult children don't want to be bothered with taking care of elderly parents. It's much easier to send them to a nursing home. I'm not saying it's never right to put someone in a nursing home. Sometimes it's necessary. I have visited many nursing homes and seen so many who never have a visitor. We also have situations when the parents hardly ever hear from their adult children. We also have parents who are visited by their adult children under a feeling of obligation, but the children aren't interested in hearing about their parent's activities. Praise God for the children who honor their parents. This commandment is more easily obeyed when the parents have taught their children when their young to respect all people. Quite often it's from not seeing the parents' example of respect for others. We must ask ourselves what kind of example we show children. Are we respectful of others around us?

Matthew 15:8 More Than Lip Service

These people honor me with their lips, but their hearts are far from me. (NIV)

More Than Lip Service

Honoring God with our lips and not meaning it is very close to using His name in vain. Many acknowledge Jesus is the Son of God, yet they do not honor Him in their hearts, minds, or lives. They may be very active in church thinking all they do is enough. So often we mistake the love of God for a love that never disciplines when necessary. God created us to love and to be loved by us. Our work is not our primary reason for being. Our primary reason for being is to be in a close relationship with our Father through His Son, Jesus, and with the help of His Holy Spirit. As Lent is ending, let's be sure we ask the Holy Spirit to show us where our hearts are. Do we love God so much that our biggest desire is to be with Him and please Him?

Matthew 15:11 Our Mouth

What goes into someone's mouth does not defile them, but what comes out of their mouth, that is what defiles them." (NIV)

Our Mouth

With all the emphasis on health through nutrition, many of us concentrate more on what goes in our mouths than what comes out. What is in our thoughts quite often will spill out of our mouths. Sometimes that happens embarrassingly fast. This is one reason we are told to "hide the words of God deep in our hearts that we won't sin against Him." The only way to do this is by daily study and meditation of His written word, the Holy Bible. This should be what we read more than any other thing. The Bible is our Basic Instructions Before Leaving Earth. Everything we need to know to live a full and abundant life that is pleasing to God is contained in its pages.

When our thoughts are on "Philippians 4:8,

> whatever is true, whatever is noble, whatever is right, whatever is pure, whatever is lovely, whatever is admirable—if anything is excellent or praiseworthy—think about such things." (NIV)

when we learn to keep our thoughts on these things, our mouths will not speak words that defile. Let us concentrate more on what comes out of our mouths rather than what we put into our mouths.

Matthew 15:28 Humble Faith

Then Jesus said to her, "Woman, you have great faith! Your request is granted." And her daughter was healed at that moment. (NIV)

Humble Faith

It matters not what gender, race, ethnicity, education, profession, or anything else we are, the only thing needed for our requests to God is faith. But we must recognize our unworthiness in and of ourselves to even ask God for anything. It is only because of His Son, Jesus, that we are given the privilege of talking with Almighty God. We cannot come to Him in arrogance or pride. We come to Him in complete humility of our sinfulness and with thanksgiving for the righteousness of Jesus. We also learn through this scripture section the importance of interceding for our children. This woman was humbling herself as totally worthless in hopes of the attention of Jesus. We now have the assurance of His attention if we have Him as Lord of our lives. Let us always come humbly before Him and recognize the equality of all who seek Him.

Matthew 16:18-19 Keys

And I tell you that you are Peter, and on this rock, I will build my church, and the gates of Hades will not overcome it. I will give you the keys of the kingdom of heaven; whatever you bind on earth will be bound in heaven, and whatever you loose on earth will be loosed in heaven." (NIV)

Keys

What God has revealed to me about these two verses may upset some people. Jesus was not referring to Peter as a person as the rock He built His church on. He builds His church on the confession of Peter saying Jesus is the Son of the Living God and the Messiah promised centuries before. When we accept Jesus, agreeing with Peter's statement of faith, we are given the keys to the kingdom of heaven because heaven is our home and those who live in the home have the keys to it. Jesus is the key. Through the Holy Spirit, who now dwells in every believer, what we bind or loose on this earth is also bound or loosed in heaven. That is one reason it is so very important to forgive others immediately. Unforgiveness binds us and others to sin. Forgiveness looses us and others. Our question is, if we are living out this statement of faith, are we picking up our responsibility of being a key holder, binding only the sin and loosing the sinner into the love and acceptance of Jesus?

Matthew 16:27-28 Take Up Your Cross

For the Son of Man is going to come in his Father's glory with his angels, and then he will reward each person according to what they have done. (NIV)

Take Up Your Cross

Yes, we will be rewarded for what we have done if what we have done is out of love for Jesus. We cannot earn our way to heaven. There is no way for any human to do enough or be good enough to get into heaven. We only get the keys to enter heaven through believing in trusting and living for Jesus in the way He showed us to live. Because of what Jesus did for us, we will also come into the Father's glory if we have lived for Him. The verses preceding this (I do hope you read the entire section) deal with taking up our cross, denying ourselves, and living for Him. This doesn't mean we don't take care of ourselves, but it does mean we love and serve others rather than wanting others to serve us. We serve others out of the love we have for God because He loves us more than we can understand and gave His only Son for us. Yes, He knew He would have His Son back but, His Son is different now that He has taken on our sins. This is love beyond our understanding. If this doesn't motivate us to "take up our cross" and follow Him in service and love to others, I have to question if we know and trust Him as our Lord and Savior.

Matthew 17:20 Mustard Seed

He replied, "Because you have so little faith. Truly I tell you, if you have faith as small as a mustard seed, you can say to this mountain, 'Move from here to there,' and it will move. Nothing will be impossible for you." (NIV)

Mustard Seed

Jesus isn't talking about earthly mountains. He is talking about our trials that seem to be as big as a mountain. He said all we need is a tiny amount of faith to move the mountain we are facing away from us. Our first problem is we fail to pray to Him in faith that He will give us the wisdom and power to remove the mountain. When we first face a problem, we usually start with complaining. We might tell a lot of others how big our mountain seems. We ask all sorts of people for advice. As the mountain continues to grow, maybe, we finally turn to God and ask Him for wisdom and power to remove the mountain. If all we do is ask Him to remove it for us, we will most likely continue to face the mountain. God has given us the Holy Spirit to give us wisdom and power in all situations, if we ask, look to Him, and believe. During this Lenten season, we have been going through the Gospel of Matthew and contemplating the words of Jesus. Hopefully, we have meditated on the words enough to start to put them into practical existence in our lives. The faith in us is a tiny mustard seed. When we plant it in the written word of God, the Holy Bible, and fertilize and water it with prayer, study, and meditation, we find the seed of faith grows. As it grows, we must exercise it while still fertilizing and watering it and it will continue to grow. Let us not end the exercising, fertilizing, and watering when lent ends. Let us continue to see to it that our faith grows more and more every day.

Matthew 18:3-4 Little Children

And he said: "Truly I tell you, unless you change and become like little children, you will never enter the kingdom of heaven. (NIV)

Little Children

Little children look to their parents for all their needs. They are not concerned about tomorrow or even the next hour. They live in the present. They are not concerned about what they wear or what they will eat. They trust the provision of their parents. They are eager to learn from their parents. They ask questions to learn, and they copy what they see their parents do and what they hear their parents say. We must ask ourselves if we are children of God the Father. Do we trust Him with tomorrow or even the next hour? Do we trust His provision? Are we eager to learn from Him? Do we ask Him questions so we can learn? Do we copy what we've read in His written word, the Holy Bible, what it says He did on this earth, and repeat and do what He said? I don't know about you, but I know I often act like I've grown up rather than continuing to learn and copy His example.

Matthew 18:6-7 Stumbling

If anyone causes one of these little ones—those who believe in me—to stumble, it would be better for them to have a large millstone hung around their neck and to be drowned in the depths of the sea. (NIV)

Stumbling

We are all little ones in God's eyes. We must consider how often we might cause someone else to stumble. We tend to put pressure on others to do what we want them to do. Something as simple as someone who is trying to lose weight. We say, come on, one piece won't hurt you. We say this because we want company in our indulgence. What we are doing is enticing and encouraging someone to do what they feel they shouldn't do. How much better would it be if we concentrated on encouraging one another to do what God has led us to do? What He leads one of us to do may not be what He leads another to do. We must each answer to God. We must encourage each other to walk in faith to what God is telling them at that time of their life. Let's not encourage gossip or anything that would cause another to stumble.

Matthew 18:14 Lost Sheep

In the same way your Father in heaven is not willing that any of these little ones should perish. (NIV)

Lost Sheep

God isn't willing for one soul to perish. Neither should we be. This means we must do all we can to be an example of God's love to all we meet. Quite some time ago, my husband and I realized all our friends and neighbors were in church. We didn't socialize with anybody who wasn't in church. We decided we needed to get out of the saltshaker if we were going to be the salt of the earth. We signed up for square dancing lessons. The first couple we met were church members. We explained why we signed up and moved on to meet other couples. Long story short, we were able to see God work in two couples we began socializing with as they started asking us questions and eventually giving their lives to God. God says to leave the 99 sheep who aren't lost and go after the one who is. This takes prayer and time. Let's ask Him to put a lost soul in our hearts and become salt and light to that person.

Matthew 18:19-20 Not Just One

"Again, truly I tell you that if two of you on earth agree about anything they ask for, it will be done for them by my Father in heaven. For where two or three gather in my name, there am I with them." (NIV)

Not Just One

After my husband went home to God, I was missing my prayer partner. Now I was just one praying. It bothered me greatly for several months. I finally asked God about what to do in this situation where there is only one. His answer? I am filled with His Holy Spirit. His Holy Spirit counts as one. Therefore, there are two praying when I pray. I pray what the Holy Spirit puts in my heart and mind to pray and because of that, we are united in prayer. I continue to see my prayers answered. It's great when more brothers and sisters gather with me to pray. God does wonderful things when we pray. But I never need to be concerned about praying alone. I am never alone. God is always with me through His Holy Spirit Who dwells in me. I pray you have let Him dwell in you also.

Matthew 19:23 Money

Then Jesus said to his disciples, "Truly I tell you; it is hard for someone who is rich to enter the kingdom of heaven. (NIV)

Money

Not everyone can manage being rich. So often the more money we have, the more we spend on things we think we want or things that will show how much money we have and the more money we want. It can be a vicious circle. An abundance of money can produce pride. When we think the money, we earn is our own because we are the ones who worked and earned it, we are so wrong. Everything on this earth belongs to God. He is the One Who made all that is on this earth. He made us and He is the One Who gives us breath and the ability to work. It is the Creator we need to seek, not the creation. When our hearts are right, God has promised to meet all our needs. We need to be mindful of how we spend God's money. All our money belongs to God. He allows us to use it. Let's use it in a way that is pleasing to Him.

Matthew 20:14 Equality

Take your pay and go. I want to give the one who was hired last the same as I gave you. (NIV)

Equality

Some think because they accepted Jesus at an early age and spent years walking in obedience and serving Him, they will reap extra rewards in heaven. What they have earned, more than those who come to know Him in their last days on this earth, was a life of abundant joy from knowing Him. All who come to know Jesus, regardless of how long they walk with Him in this life, have equal access to the throne of God and eternal life. We are equally covered in the righteousness of Jesus. Granted there are rewards in heaven but thinking our work on earth makes us more valuable to God than those who have done less is putting us in the middle of the pride of sin. We serve out of love for God, not out of the hope of rewards or being more in favor than others. Because of our love for God, we love others and want only God's best for them. Let us reflect on our attitude both to whatever ministry God has called us to and to others around us. Let us ask the Holy Spirit to fill us with pure love not only for God but also for all humanity, wanting only His best for all.

Matthew 20:32 Specific

Jesus stopped and called them. "What do you want me to do for you?" he asked. (NIV)

Specific

Many prayers go unanswered because we don't pray specifics. We learned that the hard way. We were in a rental house while we were building a new house. We gathered around the breakfast table and prayed, "Lord, give us an abundance of water." That's all we asked. I was going to meet the well digger at our land, and we wanted him to find a good well on the first dig. He dug and found a good supply of water. It didn't take him very long. I rejoiced and drove back to the rental house. As I opened the front door, I heard what sounded like our aquarium pump. Then I remembered that was in storage. As I stepped in, I was ankle-deep in water. The water heater located in the kitchen had rusted out and water was all over the house since no one was there to turn it off. God gave us an abundance of water that day. Along with showing us His sense of humor He also taught us to be specific in what we asked Him.

As a hospital chaplain, I ask the patients and/or family members present, if there is something specific, they would like to ask God. Sometimes it isn't for physical healing. Sometimes they have a more pressing emotional, spiritual, or other need. God wants to meet our needs. He also wants us to know what our needs are. Let's learn to be very specific when we pray.

Matthew 20:26 Serving

Not so with you. Instead, whoever wants to become great among you must be your servant, (NIV)

Serving

So many like to be served. We like to wait for others to do the work. Parents hear children say, "It's not mine. I didn't drop it." When they're asked to pick up something. We have this misconception that being the one doing the serving demeans us. Jesus set the example. When we continue reading this section of scripture we read, "I didn't come to be served but to serve." Of all who have ever walked this earth, Jesus deserves and has the right to be the one who is served. When we look honestly at ourselves, how can we ever imagine we deserve to be served? As we learn to be the server, we learn to enjoy being the server. Serving is a form of giving and it is a great joy to be a giver. When we see a need, let's learn to serve and fill that need. Something as small as picking up a piece of trash left carelessly by someone else can put joy in our hearts when it's done in the right attitude; an attitude of doing it unto our Lord Jesus Christ.

Matthew 21:9 Crowd Mentality

The crowds that went ahead of him and those that followed shouted, "Hosanna to the Son of David!"

"Blessed is he who comes in the name of the Lord!"

"Hosanna in the highest heaven!" (NIV)

Crowd Mentality

There is a crowd mentality. We don't want to stand out alone. When we see a crowd gathering, the normal human tendency is to join the crowd, see what's going on, and join in with them. A good many of the people in this crowd didn't even know who Jesus was. They just joined in with the rest of the crowd. There is also a church mentality today. Many people think if they join in with a church group that means they are a Christian. They do as the rest of the church members do, thinking that copying their actions and their way of speaking seals them in good standing with God. Jesus said otherwise. He said we must be born again. We are born again by accepting Jesus into our hearts, minds, and lives as our Lord and Savior and following the example of living He demonstrated when He walked this earth. Just acknowledging the fact that He is the Son of God doesn't do it. Satan acknowledges that fact. We must ask Jesus to live in and through us. Let us take time to be sure we have a personal relationship with the Son of God, Jesus. Let us also ask our family members and friends about their relationship with Jesus. Coming through Jesus is the only way into the family of God.

Matthew 21:13 Money Changers

"It is written," He said to them, "'My house will be called a house of prayer,' but you are making it 'a den of robbers.'" (NIV)

Money Changers

Granted we don't have money changer tables in our churches anymore, but there are a lot of things that go on in our churches that would probably upset Jesus if He were to walk into them physically now. Many churches have become big social clubs. It's fine to have things of fellowship and good activities for the church members but we must remember our primary reason for a church is to worship God, feed the sheep, and equip the sheep to go outside of the church into the community and make disciples. When we are in the church with other believers, we are to encourage each other to go out the doors of the church and get to work in the community. I've written about this before. We must be salt and pour ourselves out of the saltshaker. We can do this as a group, and we can do this as individuals. We must ask ourselves what we are doing to bring new disciples into the kingdom of God. Where are our neighbors concerning Jesus? Where are our business associates in relationship to Jesus? Do they know where we are? Are we being salt and light?

Matthew 21:24 Under Authority

Jesus replied, "I will also ask you one question. If you answer Me, I will tell you by what authority I am doing these things. (NIV)

Under Authority

The religious leaders were jealous and felt threatened by Jesus. They wanted to discredit His teaching but had nothing to discredit. You can't discredit what you know is true. Therefore, they were not able to say anything when Jesus asked them about John the Baptizer. They knew the truth but preferred to live under their lies and dreams of self-importance and power over others. We, as believers, have the Holy Spirit indwelling in us. This gives us the authority to speak God's Word. But we must be cautious and be sure our hearts are right. We don't speak to be honored by men. We don't speak to have people acclaim us. We speak out of love of God and a desire to serve Him, obey Him, and make disciples for Him. Every time I preach, I spend time trembling in prayer. I know I have nothing of my own to say worth anybody listening. But I also know I've given myself to be a vessel for God to pass His love to others so that they may know, love, and serve Him. This is for all believers. Be it preaching before thousands or talking to a neighbor or friend in need, it is all the same. We are under the authority of God and through Jesus we have His authority to speak and make disciples. We must ask ourselves if we are obeying Him out of love and obedience.

Matthew 26:35 Denial

But Peter declared, "Even if I have to die with you, I will never disown you." And all the other disciples said the same. (NIV)

Denial

We judge Peter harshly. He says he will be faithful to Jesus and stand with Him and then he turns his back. Not only does he turn his back, but he also actually denies even knowing Him. We must look at ourselves. How many times have we denied Jesus through our actions, our words, and our thoughts? Think not? Judging someone else is putting yourself in the place of God. There is only one Judge and one God. Taking His role is denying Him. Disobeying His word is denying Him. Looking to the world to meet our needs instead of to Him is denying Him. We are all in the same boat as Peter. We all deny Jesus. But we will see that after His resurrection, Peter is filled with the Holy Spirit he turns from denial to complete obedience and service to his death for the glory of God. We have the Holy Spirit in us. Let the Holy Spirit change us as completely as it changed Peter. Peter gave his all. Should we give less?

Matthew 26:38 Can't Repay

Then he said to them, "My soul is overwhelmed with sorrow to the point of death. Stay here and keep watch with me." (NIV)

Can't Repay

We tend to romanticize the crucifixion. We don't understand how very harsh and inhumane it was. Jesus knew He was headed for crucifixion. He grew up seeing people nailed to crosses. He knew the intense pain and humiliation He was about to face. No clothes were worn on the cross. People were nailed there fully exposed for all on the major road to see. He didn't look forward to it. He even asked His Father if there was any other way possible to pay for our sins for all eternity. Despite his dread and intense sorrow, love for the Father and love for us prevailed and He went forward. He could have come down from the cross like the crowd jeered Him to. If He had come down, we wouldn't be here. We wouldn't have God's mercy, grace, forgiveness, or the Holy Spirit. Let us reflect on a cost we cannot understand because we will never have to pay such a cost. Let us give Him praise and thanksgiving for taking our place.

Matthew 27:59-60 Hopeless

Joseph took the body, wrapped it in a clean linen cloth, and placed it in his own new tomb (NIV)

Hopeless

We find the Sabbath day. Many of the friends of Jesus have gathered. They talk in quiet voices. They are scared. They are disappointed. They are sad. They are confused. They thought Jesus was the Messiah and they would be free from Roman rule. Now Jesus is dead and sealed in a tomb. Their hope has died. It is hard for us to relate because we know what happens the next day. They don't know. They saw Jesus raise Lazarus from the dead, but they watched Him die a horrible death on the cross. There's no coming back from such a death. On the day between Good Friday, the crucifixion, and Easter Sunday, the resurrection, think about how hopeless they felt. We can be thankful we never need to be hopeless. We have the Holy Spirit dwelling in us since we accepted Jesus into our hearts, minds, and lives as our Lord and Savior. God had to turn away from Jesus as He took on all the sins of humanity. Because of that, God will never turn away from us. When He looks at us, He doesn't see sin. He sees the righteousness and the blood of His Son, Jesus. We can stand forgiven in His presence by His mercy and grace. Let's praise and thank Him in preparation for the celebration of His resurrection and the expectation of His coming back to this earth to gather His Bride, the children of God through Jesus.

Matthew 28:6 Alive

He is not here; he has risen, just as he said. Come and see the place where he lay. (NIV)

Alive

He is alive. Jesus rose from the dead. The tomb is empty. Though He rose from the dead, He returned to His Father in heaven. But He hasn't left us alone. He sent His Holy Spirit to dwell within every believer. He now lives on this earth inside and through every believer. We must ask if Jesus is alive in us. Do we push Him out? Do we ask for a renewal of the Holy Spirit in and through us every day? Do others see Jesus in and through us? There is much to contemplate today. Let us be sure He is resurrected in us. Let us be sure we allow His Holy Spirit to live in every area of our lives. Let us be sure when others see and hear us, they know Jesus is alive. Praise God. Jesus lives.

Matthew 7:13-14 One Passage

Enter through the narrow gate. For wide is the gate and broad is the road that leads to destruction, and many enter through it. But small is the gate and narrow the road that leads to life, and only a few find it. (NIV)

One Passage

When the Apollo astronauts would return to Earth's atmosphere after their very long journeys, they had a narrow door to reenter. The passage was less than forty miles wide. Coming from such a great distance at such a great speed it is like trying to thread a needle with a narrow thread from several feet away from the eye of the needle. Many people think there are multiple ways to enter heaven. Jesus, whose home was heaven and Who was very familiar with it said there is only one door into heaven. He said He is the door, and no one can enter heaven except by going through Him. It may not sound like a loving God but that doesn't change the fact of how heaven and earth were created. But, since God is loving, He provided a way for us. He sent His Son, Jesus, the Door to heaven, to walk on this earth and demonstrate love. This is the highest form of love there is.

John 20:16 First One

Jesus said to her, "Mary." She turned toward him and cried out in Aramaic, "Rabboni!" (which means "Teacher"). (NIV)

First One

The first person to see Jesus risen from the dead was Mary Magdalene. All we know about this Mary is that she seemed to have a sordid past, she had no home obligations to keep her, and she had enough money to follow and serve Jesus. That Jesus would choose a past sinner to be the first to see Him resurrected is appropriate seeing as His purpose in coming was to save the sinner. What we notice in this verse is that she didn't recognize Jesus by sight through her grief and tears, but she did know how He said her name and immediately recognized Him when He called her name. He still calls the names of the sinners. Our question is do we hear Him call our name? Mary turned toward Jesus when He called her. He's calling us to turn toward Him. Let us be sure to not only turn toward Him but to keep our eyes, hearts, and minds on Him throughout every day.

Acts 1:3-4 Limits

After his suffering, he presented himself to them and gave many convincing proofs that he was alive. He appeared to them over a period of forty days and spoke about the kingdom of God. (NIV)

Limits

There is much proof Jesus lived, was crucified, died, was buried, and arose from the dead appearing to, be touched by, speaking and teaching, and eating with many witnesses. This proof is not my purpose today. What I want to point out is He appeared at various times to various people doing and saying various things. No one knew when He would appear, where He would appear, or what He would do or say when He did appear. The same is true today. These people whom Jesus appeared to be going about their daily business. We are to go about our daily business. The business He charged us with was to go and make disciples. That is more than going and seeing. That is teaching, encouraging, and enabling those around us to not only believe in Jesus but to follow Him and obey Him in all we do. Jesus appears every day through His Holy Spirit in His followers. It is through us He is seen, heard, and taught. It is not recorded every time He appeared during the 40 days He remained, physically on this earth nor where He went. He is no longer limited to the physical. He is only limited by our willingness to go, act, and speak. Our question is are we limiting Jesus from going into all the world making disciples?

Acts 1:8 Power

But you will receive power when the Holy Spirit comes on you, and you will be my witnesses in Jerusalem, and in all Judea and Samaria, and to the ends of the earth." (NIV)

Power

Jesus said we would receive power when the Holy Spirit comes on us. This is one of the major reasons and purposes of the Holy Spirit in us. It is to give us power to be Jesus' witnesses on all the earth. It's nice to have the power to command sickness to leave a body but that isn't our primary task. We have been commanded to make disciples. We have the power of the Holy Spirit to make disciples through our witness. Our question is are we doing this? We must each ask ourselves how many disciples we have made. This is not the job of paid church pastors. Their job is to feed us, the sheep of God's flock. Our job is to digest the food, go out from the church walls into the world, and make disciples for Jesus. We do this through the power of the Holy Spirit as He witnesses through us in our words and actions. Let us go forth. Let us not only digest the food of God's word for our growth. Let us use it to feed the hungry and lost. Let us make disciples for Jesus.

Acts 1:4 Not Without Power

On one occasion, while he was eating with them, he gave them this command: "Do not leave Jerusalem but wait for the gift my Father promised, which you have heard me speak about. (NIV)

Not Without Power

Jesus told His disciples to wait. They were not to go make disciples until they received the Holy Spirit. Working on our power doesn't accomplish much. We may have all the intelligence and physical capability available but without the power and wisdom of the Holy Spirit our work for God's kingdom is in vain. We can do all sorts of seemingly marvelous things in the material world but nothing in the spiritual world without the Holy Spirit. The disciples were full of fear, even after seeing, talking, listening, and eating with the resurrected Jesus. Fear didn't leave until they received the Holy Spirit. It was then they were able to have faith instead of fear and speak the truth of God with boldness. We can do all sorts of work for charity and all sorts of work in and through our churches but if we are not allowing the Holy Spirit to work through us our work will be lacking. It is imperative to ask for a fresh infilling of the Holy Spirit at the start of each day and depend on Him to give us wisdom and power for any task at hand. Let us go forth in His power and wisdom making disciples throughout our homes, schools, churches, places of work, neighborhoods, and the world.

Acts 2:17a No Limits

In the last days, God says, I will pour out my Spirit on all people (NIV)

No Limits

All people who believe in, worship, and follow Jesus have the Holy Spirit. Not just a little. God pours out His Spirit. He doesn't sprinkle His Spirit or meter the Spirit but pours the Spirit out on us. What we must consider is how much room we give the Holy Spirit within us. Are we too busy? Are we too consumed with worldly things? What is our priority? Are we staying busy without really accomplishing anything? Joyce Myers says she's not busy, she's fruitful. We have the option of having as much of the Holy Spirit as we want to receive. God doesn't limit Him. Let us meditate on how much room we are willing to give God and His Holy Spirit in our hearts, minds, and lives.

Matthew 28:19-20 Go

Therefore, go and make disciples of all nations, baptizing them in the name of the Father and of the Son and of the Holy Spirit, and teaching them to obey everything I have commanded you. And surely, I am with you always, to the very end of the age." (NIV)

Go

Let's look closer at what we now call the great commission that Jesus gave before He ascended to heaven. The first verb is "go." Go is an action word. We are not to stay in our churches. The lost do not come to church. Church is for feeding and encouraging the believers. We are to eat from God's Word at church and then go out. When we go out, we are to make disciples. This is more than making converts. We must continue to nurture and feed the new believers that they, too, will be able to go out. We are to teach them all that Jesus said and encourage them to obey. Jesus ends with the promise He is and will always be with us as we go. Are we going? Are we making disciples? This is for the believers, not left to those who are paid pastors of churches. Let us go.

Acts 2:14 Know Him

Then Peter stood up with the Eleven, raised his voice and addressed the crowd: "Fellow Jews and all of you who live in Jerusalem, let me explain this to you; listen carefully to what I say. (NIV)

Know Him

Remember Peter. He was the one who claimed vehemently he didn't even know Jesus. He spent three years with Him, eating, laughing, learning, traveling seeing miracles. Then he cowers and denies Him. What changed? After the crucifixion, he hid with the other disciples. After the resurrection, he stayed hidden. Now he is standing in front of a crowd of people telling them about Jesus. What a change. From a coward denying to a bold witness. The difference is Peter is no longer alone. He is filled with the Holy Spirit. The Holy Spirit gives us knowledge, wisdom, and boldness when we are open to receiving those gifts. All believers have the Holy Spirit. Our problem is we don't avail of His power in and through us. There are Christians in countries who are being persecuted and threatened with death who are standing firm and bold because they know the Holy Spirit within them. Jesus came not only to die and take our sins on Himself, but He also came for us to intimately know and fellowship with God the Father, God the Son, and God the Holy Spirit. We must know and welcome the Holy Spirit and live and stand with boldness. Open your Bible software and search the Holy Spirit. Read all the references and get personally acquainted with Him. Then go and make disciples.

Acts 2:39 Who Are Far Off

The promise is for you and your children and for all who are far off—for all whom the Lord our God will call." (NIV)

Who Are Far Off

Just in case you are still not very sure all Christians, including you, have the Holy Spirit within them, here is yet another verse of promise. We are far off in generations from the first disciples of Jesus. If we are believers and followers of Jesus, we are because He has called us to follow Him. We are each called at different times of our lives and in different ways, but we are all called, and we are all filled. The original word for filled with the Holy Spirit is of the continuing verb form. The continuing verb form is a word of continuing action. Being filled with God's Holy Spirit is a continuing thing. We pray every morning for a fresh refilling of the Holy Spirit. We were baptized and received the Holy Spirit when we accepted Jesus into our hearts, minds, and lives but we are continuing to be filled. The only limit of the refreshing or refilling of the Holy Spirit is the limit we set. Let us be sure to be open every day for all the Holy Spirit's filling in us. Then we have the power and boldness to go out into the world and make those disciples.

Acts 2:46-47 Meeting Together

Every day they continued to meet together in the temple courts. They broke bread in their homes and ate together with glad and sincere hearts, praising God and enjoying the favor of all the people (NIV)

Meeting Together

The people in the early church recorded in Acts met together every day. They met in the temple, and they met in their homes. When together they praised God. Meeting together created encouragement to follow in what was called then, "The Way." Today we tend to meet once a week, some not even that often. If you read the next verse, not quoted here, you will see their numbers grow daily. Meeting together, enjoying fellowship together, worshiping, and praising God together are like vitamin pills to our faith. You know the saying, a hot coal left by itself will soon go out. Faith needs encouragement to grow. We must not only meet together in churches, but we must also meet together during the week. Sometimes it is by phone, at work, and sometimes for a meal. We must be careful to avoid isolationism. Let's build relationships with other believers, encouraging one another and fellowshipping with one another, sharing the insights God gives us during our devotions.

Acts 3:16 Seed Growth

By faith in the name of Jesus, this man whom you see and know was made strong. It is Jesus' name and the faith that comes through him that has completely healed him, as you can all see. (NIV)

Seed Growth

In and of ourselves we have no faith. We, as sinful humans, are full of doubt. Faith in God can only come through Jesus. It is Jesus who fills us with His Holy Spirit to give us faith. When we pray in the name of Jesus, we are praying in the faith He gives us. He gives us the faith of a tiny mustard seed. When the seed is planted, it grows into a tree. When Jesus plants the seed of faith in us, He expects us to nourish it so it will grow. It is for us to nourish the seed of faith. We nourish it in a combination of several ways: Bible study, meditation, prayer, gathering with others of faith, speaking of all God does for us, and witnessing and making disciples. Just like our bodies need a balanced diet to grow and be healthy, faith needs a balanced diet to grow. Let us work on growing the seed of faith planted in us by Jesus and His Holy Spirit.

Acts 4:12 One Door

Salvation is found in no one else, for there is no other name under heaven given to mankind by which we must be saved."(NIV)

One Door

Many people think they can earn their way to heaven by being good. Others think they go to heaven through some form of religion. Jesus said there is only one door which leads to heaven. He said He is the door. There is no other way. Many people think that because God is love He wouldn't exclude anyone who tries to be good from entering heaven. Jesus said man's goodness is like filthy rags. There is only One Who always existed with God the Father. He is Jesus. Jesus is the Word through which the Father created all things. The Father sent the Word to earth through a virgin woman to demonstrate His love for man and to take away the sins of man (the desire to worship himself and other things other than God) on Himself so man could be covered with the righteousness of the Word, Jesus, and dwell in the presence of God for all eternity. It is not a lack of love that there is only one way to heaven. It is pure, perfect, and divine love. It is a love beyond the comprehension of sinful man. As we open ourselves to such a great love, we are moved to bring others to that love. Let us go forth and spread that love to others.

Acts 4:20 Can't Help It

As for us, we cannot help speaking about what we have seen and heard." (NIV)

Can't Help It

The disciples were successful in building up the Bride of Christ (the church of believers) because they couldn't help but speak about what they had seen and heard, we have also seen and heard from God. We see miracles if we have eyes to see, every day. We see miracles of creation, of lives turned around and so many other things if we would just look. We hear God speak to our inner selves, we hear Him as we read the Bible, and we hear Him through the mouths of others if we will just open our ears. Our problem is distraction. We get too involved in things that don't last. We allow those things to sap our energy and forget how excited we were when we first realized God loves us. We need to reaffirm God loves us the first thing every morning. Say it aloud. Keep saying it until we believe it. When we believe it, we should be excited. When we believe something and are excited about it, we want to share it. Let us be like the early disciples. Let us speak about God the Father, God the Son (Jesus), and God the Holy Spirit Whom we see and hear.

Acts 4:29 Silent Minority

Now, Lord, consider their threats and enable your servants to speak your word with great boldness. (NIV)

Silent Minority

So many Christians are in the "silent majority" which is quickly becoming the "silent minority." We have kept our mouths shut while prayer and Bible reading were taken out of our schools and out of many civic meetings. We've not spoken up for freedom of religion and allowed freedom from religion to take a firm hold in our courts and nation. We've not prayed for boldness to speak up in the governing of our nation. Let us pray and be willing to move with boldness into the vocal majority. After we pray, we must be willing to put feet, voice, and action in faith that God will give us the boldness and the right words to speak. Let us take this nation (any nation where you live) back for God and His glory.

Acts 4:32 One in Heart

All the believers were one in heart and mind (NIV)

One in Heart

I am distressed over denominationalism. It is a bad witness. They compete. And within the denominations, the individual churches seem to compete with each other. But this attitude is not new. It happened in the early church. The church in Ephesus was different from the church in Rome and the church in Corinth. This is because the churches are made up of sinful humans. We make up for our feelings of being inferior by criticizing others. This started with Adam and Eve pointing the finger elsewhere for their disobedience. We now have the Holy Spirit. We should be able to allow the Holy Spirit to love all others through us. We agree Jesus is the Son of God, came to earth to show us the love of the Father, died on the cross to take our sins on Himself, and rose from the dead to give us eternal life. Beyond this, it doesn't matter how we choose to worship or show His love. What counts is we do worship and we do show His love to all others. Let us learn to avail ourselves with the power of that love and put judgment and criticism aside.

Acts 10:34-35 No Favorites

Then Peter began to speak: "I now realize how true it is that God does not show favoritism (NIV)

No Favorites

We like to wear titles. Titles give us identity. We judge some titles to be more important and impressive than others. We have made a grading system for people who are to be treated more favorably. God has no favorites. He loved each one of us to equally die on the cross to forgive each of our sins. We are each forgiven to the extent we forgive others. The same amount of forgiveness is there for each one of us (total forgiveness), but it is our choice by our willingness to forgive others which determines our forgiveness from God. This is not favoritism. This is our openness and willingness to receive from God. Let us put jealousy aside when looking at others for we are all equal. Let us encourage one another to avail ourselves of all God has for us through His Holy Spirit.

Acts 11:17 One in Christ

So if God gave them the same gift he gave us who believed in the Lord Jesus Christ, who was I to think that I could stand in God's way?" (NIV)

One in Christ

Who are we to judge or criticize how anyone else worships God? God made each of us unique. When Jesus prayed for us to all be one in Him and in each other just as He and the Father are one, He didn't mean we were to do everything the same way. We are to be one in love. One in wanting God's best for each other. One in encouraging each other to walk the path God has for them in joy and boldness. Let's put aside our competition with each other and our criticism of each other and enjoy our uniqueness in the love of God. This must be more than lip service; we must learn to have the mind of Christ and only have love in our hearts, words, and minds. We are all one in Christ.

Acts 12:16 Expectations

But Peter kept on knocking, and when they opened the door and saw him, they were astonished. (NIV)

Expectations

The new church was afraid. They were huddled in a room praying. Peter had been arrested and was in prison. They were praying intently for Peter to be freed. When the woman went to the door to see who was knocking, she was shocked to see Peter, closed the door on him and went to tell the others. So often we pray for things, but we don't expect the prayers to be answered. Because of our lack of expectation, we quite often miss the answers. They might be right in front of our faces, but our doubts blind our vision to the answers. The woman thought it was too good to be true. How can we doubt the promise of Jesus that God hears our prayers and answers them? When we pray, let us fill our minds with the promises recorded in Scripture. Fill them until there is no doubt God will answer our prayers. Then pray with the confidence God will do what He promised. Keep praying with thanksgiving and watch to see what God will do.

Acts 13:22 Heart for God

After removing Saul, he made David their king. God testified concerning him: 'I have found David son of Jesse, a man after my own heart; he will do everything I want him to do.' (NIV)

Heart for God

This is God Who said David was a man after His own heart. What made David a man after God's own heart? One thing is written here. David will do everything God wants him to do. Reading the scriptures about David and the Psalms he wrote we can see other reasons. David enjoyed worshiping God. He worshiped Him with all his being. David didn't sit in judgment of those God had anointed (refusing to kill Saul even though Saul was trying to kill him). David admitted and repented when he sinned when he became aware of it. (Killing Uriah) We must look at our lives. I'm sure everyone would like God to say they are after His own heart. Do we do everything God wants us to do? Do we even know what God wants us to do? We can't know if we don't ask Him and listen to Him. Are we open to accepting our sins and repenting? Do we worship God with our entire being? After we get over the sting of having to answer, "not all the time," let's take some time to ask the Holy Spirit to work in us the kind of heart David had along with his obedience and willing to repent.

Acts 16:25 Attitude Adjustment

About midnight Paul and Silas were praying and singing hymns to God, and the other prisoners were listening to them. (NIV)

Attitude Adjustment

Paul and Silas were in jail. The jails then were not like our jails. They were stone and dirt. They had no plumbing and were full of excrement on the dirt floor. They didn't have freedom of movement as the chains on their wrists and ankles were attached to the stone wall. Yet with all this, Paul and Silas weren't complaining and moaning feeling sorry for themselves. They were praying and singing hymns to God. We must examine ourselves. What inconveniences do we complain about? What things do we consider inconvenient and get upset about? Nothing like what Paul and Silas were facing. Yet, because of their attitude they saw a miracle take place. God broke their chains loose and opened the door. Still, they stayed in the jail. Miracles God performs aren't for the believers alone. They are for those who don't believe. The jailer saw the miracle and saw all the prisoners still there and became a believer. Maybe the reason we don't see mighty miracles happen is our attitude. Let's as the Holy Spirit to help us do an attitude adjustment. Let's remember we remain on this earth to serve God and show His love and light to others that they, too, may come to know Him.

Acts 17:11 Examine the Scriptures

Now the Berean Jews were of more noble character than those in Thessalonica, for they received the message with great eagerness and examined the Scriptures every day to see if what Paul said was true. (NIV)

Examine the Scriptures

The noble character was related to great eagerness for the message of salvation along with a determination to examine the Scriptures every day. We cannot depend on other teaching or preaching as our only means of examining the Scriptures. We must examine them for ourselves. I've learned to look up the history at the time where the Scripture was written and to whom the Scripture was addressed. The book of Romans, for example, was written at a time when the churches in Rome were very much like the churches in the United States today. Read Romans and check it out. Reading about the period makes the Scripture more real. We need to examine the people mentioned in Scripture. Doing this helps us relate to them. Having others do it for us and presenting it to us doesn't take the place of our examination. Let us choose to examine and study the Scriptures like that is the most import thing for us to know. It is. It will bring us to a greater knowledge of the God we serve.

1 Corinthians 1:5 Made Perfect

For in him you have been enriched in every way—with all kinds of speech and with all knowledge (NIV)

Made Perfect

What a wonderful fact. In Jesus we are enriched in EVERY way. Our speech and our knowledge are enriched when we are in Jesus. When we are in Jesus we are filled with His Holy Spirit. When we learn to listen to the Holy Spirit, we will be given knowledge and with the knowledge be able to speak the truth of God to others. The knowledge comes through the written Word, the Holy Bible as well as through experience of our walk with God and our conversations and meditations with God. We need all of these to grow and to learn to use the enrichment He gives us. When we begin to put ourselves down because we have made a mistake, we are to remember Whose we are and Who dwells within us. Putting ourselves down is calling God a liar because He says we are precious in His sight, and we are perfect in Him. Perfect doesn't mean we will never make a mistake or sin but, because Jesus is perfect and His Holy Spirit is within us, we are perfectly in Him. Let us avail ourselves of the knowledge He has for us and then share it with others.

1 Corinthians 1:30-31 Because of Him

It is because of him that you are in Christ Jesus, who has become for us wisdom from God—that is, our righteousness, holiness, and redemption. Therefore, as it is written: "Let the one who boasts boast in the Lord (NIV)

Because of Him

We humans think we're so smart; we have so much wisdom; we are so very proud. We even pride ourselves on how religious we are. None of these things are anything but filthy rags compared to Jesus. It is only when we invite Jesus into our hearts, minds, and lives that we can gave even a little wisdom and righteousness or holiness. That is because of the grace and mercy of God. We can, of ourselves, do nothing to gain or earn it. It is only God's love and mercy that can call us to come to Jesus and be given the Holy Spirit with His wisdom, Holiness, righteousness, and redemption from our human pride. When we are praised by others for something God does through us, we must be sure to give God the credit. Without God, we are nothing but creations of His walking around in a sinful world as a sinner. With Jesus we become more than creations. We become God's children and joint heirs with Jesus covered in His righteousness and holiness. Therefore, we are allowed to call God our Father. There is nothing better than this. Let's thank Him every day.

1 Corinthians 2:10-16 Thoughts

These are the things God has revealed to us by his Spirit. The Spirit searches all things, even the deep things of God. For who knows a person's thoughts except their own spirit within them? In the same way no one knows the thoughts of God except the Spirit of God. What we have received is not the spirit of the world, but the Spirit who is from God, so that we may understand what God has freely given us. This is what we speak, not in words taught us by human wisdom but in words taught by the Spirit, explaining spiritual realities with Spirit-taught words. The person without the Spirit does not accept the things that come from the Spirit of God but considers them foolishness and cannot understand them because they are discerned only through the Spirit. The person with the Spirit makes judgments about all things, but such a person is not subject to merely human judgments, for, "Who has known the mind of the Lord so as to instruct him?" But we have the mind of Christ. (NIV)

Thoughts

It is important to read this entire paragraph. Not just read it but slow down and pause on each phrase and meditate on each one. To know our own thoughts, we must allow our spirit to search our minds completely. This takes a willingness to be honest with ourselves. Then we must allow God's Holy Spirit into our minds and put in them (renewing our minds) the thoughts of God which we are ready and able to receive. We are not to judge things with our own mind but with the mind of Christ which the Holy Spirit implants within us. How do we know if the thoughts we have are from God? We judge these thoughts with the Holy Bible. Only the thoughts which agree with Scripture are from God. We must read, study, and meditate on His written word to keep His thoughts speaking to us louder than our own carnal and worldly thoughts. We have the mind of Christ. Let us learn to listen and obey those thoughts.

1 Corinthians 10:31 Glory of God

So whether you eat or drink or whatever you do, do it all for the glory of God. (NIV)

Glory of God

One book which had a powerful impact on my life was "Practicing the Presence" by Brother Laurence. He was a dishwasher in a monastery. He believed everything he did was important to God and should be done in an attitude of joy of serving and doing his best for God's glory. Reading this book changed my attitude toward doing the things necessary but which I considered boring, repetitive, and mundane. I didn't learn to change my attitude overnight, but I did start praying about each thing I did and asked God to help me do it with a grateful heart. After a while, a joy I hadn't experienced began to stay in me. Even taking garbage out became a joy. It's amazing what a grateful heart does to one's entire being. It doesn't matter if we are preaching a sermon to thousands of people or cleaning out a commode. We are here on this earth to bring glory to God, to fellowship with Him and to bring lost souls into God's family. Every task we do, whether considered great and important or one not even worthy of consideration is a task worth doing to our best and done for the glory of God. Let's ask the Holy Spirit to help us remember to choose a thankful attitude in all we do.

Psalms 43:5 In All Things

Why, my soul, are you downcast? Why so disturbed within me? Put your hope in God, for I will yet praise him, my Savior and my God. (NIV)

In All Things

In life we will have times of discouragement and sadness. David certainly had his share. But David refused to stay in a state of discouragement or sadness. He knew His life was in the hands of God. How did he change his emotional state? He chose to praise God. We may not feel like saying or singing words of praise when we are discouraged but we do have a choice. When we start verbalizing the positive such as praise to God, eventually we really start to put our mind on the power and love of God rather than dwelling on the source of our discouragement. Gradually we find God's joy enveloping our mind and changing the way we feel. When we have turned from discouragement to joy through praising God, we open our hearts and minds to God's answer for the situation which brought us down to discouragement. The Bible is full of instructions to praise God in all things. Let us stop the "woe is me" attitude and remember to always give praise to God in all circumstances. This tunes our spiritual ears to really hear the way God will lead us through any situation.

Acts 27:31 Press On

Then Paul said to the centurion and the soldiers, "Unless these men stay with the ship, you cannot be saved." (NIV)

Press On

They were in the midst a storm and were afraid. Paul knew God wanted him in Rome. Storms, shipwrecks, or snake bites wouldn't be able to prevent what God wanted. So often we start out on a ministry God has ordained but when things get tough, we think maybe we were wrong, and we jump ship. Just because God calls us to do something doesn't mean it will be easy. The evil in this world will do everything to divert us from God's leading. When we hear the call from God and it's confirmed, we should persevere. Paul did. He and all with him survived the shipwreck. Paul survived the poisonous snake bite. Paul got to Rome and delivered God's message. What is stopping us from persevering in what God has called us to do? Is it inconvenience, fear, reputation, or anything else? We must examine our hearts, confess our lack, ask the Holy Spirit to renew our faith and commitment and press on with God's calling on our lives.

Matthew 26:8-13 Extravagance

When the disciples saw this, they were indignant. "Why this waste?" they asked. "This perfume could have been sold at a high price and the money given to the poor. "Aware of this, Jesus said to them, "Why are you bothering this woman? She has done a beautiful thing to me. The poor you will always have with you, but you will not always have me. When she poured this perfume on my body, she did it to prepare me for burial. (NIV)

Extravagance

Sounds spiritual when the disciples said it's to extravagant and should go to help the poor. But Jesus said it was to prepare Him for what was waiting ahead for Him. Many of us forget we are precious to God and are worthy of a little extravagance from time to time. There are many hard roads to travel in this life. When there is an occasion for a little extravagance it lifts our spirits and prepares us to face more rough roads. Yes, we are to give to the poor. But if we neglect ourselves, we become unable to give to the poor for we sink into depression from the hard times without celebrating the victories. This woman showed her priorities. Jesus was so precious to her that spending an entire year's income on Him to show Him how precious He was to her was more important. I would imagine this helped Jesus remember it was for His great love for us that He was going to face the hardest and most painful ordeal anyone has ever faced. Let us remember since Jesus loves us that much, we should love ourselves in addition to loving others.

Isaiah 40:31 Entwined

But they that wait upon the Lord shall renew their strength; they shall mount up with wings as eagles; they shall run, and not be weary; and they shall walk, and not faint. (KJV)

Entwined

There are many different Greek words which are translated in English as "wait." In this verse, the Greek word which is translated as "wait" actually means "to be entwined." When string is entwined to make a strong cord, it is braided or wrapped around several strands to become stronger. We are to be entwined or wrapped up in God to be strong and to soar and not be weary or faint. How do we become entwined in the Lord? We read, study, and meditate on His written word, putting it deep in our minds and hearts. We practice what we read in His written word. We communicate regularly with God being sure to spend more time listening than talking. Jesus prayed for us to become one with God as He is One in God and to be one with other believers. Let us work toward our oneness in God through obedience and with one another by putting our petty differences aside and worshiping and walking with God through His Holy Spirit.

Deuteronomy 8:2 Testing

Remember how the Lord your God led you all the way in the wilderness these forty years, to humble and test you in order to know what was in your heart, whether or not you would keep his commands. (NIV)

Testing

When we walk through a wilderness time in our lives it is a time of testing and learning for us. The testing is not for God to know what is in our hearts. He knows. It is for us to know what is in our hearts. When we murmur and complain during a time of testing it hampers our ability to listen and learn what God is showing us. Testing is often a pruning time. In the wilderness or trial of struggle the things that are separating us from becoming one with Christ are lopped away if we will walk through the testing with an open heart and mind. When we find ourselves facing a difficult time, let us remember these times are for us to learn. We learn more about the power of God. We learn more how dependent we are on Him. We learn more about our own weakness. We learn more how to look to Him for all our answers. Let us put our complaints about our difficulty aside and fully participate in God's schooling of testing for our benefit and for His glory.

Job 42:2 Purpose

I know that you can do all things; no purpose of yours can be thwarted. (NIV)

Purpose

This is a guarantee. No purpose of God's can ever be stopped. Since that is true, I would think all of us would rather cooperate with God's purpose than be on the losing team and try to be against His purpose. We might ask, what is God's purpose? His purpose is plainly recorded in His written Word, the Holy Bible. As we read, study, and meditate on it His purpose will gradually become clear. He created us to have fellowship with Him. Are we really in fellowship with Him? If not, what's stopping us? He desires all to be in fellowship with Him. Are we doing our part to help all others be in fellowship with Him? If not, why aren't we? These are questions we all must take to heart in an honest way. With God it is all or nothing. We are either for Him or against Him. We cannot be part-time children. God is love but His love is serious, not flippant. I pray we all realize time is getting short, we are here to love, fellowship and serve God and we need to invest our time, hearts, minds, and lives in Him.

Exodus 13:22 Following the Pillars

Neither the pillar of cloud by day nor the pillar of fire by night left its place in front of the people. (NIV)

Following the Pillars

The Hebrews didn't wander in the wilderness. They were led by the pillar of cloud by day and by the pillar of fire by night. When the pillars moved, the Hebrews moved with them. They could have chosen to stay in one place, but they moved forward with the pillars. We are led by God's Holy Spirit Who is our pillar of cloud and fire. Are we moving with Him? It's comfortable to stay in one place or to worship in one traditional way. We must make a choice. We can stay in one place, do things in one way, or be open to the leading of the Holy Spirit and move with Him. We can say, "We've never done it that way before." Or we can say we will go and do in whatever way the Holy Spirit leads us. We must ask ourselves if we're moving forward with God or if we are content to stay in a comfortable rut.

Exodus 15:23 Bitter Water

When they came to Marah, they could not drink its water because it was bitter. (That is why the place is called Marah.) (NIV)

Bitter Water

God led the Hebrews to the bitter water for a reason. The waters had the same elements as the drink we must take before a colonoscopy to purge our system. God wanted to purge the systems of the Hebrews from the Egyptian diet they've eaten over the years. But the people rebelled so the Egyptian diet along with other not-so-good things of Egypt stayed with them for quite a while. Sometimes God leads us through things that are bitter. There is always a reason. Instead of complaining we should ask Him to reveal the purpose, learn what we need to learn and walk through the bitterness with thanksgiving that God loves us enough to want His best for us. To have His best, we must have the things that separate us from Him purged from our hearts and minds. Let us not have complaints on our lips nor in our hearts and minds. Let's remember nothing can touch us without first passing through our Father's hand and praise Him as we walk, He has prepared for us.

Jude 1:20-22 Building Up

But you, dear friends, by building yourselves up in your most holy faith and praying in the Holy Spirit, keep yourselves in God's love as you wait for the mercy of our Lord Jesus Christ to bring you to eternal life. (NIV)

Building Up

We are told to build ourselves up. Many of us put ourselves down. We don't like the way we look or talk or how we do certain things. We condemn ourselves when we make a mistake. This is not building ourselves up. We forget we are so very special to God. How do we build ourselves up and accept how special we are in God's eyes? We pray. That is, we communicate with God. Communication is a two-way process. We talk then we listen. We can't listen if we have distractions around us. We can't meditate on the Bible if we have distractions around us. We are accustomed to living in noise. We get nervous with quiet. We are out of practice of really listening. When we really spend time with God, listening to His quiet voice through His Holy Spirit in us, we will hear words of love and encouragement. Not only does God love us, but He also wants us to love ourselves. To not love ourselves is to deny God's love for us. Instead of condemning ourselves let's immerse ourselves in God through Bible reading, meditation, study, and prayer.

Matthew 16:23 Stumbling Block

Jesus turned and said to Peter, "Get behind me, Satan! You are a stumbling block to me; you do not have in mind the concerns of God, but merely human concerns." (NIV)

Stumbling Block

From a human perspective, we agree with Peter's effort to keep Jesus from any harm. Jesus had a unique perspective. Most often we don't understand why God allows us to walk through hard trials. A child dies young, Christians are tortured and so many other things we consider to be terrible. We can't see God's perspective. We can only trust God will turn all things to the good for His children. Jesus had to go through horrible torture and then wait 3 days before He was resurrected. Sometimes our wait seems non-ending, but God will show us His victory and glory. Our job is to trust. Trust is a choice. Emotions don't always agree with the trust. Emotions come and go but the choice of trust can remain steadfast. As I watch a dear friend go through a most difficult time, I pray for peace to come with the trust and eventually the joy of seeing God's victory through the trial. Let us not be stumbling blocks but let us speak words of encouragement as we watch others walking through trials.

Numbers 21:4-9 The Snake

They traveled from Mount Hor along the route to the Red Sea, to go around Edom. But the people grew impatient on the way; they spoke against God and against Moses, and said, "Why have you brought us up out of Egypt to die in the wilderness? There is no bread! There is no water! And we detest this miserable food!" Then the Lord sent venomous snakes among them; they bit the people and many Israelites died. The people came to Moses and said, "We sinned when we spoke against the Lord and against you. Pray that the Lord will take the snakes away from us." So, Moses prayed for the people. The Lord said to Moses, "Make a snake and put it up on a pole; anyone who is bitten can look at it and live." So Moses made a bronze snake and put it up on a pole. Then when anyone was bitten by a snake and looked at the bronze snake, they lived. (NIV)

The Snake

To learn this lesson, we must read and meditate on the entire paragraph. The Hebrews, after experiencing many miracles of God, were complaining. They were looking back to the land of sin where they had become comfortable. God needed to get their attention. He wanted them to not only look to Him but also to trust Him. The snake on the pole was to get them to look up. Our question we must ask and answer for ourselves is who do we look to for our source? When we first notice a problem do we look to our own human wisdom? Do we look to another person? Do we look to drug or food? Our first response to any situation should be to look to God. When we look to God first, He will guide us through our problem. He may send us a friend, or He may tell us directly what to do. The main thing is for us first to take our problem to God without complaint but with faith and thanksgiving for His faithfulness, grace, and mercy to guide and provide for us through everything He allows to pass through His hands to us.

Matthew 6:26 Make Time

Look at the birds of the air; they do not sow or reap or store away in barns, and yet your heavenly Father feeds them. Are you not much more valuable than they? (NIV)

Make Time

I had some free time yesterday and was sitting on the porch watching the birds. They were flitting from tree branch to tree branch and singing the unique song God had given each one. Though they were alert to danger, they were content doing what God created them to do. They seemed to do it so naturally. It made me think about me and other humans. We tend to forget what God intended us to do. He created us for fellowship. Fellowship with Him and fellowship with one another. Fellowship is our main business, yet we always seem to busy. It seems we want to be too busy. We mistakenly think our worth is tied to how much we get done rather than our relationship with God and each other. Our priorities get out of order so easily. What do we do about this? We learn to start our day with fellowship and worship with and of God. We ask Him to help us keep our priorities straight. We think twice before we tell someone we're too busy to be or talk to them right now. We choose to make time. Let us make time for God and for each other.

Matthew 6:34 Move

Therefore, do not worry about tomorrow, for tomorrow will worry about itself. Each day has enough trouble of its own. (NIV)

Move

God told Moses His name is I Am. "Am" is in the present tense. Though God knows the future, He is in the present and He expects us to be in the present. Yesterday is in the past. It cannot be changed. Just because God told us to do something yesterday in a certain way doesn't mean we are to do the same thing in the same way today. God is on the move. Our question we must answer is are we on the move with Him? Humans tend to get in habits which become very comfortable. The only habit we should have been fellowship with God. We must choose to be open to His movement and be willing to move with Him. The old is comfortable. The new sometimes makes us feel insecure. Our security is in God. He is faithful. He will give us what we need to move with Him. The only standing we should do is stand on the faith God gives us. He is faithful. Are we?

Matthew 7:1-2 Our Thoughts

Do not judge, or you too will be judged. (NIV)

Our Thoughts

I constantly fight this one. I seldom judge or criticize out loud but in my thought pattern I do. I'm sitting at a restaurant eating and criticize in my mind how someone's dressed or how much they're eating. Even in church, I find myself criticizing how someone is dressed or their hairstyle. I criticize a slow driver without knowing the reason why they're driving slower than the speed limit. I could go on and on. As I catch myself doing this, I ask God to forgive me for judging and criticizing someone He loves and died for and ask Him to help me stop doing this. God not only cares about our actions, but He also cares about our thoughts for our thoughts reflect our hearts. He wants us to love our neighbor as ourselves, not critique them. I still do it but I'm catching myself in mid-thought now. You might want to reflect on how you're doing with this command of God.

John 9:5 Shine the Light

While I am in the world, I am the light of the world."

Matthew 5:14 "You are the light of the world. A town built on a hill cannot be hidden. (NIV)

Shine the Light

Jesus shined His light while He was walking in this world. When He sent His Holy Spirit to the believers, He also sent His light. We are His light in this world. We are to let His light shine for all to see. To know how to let the light shine we must study the scriptures and become very familiar with how Jesus let His light shine. He showed His love and concern for all people regardless of age, gender, race, status, education, or any other characteristic. He touched, spoke, shared God's commandments, and healed. He met people where they were at and never talked down to them. We must look honestly at our light. Our light is the reflection of Jesus and His love. How much does it shine? Do we let it blink on and off depending on our circumstances? How far does it shine? Have we allowed it to become dim? Let's clear of anything that shades it and let His light in us shine out bright to all.

Matthew 7:16 Known by Fruits

By their fruit you will recognize them. Do people pick grapes from thorn bushes, or figs from thistles?

Galatians 5:22-23 But the fruit of the Spirit is love, joy, peace, forbearance, kindness, goodness, faithfulness, gentleness, and self-control. (NIV)

Known by Fruits

It's important to notice it is by our fruit, not by our works. We tend to judge people by their works. Good works are not only done by Christians; they are done by people of various religions or even no religion. From the verse in Matthew, we must look at the verse in Galatians to determine to what fruits Jesus is referring. If good works lack these fruits, they are really nothing more than filthy rags to God. God looks at the heart, not the works. Someone full of the Holy Spirit and growing in these fruits will do good works because of the fruits. We must pay attention to each fruit and see which ones we've not permitted to grow in us. Let us be diligent to feed all these fruits through meditation on the written word and conversations with God.

Deuteronomy 1:22 Return to the Wilderness

Then all of you came to me and said, "Let us send men ahead to spy out the land for us and bring back a report about the route we are to take and the towns we will come to."

Deuteronomy 1:32 In spite of this, you did not trust in the Lord your God, (NIV)

Return to the Wilderness

The Hebrews saw how good the land was which God promised to give them. They also saw the people and their fortifications in that land. They saw them as a big problem and, instead of trusting God to fulfill His promise, they fixed their eyes on what they saw as a problem. Because of their lack of trust, they were left in the wilderness for a full generation. We can't judge them without looking at our own personal history. How many times do we wallow in a problem without trusting the promises God has given us? He said He will be always with us in and through all things. He said just ask and we will receive. He said all things are possible for us through His power and might. We must think about the times we lacked faith and trust then ask His forgiveness and resolve to choose trust in and through each experience God allows to come our way.

John 8:7 God Up

When they kept on questioning him, he straightened up and said to them, "Let any one of you who is without sin be the first to throw a stone at her." (NIV)

God Up

One thing we humans are very good at is blaming others for our problems. We don't like to admit we might be wrong. We don't like to even think any problem we have is because of our own choices. It is so easy to blame others not only for our own problems but for any problem we see. There is a saying, "When you point one finger at someone else there are 3 fingers point back at you." We don't like to take responsibility for our own actions or our feelings. It is so much easier to blame others. Jesus is telling these people here to stop judging others. We like to put our own standards on others and when they don't meet the standards we've set, we judge them to be wrong. There are many who don't want to read this. Those are the ones who would rather blame all their troubles on someone else. Some excuses for our blaming others are: had a bad childhood, not understood by others, can't help the way I am, someone else made me do it and on and on. There's a new phrase going around. It's, "man up." I would rather say, "God up." Let's be open and honest with God and acknowledge our own responsibility for our actions and feelings and relationships with others. Let's ask Him to heal our hurts and put them behind us, choosing to act in love in our relationships with all others. Their response or reactions are not our responsibility, but our actions and responses are our choice and accountable unto God.

Isaiah 40:31 Soar Like Eagles

but those who hope in the Lord will renew their strength. They will soar on wings like eagles; they will run and not grow weary, they will walk and not be faint. (NIV)

Soar Like Eagles

Eagles are fascinating birds. They have been spotted soaring as high as 20 thousand feet. They can do this because they find the up-air currents and hold their wings out letting the air currents lift and keep them up. This is what putting our trust in God does for us. When we put our trust in God, we can soar through our trials, resting on the currents of the Holy Spirit and the power of God's Word. As we rest on God's Word our strength is renewed. When we run to God and His Word we are refreshed and will not grow weary. When we walk firm, standing firm on God's promises, we will not faint. We must know the written Word of God so we can stand firm on it through all circumstances and soar as the eagles soar through the sky.

An Extra fact:

Eagles can also see 50 miles. We can't do this without the aid of high-powered telescopes. But God's vision is limitless. If we ask Him, He'll enable us to see what we need to see.

2 Timothy 3:16 Living Word

All Scripture is God-breathed and is useful for teaching, rebuking, correcting, and training in righteousness, (NIV)

Living Word

Scripture, the Holy Bible, is the Logos, or the written word of God. Anyone can read the scripture. There was a time in China they used the Bible to teach English. That was all the Bible was to them. There is another language needed to understand the Bible. This is the Rhema, the spoken word of God through His Holy Spirit. Without this the Bible is only a book of history. With the Holy Spirit the Bible becomes the living word of God. Remember the two disciples walking on the road when Jesus came after his resurrection and joined them. He was explaining or interpreting the written scripture and making it a living scripture which spoke to them and gave them understanding. When we sit down to read God's written word, we must first ask His Holy Spirit to speak to us through that word. We can read the same passage at different points of our life, and it will say different things to us. Therefore, it is the Living Word. It is always for the now and always gives us life. Let us thank God for His written Word, for the interpretation of the Holy Spirit, and for His quiet voice within us when we are willing to be quiet and listen. May we always be listening.

Romans 3:10-12 It's a Fact

As it is written: "There is no one righteous, not even one; there is no one who understands; there is no one who seeks God. All have turned away, they have together become worthless; there is no one who does good, not even one."

It's a Fact

This is a description of mankind in comparison to God. It is not harsh. It is very factual. In comparison to God, we are despicable. But God provided a way to change this. He sent part of Himself, His Son, Jesus, to walk where we walk and show us how to live and talk. Then He paid the ultimate price for our sin by shedding His blood on the cross. After He paid the price, He physically rose from the dead to show and give us new and eternal life through Him. There is no other way to God because no other being has ever been totally righteous, shed blood for our sins and after death come back physically to life and after being witnessed by hundreds physically ascended to heaven. It isn't prejudice that says Jesus is the only way to God's righteousness. It is pure fact. Only God is righteous, and we must have His righteousness within us to be able to be in His presence. We must ask ourselves if we have fully welcomed Jesus into our minds, hearts, and lives. Without Him, we are doomed to sin regardless of how much we try to do what seems good. I pray all who read this have invited Jesus into their minds, hearts and lives and will share this fact with all others in their path.

John 14:16 Advocate

And I will ask the Father, and he will give you another advocate to help you and be with you forever— (NIV)

Advocate

An advocate is defined as "one who pleads another's cause, who helps another by defending or comforting him." (Eston's Bible Dictionary) The original Greek word is "kietos" which is a verb translated as "to call," The Holy Spirit is within the believers and followers of Jesus to be called on at any time. He is here to stand beside us, to intercede for us when needed, to advise us when asked. Our question is do we make ourselves available for our advocate? When we face a situation how long is it before we ask the advice of the Holy Spirit? He is within us, waiting to be invited to defend, advise, and work on our behalf. Our human nature is stubborn. We want to "do it ourselves." This attitude of pride only gets us in trouble. We need to humble ourselves before the Lord our God and acknowledge we are nothing and can do nothing in and of ourselves. It is only God, in and through us, that any good or righteous thing can be accomplished. Let's not start another day without inviting the Holy Spirit to be active in our hearts, minds, and lives.

2 Corinthians 12:10 Impact of Trials

That is why, for Christ's sake, I delight in weaknesses, in insults, in hardships, in persecutions, in difficulties. For when I am weak, then I am strong. (NIV)

Impact of Trials

Enduring and passing through trials isn't only for our own learning experience. Read about the people in the Bible. Without Paul being in prison, many of the letters in the New Testament wouldn't have been written. Without John in prison on the island, Revelations would not have been written. Without David being hunted down by Saul many of the Psalms wouldn't have been written. Trials have an impact on the kingdom of God on this earth. Trials carry His word further. The next time we are going through a trial let's not only ask God what we are to learn in and through it, let's ask Him how we can impact His Kingdom in and through it.

1 Corinthians 2:16 Mind of Christ

For who has known the mind of the Lord so as to instruct him? But we have the mind of Christ. (NIV)

Mind of Christ

This verse seems at odds with itself. We must look at the tenses of the verbs. The first part is "Who has known." The verb has known is past perfect. It is in the past. Before God sent His Holy Spirit to come into the believers in His Son, Jesus, it was impossible to know the mind of God. Now we have the Holy Spirit. With His interpreting, the written scriptures and making them real as we meditate on them, we can come to know the mind of Christ. We do this by reading carefully all that Jesus did and said as He physically walked this earth. All that He said and did was to honor the Father and extend the Father's love to all. As we read and meditate on the words and actions of Jesus, we need to visualize all that was occurring and put ourselves in the situation. Doing this makes the written word alive in us. As we get to know Jesus better, we will get to know His mind. This will be a life-long process. Let us be sure to do our part by allowing the Holy Spirit to work within us.

Philippians 3:20 Citizenship

But our citizenship is in heaven, and from it we await a Savior, the Lord Jesus Christ, (NIV)

Citizenship

The original Greek word from which "citizenship" is translated is "politeneu" which means good citizen. Paul is encouraging the Romans in Philipi (a Roman city) to be good citizens of Rome. Paul was proud to be a Roman. But he reminded them that before this world's citizenship comes the citizenship, we have through Jesus in God's throne room. We must learn to be good citizens of both. Of this world where we currently live, we are to pray and intercede for our government and the leaders and people. Of our citizenship in the eternal kingdom, we are to obey our King and spread His light and love through us to all we meet. We must be honest with ourselves as we look over our actions to see if we are really being good citizens both here and in God's kingdom. We must ask ourselves if His kingdom is really within us like He said it could and should be.

Psalms 99:5 Footstool

Exalt the Lord our God and worship at his footstool; he is holy. (NIV)

Footstool

On our 10th wedding anniversary, our first one after we accepted Jesus as Lord of our lives, my husband and I, without each of us knowing what the other was doing, gave each other a gift. His was a ring I designed. It had a throne with the cross that represented Jesus on it and below it was a footstool with my husband's initials. He designed a very similar thing on a pendant for me. We had both come into the realization that believing Jesus is the Son of God wasn't complete if we didn't take Him into our minds, hearts and lives as our Lord and King. Satan knows Jesus is the Son of God, but he doesn't have Jesus as Lord and King. It takes more than belief to enter the narrow way of Jesus and come before the throne of God for all eternity. It takes obedience out of love. We must ask if we are on the throne of our lives and have Jesus on the footstool in case of emergencies or if we have Him on the throne of our lives where He belongs, and we are on the footstool.

Luke 4:18-19 Job Description

"The Spirit of the Lord is upon me, because He has anointed me to proclaim good news to the poor. He has sent me to proclaim liberty to the captives and recovering of sight to the blind, to set at liberty those who are oppressed, to proclaim the year of the Lord's favor." (NIV)

Job Description

This is the first sermon or teaching of Jesus. This was His job description. It is also our job description. What does it say we are to do? We are to proclaim the good news. The good news is forgiveness of sins and salvation to eternal life with God through His Son, Jesus. We are to proclaim this to the poor. This isn't limited to financially poor people. We are all poor in our lives, minds, and hearts without experiencing the love and forgiveness of God. We are to proclaim liberty to the captives. The captives are people living in the captivity of sin. We are to help the blind recover their sight. Without Jesus in our lives, we are blind to God, His grace, His mercy, His salvation, His forgiveness, and His love. We are to set at liberty those who are oppressed. All sinners are oppressed for joy is not possible without the love and forgiveness of God. We are to proclaim the year of the Lord's favor. All years living with God's Holy Spirit in us as believers and followers are years filled with the favor of God. Are we doing all that is in our job description?

Colossians 2:2 Aspen Grove

My goal is that they may be encouraged in heart and united in love, so that they may have the full riches of complete understanding, so that they may know the mystery of God, namely, Christ, (NIV)

Aspen Grove

Aspen trees are fascinating. Their root systems are all united together underground. They grow and function as one. We are to be like the aspen trees. We are to be united through Jesus. We are not to be divisive. We are to function as one. When one hurts, we all are hurt. When one is killed because of belief in Jesus, part of all of us is killed. Let us learn to encourage one another. Let us learn to pull together. Let us not be divisive but function in the love of God through the Holy Spirit. When we don't agree, let us move on together in love and accept one another's differences. Our root system of love is underground deep through the love, grace, and mercy of our God. Let us always remember we are only as strong as the weakest one among us. Let us build up, unite in Christ Jesus, and help in bringing His Kingdom on this earth as it is in heaven.

Numbers 11:15 Help

If you will treat me like this, kill me at once, if I find favor in your sight, that I may not see my wretchedness." (NIV)

Help

Moses was extremely tired. Nothing God did please the Hebrews in the wilderness. After the start of every miracle, they wanted more and longed to be back in the bondage to which they were accustomed. Moses was looked to for every complaint and to settle every disagreement. Then God told Moses to get some help. He didn't need to face so many problems by himself. Read all of Numbers 11 to get the entire story. What this tells us today is, that when things get a little tight for us, when we start to feel overwhelmed, we are not to assume other people can read our mind and offer help unasked. We need to speak up. When we are under pressure, ask for help. Moses was recommended to choose his help carefully and so must we. We don't "blab" our problems to anyone who will listen. We ask God who we should go to and ask for help. I have a friend who complains things are hard and no one will help, visit, or call. The friend needs to ask rather than complain about it. If Moses needed help and God agreed, we are not inadequate for needing help ourselves. Next time we start to feel a little too much pressure, ask God and then ask the one He leads us to for help. As the roots of the Aspen trees (yesterday's devotion) are connected, we are connected. Whether the helper or the one being helped, it's all the same. It is God working through us.

Matthew 28:20 Always a Light

And surely, I am with you always, to the very end of the age." (NIV)

Always a Light

We were at the beach on the East Coast waiting to watch the sun rise. There was a storm brewing, and the sky was dark with clouds. Gradually we could see a touch of pink being reflected in a small cloud. Then I noticed a bright hole surrounded by the dark clouds. As I meditated, God reminded me no matter how bad a storm or how dark things were, there was always a bright light to look and see if we would only remember to look to Him. The sun was rising though we couldn't see it. But we could see the evidence of the sunrise and, when we look, we can see the evidence of God with us. Let us always be looking.

Isaiah 55:11 Not Return Empty

so is my word that goes out from my mouth: It will not return to me empty but will accomplish what I desire and achieve the purpose for which I sent it. (NIV)

Not Return Empty

Jesus is the Word of God. He was sent out by God to bring salvation to all people, and He accomplished this on the cross by taking on our sins for all eternity. He returned to God the Father achieving the purpose for which He was sent. But it takes more than what Jesus did to accomplish His purpose. It takes us hearing and receiving Jesus and accepting what He did for us on the cross. After we accept this, we become joint heirs with Jesus for all of God's blessings and for anything God plans to accomplish. It is now our responsibility to see that His Word, Jesus, is heard by all others. We do this by our actions and with our mouths. Our question is, what are we doing to share God's Word, Jesus, with others?

1 Corinthians 2:10 Searching

these are the things God has revealed to us by his Spirit. The Spirit searches all things, even the deep things of God. (NIV)

Searching

This verse can be confusing if not read through the interpretation of the Holy Spirit. The Holy Spirit is God. He doesn't need to search all things, even the deep things of God for Himself. He already knows all that is to know. He searches all things in us for us to know even the deep things of God. He is in us, wanting us to plug into His searching for us. Our question is are we allowing Him to search within us to reveal to us the deep things of God? It is such an exciting and glorious search when we allow ourselves to connect with Him and embark on that search. We search through allowing Him to interpret the scriptures for us and meditate on what He shows us. We search through seeing what God does in and around us through nature and other people. The search is so enjoyable and fills us with the deepest joy possible. Let us get serious and disciplined in the search through God the Holy Spirit.

Matthew 25:10 Keep the Wicks Burning

But while they were on their way to buy the oil, the bridegroom arrived. The virgins who were ready went in with him to the wedding banquet. And the door was shut. (NIV)

Keep the Wicks Burning

It is my prayer before you read any further you will open your Bibles and read Matthew 25 starting at verse 1. The virgins represent the believers in Jesus. The oil stands for the Holy Spirit. Ten of the virgins didn't refresh their lamps with oil. They had to find someone with oil to refresh them. The other ten had a daily supply of oil. We have the option of having a daily supply of oil. We can ask God to refill us every day. We can't afford to go one day without the re-infilling of the Holy Spirit. No man knows the day or time of Jesus' coming back for the believers. Jesus said He didn't even know the day or time. Only the Father knows. We must be continually ready. We dare not sleep and let our flame, the flame of the Holy Spirit, the Light of God, burn out within us. He must be the priority in our hearts, minds, and lives. We need to be continually filled with the Holy Spirit. This takes discipline in obedience and meditation in communion with God the Father. Let not a day go by without the re-infilling of the Holy Spirit to enable us to keep the wicks of God's light burning within us.

Philippians 2:6-7 Not Equal

Who, being in very nature God, did not consider equality with God something to be used to his own advantage; rather, he made himself nothing by taking the very nature of a servant, being made in human likeness. (NIV)

Not Equal

Jesus came to earth to glorify the Father. He didn't consider Himself equal to the Father even though He and the Father are One. We tend to forget we are here not for our glory but here to glorify God. We forget and our prayers reflect our attitude of "God serve me, God bless me, God do this for me." We forget to ask, "God what do You want to do through me." This attitude also shows in our relationship with others. We put our desires before those of others. We want to be served rather than to serve. We like to think we are putting others and God first but when we're honest with ourselves we see our lack. It takes the Holy Spirit in us to be willing to trust God enough to put Him first in our lives. It takes the Holy Spirit in us to be willing to put others first and be willing to serve them, not out of pure obedience but out of our love for God and His glory. Let us work toward that goal. The Holy Spirit works within us to truly put God first in our minds, hearts, and lives, not out of obedience but because of the love He has for us and the love we have for Him.

John 10:27 God Doesn't

My sheep listen to my voice; I know them, and they follow me.

God Doesn't

God doesn't need to speak to us in an audible voice. He doesn't need to speak to us through mighty miracles. He's given us His written word and His Holy Spirit to speak to us. The only reasons we don't hear Him is we don't listen, or we don't obey. He says to hear we must listen. He says for forgiveness we must forgive. He says to get we must give. He says to be loved we must love. If we aren't hearing God speak to us daily, it is our fault. God is always speaking. We aren't always listening, and we aren't always obedient. We must open His written word and do more than read it. We must chew on it and digest it until it becomes part of us. We have nothing to complain about for God has given us the power to be victorious in our life in this world. Let us put our excuses and complaints behind us and move on in obedience with a listening ear, eating and digesting His written word that we may hear, obey, and glorify our God.

Genesis 1:1-4 Eat and Digest

In the beginning God created the heavens and the earth. Now the earth was formless and empty, darkness was over the surface of the deep, and the Spirit of God was hovering over the waters. And God said, "Let there be light," and there was light (NIV)

Eat and Digest

I've been led to give an example of how to eat and digest God's written word. Read these first three verses of Genesis, the beginning of God's written word. Read it slowly before you read what it says to me.

At the very beginning of creation, God already was. God wasn't alone. God, the Father of all that was, is, or will ever be also has the Spirit. But there was another with God from the beginning. The Word. Later in the written Word we read the Word is Jesus, the only begotten Son of God. There were always and are always three in the person of God. We call Him One God for the three are interdependent. God the Father is the decision maker. He speaks through the Word, Jesus, His Son. Life is through His Holy Spirit. As I read over what I've received from these 3 verses I read it several times. I also praise God for Who He is and thank each part of His Godhead for what they each do.

Psalms 119:11 I have hidden your word in my heart that I might not sin against you.

Job 42:2 Mistakes are Okay

I know that you can do all things; no purpose of yours can be thwarted.

Mistakes are Okay

Many are afraid to think they might have heard God speak to them for they are afraid they might be wrong. I had a choir director say, "Sing out loud enough to hear or you will never know if you are making a mistake and then you can't correct it." God is bigger than any mistake we can ever make. What counts is our heart attitude. When we are looking to Him and trying to hear Him and we know scripture agrees with what we think we heard, we need to be bold and act on what we heard. If we are wrong, God can and will take it and turn it into good. Mistakes are a wonderful teacher when we let them teach us.

1 Timothy 4:15-16 Diligence

Be diligent in these matters; give yourself wholly to them, so that everyone may see your progress. Watch your life and doctrine closely. Persevere in them, because if you do, you will save both yourself and your hearers. (NIV)

Diligence

I love the books of Timothy. They are so full of sound advice for growing in our relationship with God. There is a temptation for those who preach, teach, and/or write to read the scripture to share with others. When we fall into this trap it hampers our growth. We are to search, study, and digest the scriptures for our growth. As we grow and display in our lives, our actions, and our words others will be drawn to us to read listen or watch and seek the reason for our growth. If we don't eat and digest the Word ourselves, we won't grow. What we say or write might be very accurate. God won't let His word come back void. Results will happen to others. We are the ones who lose out. The matters the above verse refers to are reading, studying, digesting, and obeying the instructions in God's written word, the Holy Bible. Let us apply ourselves to the sound advice Paul gave to Timothy.

2 Timothy 2:15-16 Do your best to present yourself to God as one approved, a worker who does not need to be ashamed and who correctly handles the word of truth.

Hebrews 10:24-25 Gathering Together

And let us consider how we may spur one another on toward love and good deeds, not giving up meeting together, as some are in the habit of doing, but encouraging one another—and all the more as you see the Day approaching. (NIV)

Gathering Together

Tomorrow is Sunday. This is the day we have chosen to gather in honor of our Lord Jesus' resurrection. We are told in the written word to gather. There are several reasons. The first, of course, is to worship our Lord together with one voice. But we are also to encourage one another in our separate walks. Our question is what do we do when we are in our respective church buildings? Do we just go in and out so we can be the first in line at a restaurant? We are to talk to one another. Ask each other how our walk is going. Pray for one another. Asking how someone's walk with God is going is not invading privacy. It is a way of showing love and encouraging, especially during trying times. Let us gather early before our services and stay a little later to pause, talk, and pray for one another.

Job 33:4 Uniquely Me

The Spirit of God has made me; the breath of the Almighty gives me life.

Uniquely Me

God has made each person. The miracle of conception and birth is not haphazard. It is only through the creation process of God and the breath of Him that we are born. Each one of us is a unique person. There is no other person made exactly like us. Even in twins or other multiple births, there is a difference. The outside of a person might look like the outside of another but inside we are each unique. Along with being formed uniquely, we each have a unique purpose on this earth. No one else can take our place. It is our responsibility to seek God and hear from Him what He has designed us to do while we walk this earth. We were all designed to fellowship with God and with each other. But each is called to do this in their God-given unique way. We are each loved by God. We are each important to Him. We don't need others to put us on a pedestal. We are loved, cherished, and important to God. Let us put our inferior emotions aside and accept and embrace our relationship with God. I wrote these words to a song and here is an excerpt.

I'm the only me God has

No one else can take my place

What joy it will be, to meet the real me

While looking in my Savior's face.

It is in looking to our God through our Savior, Jesus, that our identity, worth and purpose is found.

Romans 8:5 Pause First

Those who live according to the flesh have their minds set on what the flesh desires; but those who live in accordance with the Spirit have their minds set on what the Spirit desires. (NIV)

Pause First

We have a choice to live by our fleshly, self-centered desires of pleasing ourselves or to live to please God. Our minds can rationalize reasons to side with the flesh. To find out what pleases God we must study the Bible. As we study, we ask the Holy Spirit to give us insight into what pleases God. When we ask the Holy Spirit in us, we are enabled to choose to please God rather than our flesh. With practice and with getting to know and experience God's love more and more our desires will gradually change. Practice pausing before speaking or acting and allow the Holy Spirit to witness or check.

John 14-17 Co-Heirs

For those who are led by the Spirit of God are the children of God. The Spirit you received does not make you slaves so that you live in fear again; rather, the Spirit you received brought about your adoption to sonship. And by him, we cry, "Abba, Father." The Spirit himself testifies with our spirit that we are God's children. Now if we are children, then we are heirs—heirs of God and co-heirs with Christ, if indeed we share in his sufferings so that we may also share in his glory.

Co-Heirs

Present Suffering and Future Glory

When we are young children, life is about us and others doing for us and giving to us. As we become adults, we take on responsibilities, both for ourselves and for helping others. It is the same as we grow in the Lord. When we first meet Jesus it's what He has done and does do for us. But we are joint heirs with Him. This means we share in the responsibility of working for the Kingdom of God. It is no longer about giving me or doing for me but using me for Your glory, God in any way You please. This is only possible through our yielding to the Holy Spirit. We must pay attention to our prayers. Are we always praying for ourselves, God I need this or please do this for me? He already knows what we need. It's okay to ask for things for ourselves but that should be a small percentage of our prayers. We are co-heirs with Jesus which means we must share not only in sufferings but in His love and desire for all to come to know His love in a personal way. Let's be about our Father's business.

Genesis 2:1-3 Resting Day

Thus the heavens and the earth were completed in all their vast array. By the seventh day God had finished the work he had been doing; so on the seventh day, he rested from all his work. Then God blessed the seventh day and made it holy because on it he rested from all the work of creating that he had done.

Resting Day

We don't know how long each day for God was for we are told later that a day can be like a thousand years. What is important for us is God divided His time into a Seven-day period. Six days were set aside for work. The 7th day was to be a day of rest. God made the resting day a holy day. It is a day to reflect on the work carried out and for us, to reflect on the Creator of all that is accomplished. The day we choose to take as our holy day is not the important thing. What is important is that we take a day as a holy and resting day. For those who work in churches, helping and leading others to worship and grow in the knowledge of God, the Creator and His Word, His Son, Jesus, that time is not resting. It is important for our physical, mental, emotional, and most importantly, spiritual health to take a day each week for just ourselves and God. It is a day to rest from our physical and mental work and deepen our relationship with our Creator. Our question is how do we use our day of rest? Are we allotting the time needed to be one-on-one with our Father?

Philippians 2:12-14 Working Out

Therefore, my dear friends, as you have always obeyed—not only in my presence but now much more in my absence—continue to work out your salvation with fear and trembling, for it is God who works in you to will and to act in order to fulfill his good purpose (NIV)

Working Out

Working out our salvation is so often misunderstood. Our salvation is a gift of grace from God through His Son, Jesus. But this salvation must continually be worked out to completion, to the time we are completely united with God in heaven for eternity. The word fear doesn't mean what we describe as fear in the English language. A more correct translation is awe and respect for Who God is. The trebling refers to our weakness. We cannot work out our salvation on our own. It takes the power of God's Holy Spirit within us to work out to complete our salvation through our Savior and Lord, Jesus. All of this comes from our choice. We can choose to remain babies in our salvation, or we can choose to grow into maturity and oneness with our Lord. The choice is ours. Let's get to work. Study the Bible, pray and meditate, digest and work.

Philippians 3:13 Only Today

Brothers and sisters, I do not consider myself yet to have taken hold of it. But one thing I do: Forgetting what is behind and straining toward what is ahead, (NIV)

Only Today

We are exceptionally good as humans to hang on to the past. That may be partly because we're not sure of the future. One of the problems of our hanging on to the past is a lack of forgiveness and resentment due to past hurts. When we keep on going back to what was past, it becomes prevalent in our minds and hearts and, though we may have forgiven or thought we had, we find anger or resentment raising its ugly head within our minds and hearts. One advantage of getting older is fewer memory cells for the past. But there is another way. We must learn to put our past under the blood of Jesus. We must not only forgive those who hurt us in the past but also forgive ourselves for our part in the hurt. Keeping our eyes on Jesus for today and our ears tuned to the gentle promptings of the Holy Spirit is what we need to do each day. We can't change what was before. We can't control what is to come. But we are children of the Creator God Who has everything in His hand. We can rest in trust and faith and live each moment He gives us on this earth in peace and trust. The straining toward what is ahead means living each moment in expectation of God's wisdom, love, protection, and guidance.

Job 38:2 No or Wait

Who is this that obscures my plans with words without knowledge? (NIV)

No or Wait

We are a stubborn and self-centered people. We want what we want when we want it. We expect when we ask God to do something, He will do it for us. We claim if we have enough faith all our prayers will be answered. This attitude is arguing with God. We don't like it when we don't see what we want and pray for. We don't understand God's "No." or His "Not yet." We forget God knows the future. We forgot He loves us enough to say no or say wait. We tend to act like toddlers wanting things now in our way. Our prayers should not be so full of give me and do for me. Our prayers should be mostly praise and thanksgiving. Then we should be interceding for the things God wants. The Bible is full of things we are to unite with heaven in our prayers so they will come about in God's way and His timing. Let us choose to grow up into mature children who love, trust, and obey our Father. When He says no or wait, let us praise Him for knowing what is best for us. As I reflect on some of the times God has said no to me, I rejoice in His wisdom for, today I can see God does know the best for me

Psalms 119:11 Lazy

I have hidden your word in my heart that I might not sin against you. (NIV)

Lazy

Every word in the Bible applies to everyone. Since Jesus quoted the written word of the scriptures to defeat Satan, how very much more we need to do the same. But, when we face temptation or choices of action, if we don't have the written word of God deep in our hearts and minds, we are at a loss. Our day of depending on electronics has weakened our desire to memorize, meditate, and get things deep in our minds and hearts. We have become mentally lazy thinking we can always do an internet search for anything we need. We all need to realize how soft and lazy we have gotten and make a commitment to God to study and show ourselves approved unto God. Yes, He loves us no matter how lazy we might be. But love is a two-way action. If we receive God's love, we will love Him back through our commitment and obedience. It's hard to be honest with ourselves. God knows what's in our hearts and minds so our honesty will not surprise Him. Let us choose to be diligent to His Word that we may walk in it with Him showing His light through our words and actions to all around us.

2 Peter 3:18 Must Grow to Live

But grow in the grace and knowledge of our Lord and Savior Jesus Christ. To him be glory both now and forever! Amen. (NIV)

Must Grow to Live

Living things (including people) must either grow or die. To be living you can't be stagnant. We've all noticed how a tree seed managed to get established in the cracks of a rock on the side of a mountain. It sank its roots deep in the crack and reached, growing toward the sun. God's love is the seed. It's planted deep in us. The written Word, the Holy Bible, are the cracks for our roots to grow down deep. Jesus is the light we are to reach for. The Holy Spirit waters us and nourishes our roots, enabling us to grow, anchored deeply in the written Word and looking up to Jesus, the Light of the World. We must check to see if our roots are centered deeply in the Bible if we are looking to Jesus and if we are allowing His Holy Spirit to water and nourish us.

Luke 10:41 All Ministries Equal

"Martha, Martha," the Lord answered, "you are worried and upset about many things, (NIV)

All Ministries Equal

I was raised to be a Martha. I was taught to take responsibilities seriously. Never walk away from a task and never stop until it is complete. But I have a Mary personality. I'm contemplative. I would rather be quiet than be at a party. Martha was upset. She knew things must be just right for her guest. There was much to do to prepare a meal for so many (Jesus was there with His 12 disciples). She was jealous that Mary was sitting at the feet of Jesus. That wasn't her place. Women were to be serving the men, not be part of their conversation. She felt righteous in her labors and her attitude. Jesus didn't say either of the sisters was wrong. He did say there is a time for everything. The sisters had a ministry. They could do their ministry for their guest and, at the same time, listen to all Jesus had to say. What we need is a heart attitude while we go about our assigned ministries. We need a heart attitude of love. Martha could have been doing her tasks with a joyful attitude while she was serving the Son of God. Instead, her eyes and mind were on what someone else was or wasn't doing. We don't know what Mary's needs were at the time. Since Jesus didn't say anything to her, we can assume she needed to do what she was doing. We are so quick to judge others by our standards and ideas about what ministry is needed when and how it is to be done. God's word says to let all we do be with joy and thanksgiving to God. No one ministry is more important than another. Let us learn to be content with what God gives us to do and leave what He calls others to do in His hands. Whether it be our mediation time, study time, or time to take out the garbage, let all we do be done keeping our eyes on God and our ears open to His bidding.

2 Chronicles 7:14 July 4th

If my people, who are called by my name, will humble themselves and pray and seek my face and turn from their wicked ways, then I will hear from heaven, and I will forgive their sin and will heal their land. (NIV)

July 4th

This is a promise from God with a few conditions. First, we must be called by His name. This means we must be followers of God's Son, Jesus. Second, we must humble ourselves. We are no better than any other person. We are each different, but each is valued and loved by God. We don't deserve God's love or blessings but through His grace and the righteousness of Jesus, we receive His love and provisions. Then we must pray, seeking His face and turning from our sin. We must admit our sins to Him, ask forgiveness, and make the choice to turn away from those sins, walking in obedience to the words of God. With those conditions, God promises to hear us. Not only does He hear us, but He also forgives our sins. Only after that will our land be healed. We certainly need the United States to be healed along with many other countries in this world. Tomorrow, July 4 we celebrate the independence of this nation which was established so people would be free to worship God in the way they choose. What a wonderful time to start praying in the way Jesus taught us to pray and committing to pray daily for our forgiveness and for the wisdom to do our part in bringing our land into the dream the first citizens desired it to be.

2 Timothy 1:7 Discipline is a Choice

For the Spirit God gave us does not make us timid, but gives us power, love and self-discipline. (NIV)

Discipline is a Choice

To be very honest, there are times I just don't want to sit down, pray, meditate, and write a devotion. Usually, it's because I'm tired. But, as I find myself resisting, I think about how Jesus didn't want to be tortured and then crucified on the cross. Yet, without a single complaint, He set His face toward Jerusalem and what lay ahead for Him. There are many things we don't want or feel like doing that we know will bring us deeper into our relationship with God. Our question is, do we love Him and want to be pleasing to Him? If we do, we must choose to put our fleshly desires aside, breathe in spiritually to get more spiritual energy, and choose to move forward with what God would have us do. I didn't feel like leaving my daughter's home during our July 4th celebration to go back to the hospital and answer a call from a patient. I did and was blessed by being allowed to assure someone of their salvation before they went into surgery. Discipline is necessary but only successful through our choices. When we choose discipline over convenience we are empowered and able to allow the love of God to flow in and through us to others. Let us choose to be disciplined in our times of prayer, meditation, Bible study, and service.

James 1:2 Joy in Suffering

Consider it pure joy, my brothers and sisters, whenever you face trials of many kinds, (NIV)

Joy in Suffering

James, the half-brother of Jesus, begins his letter talking about suffering. He grew up with Jesus saw how Jesus lived and heard Him talk. He didn't believe or understand Who Jesus was until close to the crucifixion but became a leader in the new Christian movement. He wrote guaranteeing followers of Jesus would suffer. Today we hear much about how, as Christians, our lives should be full of blessings. Little is said about suffering unless it is tied to sin. God does bless His children. He also allows us to go through the school of suffering. Without suffering ourselves we can't relate to the world and minister God's love. Suffering is used for our benefit as well as the benefit of others watching how we walk through suffering. When I had cancer, I published letters that went around the country. I heard from ministers who read my letters to their congregation and were blessed. We are here to fellowship with God and to allow Him to work through us to bring others into His Kingdom. We are not to dictate to God how He is to use us. When we walk through a suffering time, we must ask Him how we are to walk through it and what we are to learn from it. Doing this, turns suffering into blessings. Let us count it pure joy no matter what we are walking through knowing it is God Who is in control of all that touches us.

John 11:40 See the Glory

Then Jesus said, "Did I not tell you that if you believe, you will see the glory of God?" (NIV)

See the Glory

Jesus makes it simple. He says if we choose to believe we will see the glory of God. No action is needed on our part other than believing. The word glory means seeing the manifestation of God. God's manifestation is all around us. We miss it because we choose not to see it. All our life is composed of choices. We choose what we look at, what we listen to, what we read, what we do, what we say, and what we believe. We can choose to be content, or we can choose to complain. We can choose to be at peace, or we can choose to be angry. Believing is a choice. Trusting is a choice. Like Job, when he said, "Though He slay me, yet will I trust Him" with his teeth clenched against not believing or trusting. Our problem is so often we allow our emotions to rule our thoughts rather than our choice to believe and trust God. Emotions change, sometimes faster than the blink of an eye. God never changes. How much better it is to choose to believe in One Who never changes rather than something that can't be trusted to remain. Belief opens our eyes to see God moving in and through our lives. Let us choose to believe in the faithfulness of God and keep our eyes open to see His manifestation through and around us.

Psalms 119:66 Good Judgment

Teach me knowledge and good judgment, for I trust your commands. (NIV)

Good Judgment

We humans are so very arrogant. We like to be the ones "in the know." We like to claim we already know anything someone else tells us. It is hard for us to be humble before others. It's even harder for us to be humble before God. We think, because we've read the words in the Holy Bible, we know and understand what is there. Knowing and having good judgment are two different things. We can have all the knowledge in the world and still not have good judgment. Good judgment comes from God through His Holy Spirit. As we follow God's commands, we need to pay attention to His Holy Spirit for good judgment in how to follow them. He wants us to do more than just obey His commands. He wants our heart attitude to be in line with His. We obey, not because we must. We obey because we love Him and want to please Him. Let us keep a check on our heart attitude as we walk through our days.

Romans 7:15-16 Be Real

I do not understand what I do. For what I want to do I do not do, but what I hate I do. And if I do what I do not want to do, I agree that the law is good. (NIV)

Be Real

So many of us Christians wear spiritual masks. We try to present ourselves as being good and righteous. This gives a false impression of who we are. This turns away those who are seekers of real meaning in their lives. Paul was being very honest in these verses. He admits he is a sinner not unlike all other sinners. The difference is he has the forgiveness of God through the blood of Jesus. We all need to learn to be real. We need to let our shortcomings show just as much as our good works. The difference is we can go through life with the peace and joy of God because we know our names are written in His Book of Life and Jesus is our advocate when we face the judgment seat of God. Let us be real. Let us allow others to relate to us so their ears, minds, and hearts will be open to the love and saving grace of God.

Luke 22:42 Always Answers

"Father, if you are willing, take this cup from me; yet not my will, but yours be done." (NIV)

Always Answers

Jesus didn't want to face the cross. He prayed intently for the Father to make another way for us to be forgiven of our sins and reborn into eternal life. He prayed so hard he sweated drops of blood. I've never prayed that intensely for anything. He did, yet His Father said no. Sometimes God does say No. No is just as much an answer to our prayers as Yes is. Sometimes it is even more of an answer. We can't see tomorrow. We seldom look through spiritual eyes. Our prayers are often from a self-motivated fleshly desire. When we don't get what we pray for it doesn't mean God didn't answer. We miss the answer because we are only listening and looking for the answer our flesh wants. Jesus submitted to the will of the Father. When we pray, it's okay to ask for anything we want to ask but we must be willing to trust our Father Who knows what lies ahead of us and all our needs. He loves us even more than we love ourselves. He might say yes. He might say no. He might say wait a while. All are answers to our prayers. He always hears. He always answers. We just don't always listen or accept His answer. Let us learn to trust and praise the Father no matter what His answers are to our prayers. He is the one Who holds our future in the palm of His hand.

Isaiah 28:23 Pay Attention

Listen and hear my voice; pay attention and hear what I say. (NIV)

Pay Attention

This is an admonition from God. We are to listen, hear, and pay attention. He has provided several ways for us to hear and listen. We hear His voice as we read, study, and meditate on His written word, the Holy Bible. We also can hear His voice through circumstances. Circumstances can encourage us in the direction we are headed, or they can shut the door, turning our direction elsewhere. We also can hear His voice through His Holy Spirit. The Holy Spirit's voice is quiet and easy to miss if we don't listen for Him to speak. We learn to hear Him as we meditate on His written word, pray, and meditate. Gradually we become familiar with the gentle sound of His voice. It is so very important for us to practice turning our ears to the gentle voice of the Holy Spirit. His voice is within us because He dwells within us from the time we accept Jesus, God's Son, into our hearts, minds, and lives. Learning to hear takes time and practice. Our question is, do we want to listen for, hear, and pay attention to what He would say to us? If so, we must choose to spend time with Him without worldly interruption. Let us be sure to go into our prayer closet regularly and hear, listen, and pay attention to what the One Who loves us so much He took our sin on Himself. Let us give Him our best time and attention. He gives us His.

1 Thessalonians 5:17 Continual Prayer

pray continually, (NIV)

Continual Prayer

When someone is beside you throughout your day, you don't spend the day ignoring them. We talk with them throughout our day, not continually, but very frequently. God is always with us. No matter where we are or what we are doing, God is with us. How often do we talk with Him throughout our day? Maybe we see a pretty tree and we can thank God for creating such beauty. Maybe it is a bird song, and we thank Him for the beautiful and varied music. Maybe we hear a siren, and we ask God to be in that situation. I think you get the gist of where I'm going. There are things throughout our day to thank God praise God or lift someone or something up before His throne of grace and mercy. Let us get into the practice of speaking with the One Who loves us most and never leaves us.

Hosea 6:6 Mercy

For I desire mercy, not sacrifice, and acknowledgment of God rather than burnt offerings. (NIV)

Mercy

Praise God that He shows me mercy. He forgives me every time I sin or miss His bidding. But forgiving me is different from me walking out the consequences of my actions or inaction. I walk out those consequences in a state of forgiveness. But do we show the same mercy to others? In something as simple as the act of driving, road rage is rampant. People don't show mercy to other drivers. The attitude is "You're not getting in front of me. I'll cut you off if you try." What about mercy to the sales clerk who isn't very helpful? We don't know what's behind their action. We are to show the same mercy to others that God shows to us. Our problem is pride. We don't like humbling ourselves. We want to be the one "in the right" and be sure everyone knows it. Let us practice showing the same mercy to others that God shows to us. Remember, showing mercy isn't preventing others from walking out of the circumstances of their action or inaction, just as God has us go through our consequences. Let us all walk bathed in the mercy of God and each other.

Deuteronomy 5:33 Obedience

Walk in obedience to all that the Lord your God has commanded you, so that you may live and prosper and prolong your days in the land that you will possess. (NIV)

Obedience

We often tell others (especially our children) to do something because we just don't want to do it ourselves. Unlike us, God's reason for telling us what to do is for our good. God wants us to grow in love and grow in Him. All His commandments and instructions in His written Word are for our benefit. The land we will possess when walking in obedience is the dream or calling God had put in our hearts and minds. When we're not feeling fulfilled, when we find no joy in our walk, it is time to check and see what instruction or command of God we are disregarding. God doesn't take blessings away because of our disobedience. The blessing just won't fit us unless we are in obedience. Let us be quick to admit disobedience and obey with joy that we can possess all the blessings of God.

James 2:17-18 True Faith

In the same way, faith by itself, if it is not accompanied by action, is dead. (NIV)

True Faith

We can have faith that a chair will hold us but if we don't sit in the chair, our faith in the ability of the chair to hold us is of no value. The same is true of our faith In God through His Son, Jesus. If our faith doesn't produce action, it is of no value. In Revelation, we read some will claim to call Jesus Lord, but He will say He doesn't know them. These are the people who claim to have faith, they claim to be believers, but their lives don't show it. Works by itself won't save us nor will faith by itself. Our salvation is by grace and mercy but our reward of life with Jesus is based on our relationship with Him. To love Him we will obey Him to please Him because we love Him. True faith will always be followed by actions on that faith. Let us work out our faith with actions according to the Word of God.

Psalms 68:1 Let God Arise

May God arise, may his enemies be scattered; may his foes flee before him. (NIV)

Let God Arise

When we first become aware of a problem we are facing, where do we look? Do we investigate our past to see how we handled a similar problem? Do we ask other people? Do we spend hours thinking about various possibilities? Any of these will eventually consume us. Before long, all we can see or think about is our problem. There is only one place to look first when we first become aware of a problem. We need to look to God first. We look to Him through prayer and giving the problem to Him for His guidance in the solution. We look to Him through the Bible to see what He said in His written word about that kind of situation and the solution. We give it to Him and trust He will provide the way and the answer. We must let God arise first in our hearts, minds, and lives. When we do that, worldly solutions that lead to more problems will scatter. We will be enabled to walk in obedience to God's statutes and His glory will show through our lives. Let's let the Word, power, and glory arise in all we think and do.

Genesis 18:23 Sodom and Gomorrah

Then Abraham approached him and said: "Will you sweep away the righteous with the wicked? (NIV)

Sodom and Gomorrah

When we listen to the news or look around us in the United States as well as several other countries, we see a playback of Sodom and Gomorrah. I do hope all readers will turn to this passage in the scripture and read the entire account. No matter how familiar we are with the event, it is important to read it over again and let God interpret it in relation to today. After we do this, I hope it will stress the dire importance of praying on behalf of the nation in which we live. The sins of Sodom and Gomorrah are running rampant in our nation. We Christians have kept our mouths shut too long and have sat back and watched Satan and his cohorts ride with free reign. It is past time for us to get serious with our prayers. We have the power through the Holy Spirit to pray against sin becoming the law of the land. We have the power through the Holy Spirit and our prayers to bring the laws of God back to our nation. What we are lacking is the fortitude to follow through. Let us not lose our nation to sin. Let us stand up after getting on our knees to God and let our prayers move mountains.

Romans 15:4 Holy Bible

For everything that was written in the past was written to teach us, so that through the endurance taught in the Scriptures and the encouragement they provide we might have hope. (NIV)

Holy Bible

Every day as I read and meditate on the words in the Holy Bible, I continue to be increasingly amazed. In those pages are the answers to everything I need to know to walk through my life with joy and in obedience to God. The depth of those words is amazing. I can read the same verses many times and, according to my circumstances needs, and willingness to listen, get a different perspective every time. That is why the Holy Bible is also called "The Living Word of God." I've preached many a sermon on the importance of really reading and meditating on the words in the Bible. There is no way to do too much. Yet, reading just to be intellectually enlightened will not suffice. Yes, we might be able to quote entire passages from memory but, if they don't have an impact on our life, if we don't make the choices that agree with them, the intellectual knowledge isn't of value to our lives. We must be sure to read and meditate with the leading and teaching of God's Holy Spirit to show us how to apply what we read. It is the Holy Spirit Who brings the words alive in our minds, hearts, and lives. To me, the Holy Bible is the most exciting collection of books to read. So much so that I must be careful not to read too late into the night or I will be too excited to sleep. If reading the Bible doesn't excite you, pray and ask the Holy Spirit to make it real and alive to you. I guarantee you will never be the same again.

Ephesians 6:18 All the Lord's People

And pray in the Spirit on all occasions with all kinds of prayers and requests. With this in mind, be alert and always keep on praying for all the Lord's people. (NIV)

All the Lord's People

I was speaking my usual complaint about the weather when the Holy Spirit stopped me. He had me thinking about God's children who have no shelter and those who are being arrested, tortured, and/or killed for standing firm in the faith. He told me to think about how blessed I am to have a house with air-conditioning and to have the freedom to tell anyone about Jesus without being arrested. Then He asked me to think about how much time I spend complaining about a little discomfort or inconvenience versus the time I spend praying for those less blessed and those persecuted for the sake of their faith in God through Jesus. Wow. That smart. In this nation of the United States, we are still free to express our faith even though some sources are trying to prevent it. We are free to work and own houses. We tend to take all our freedoms for granted and complain about trivial things. I'm working on changing my attitude to discomfort or inconvenience. When I feel the discomfort or inconvenience that is the time, instead of complaining, to lift those who are hurting and those who are being persecuted before God's throne of grace. How about joining me in more consistent prayers for our brothers and sisters everywhere?

John 13:17 Blessed in Doing

Now that you know these things, you will be blessed if you do them. (NIV)

Blessed in Doing

We are blessed in the way we do the things Jesus said we were to do. If we open our Bibles to John 13 and read the verses preceding verse 17, we will find Jesus is talking about our attitude of not being better than anyone else and serving others. The custom in those days was for a servant to wash the feet of the guest. They wore open sandals and their feet were dusty and dirty. Feet were near the low tables and wouldn't be pleasant near food with their dirt and dust. Jesus, the Son of God, bent down and did the job of a lowly servant. So often we tend to classify jobs. We see some trash on the floor at church but we're not the custodian and we didn't put it there, so we have the attitude it's not our job and we walk on by. This is precisely what Jesus is talking about. No job our eyes see is beneath us. If we see it, we are called to do it. We must do an attitude check. Are we willing, or yet, even eager, to do all Jesus allows us to see that needs attention or do we want to pretend we didn't see a need and move on? The blessing we can receive is up to us. It is there if we do our part. Let us enjoy blessing as we reach out doing all God puts in our path with joy and thanksgiving.

Matthew 17:20 Faith and Obedience

He replied, "Because you have so little faith. Truly I tell you, if you have faith as small as a mustard seed, you can say to this mountain, 'Move from here to there,' and it will move. Nothing will be impossible for you." (NIV)

Faith and Obedience

I was in my kitchen on my knees scrubbing the floor when I heard God whisper to me, "Go to the hospital and pray for…" Then I heard Him say the name of my husband's boss. She was in the hospital just having had a baby. While she was in labor, they discovered a large mole on her leg and biopsied it. I was melanoma. She was scheduled to have it removed the next day. Her husband was not only not a Christian, but he was also very much anti-Christian and gave my husband a hard time at work. I called my husband and shared what I heard God tell me. He said if God said it, I better do it. I changed my clothes and went to the hospital thinking her husband would be a work. When I got to her room, her husband was there. We did small talk for a while (I thought he would leave at any minute for work) and I finally realized her husband was not going to leave. I finally said, "Would you mind if I held your hand and prayed for you?" She was very polite (her husband laughed) and said that was fine. I held her hand and said, "Father God, in the name of Your Son, Jesus I speak healing. No cancer cells can be present in this body." I said Amen and goodbye and left. I was obedient to what God told me to do. The result was up to Him. The next morning when they took her down for surgery, they looked at the mole and decided they better biopsy it again. There were no cancer cells. We heard nothing about it. A few months later her husband was fired. Several years later my phone rang. It was this lady. She said, "Ginger, I'm not sure if you remember me, but I want you to know as a result of your prayer, not only was I healed, but my husband and I received Jesus as our Lord and Savior, and we are in full-time ministry."

I share this to demonstrate faith and obedience is the same. We can't have faith without being obedient and we won't be obedient if we don't have faith. When we hear God telling us to do something we don't need to weigh the pros and cons of our abilities, we only need to be obedient to His word and act on what He says to do.

John 1:18 Face of Jesus

No one has ever seen God. The One and Only Son —the One who is at the Father's side — He has revealed Him. (NIV)

Face of Jesus

Recently I saw two movies on ITBN about a face-to-face encounter with Jesus. One was in a restaurant and one on a plane. Later, a Christian novel I started reading was about a face-to-face encounter with Jesus while driving on the road. I got to thinking, that would be beyond wonderful to have a real face-to-face encounter with Jesus and be able to ask Him all my questions. Then I remembered I have a face-to-face encounter with Him every time I open and read the written Word of God, the Holy Bible because Jesus is the Word. He was made flesh to come down in a physical form to this earth to show us the Father. Now we see the Father and Jesus in the recorded Word of God. I also see Him face to face as I look and live in the creation He made. We can also see Jesus face-to-face with other believers and followers of Him. We see Him in their smiles, their eyes, and their actions and words. But, as wonderful as that is for us, we must ask ourselves if others see Jesus's face to face when they look at or listen to us. In the Christian novel I read, seeing Jesus's face to face on the road was the second time this happened to this man. The first time was four years earlier. The encounter faded. Just as Jesus said when He was physically walking this earth, witnessing miracles won't change the heart. For keeping the face of Jesus before our eyes, minds, and hearts we must continually talk with and listen to Him.

We do this through our reading and meditation of the Bible, through our conversations with Him throughout the day, and through our fellowshipping and sharing with fellow believers and followers. Let us continually investigate the face of Jesus in every way available to us.

Mark 1:11 Now

And a voice came from heaven: "You are my Son, whom I love; with you I am well pleased."

Now

One of my conversations with God.

Father, I blew it again. I know You aren't pleased with me right now. I'm so sorry. Please forgive me and help me do better.

"My child, I AM pleased with You. You are my child. You have given yourself to My Son. I AM always pleased with you. Your sins were forgiven when My Son died on that cross. I AM God. I AM Present. There is no past or future for all is Present with Me. You only need to confess your sins so you know and can turn away from them. Forgiveness is already given. You only need to forgive yourself and move forward with My Holy Spirit guiding you. When I look at you, I see My Son for you and He and I are all one because of what He did for you."

He said more but it needn't be shared. The point is God is God of Now. It is always now. We are to live in the now with God and in God. The past and the future are under the blood of Jesus. We only have now. Our question is what are we doing with our now?

2 Timothy 1:7 Set Our Face

For the Spirit God gave us does not make us timid, but gives us power, love and self-discipline. (NIV)

Set Our Face

There are some days I just feel lazy. I'm either tired physically or emotionally and just want to curl up with a good Christian fiction novel for the day. Sometimes I just don't want to write, let alone pray about a devotion. But then I think about the discipline it took for Jesus to head to Jerusalem. Scripture says He set His face toward Jerusalem. He knew what lay ahead yet He was determined to obey His Father no matter how He felt or what it took. How can I not discipline myself to do something so very little in comparison to what My Savior has done for me? God sets His Holy Spirit in us for many things. Yes, we feel His love, hear His voice, receive His comfort, and hear His directions but He also will give us the strength to discipline ourselves to be obedient to follow His instructions. We must each hear His word for us as individuals every day. Then we must be sure to follow through. It is only the first few steps that are hard and take discipline and determination. After that, we are back in sync enjoying the fact that He loves us and wants to share His work with and through us.

Joshua 1:9 Strength and Courage

Have I not commanded you? Be strong and courageous. Do not be afraid; do not be discouraged, for the Lord your God will be with you wherever you go." (NIV)

Strength and Courage

For background read the thirteenth chapter of Numbers. Ten people without strong faith, therefore courage, in the promises of God, were enough to defeat the two who stood strong with courage on the promises of God. So often so many of us come so close to receiving the fruition of some of God's promises and, though we are so very close, we miss it. When we look at the circumstances instead of the promises of God, courage fades and we turn away. We can look at our finances and sink in despair or we can look at God's word about finances, follow His instructions, and walk forward with confidence that we will see the promises of God come about. Our problem is where we are looking and if we are walking in obedience to the conditions God has set in His instruction manual (the Holy Bible). Regardless of the dream, vision, or promise God has given us, we must meet His conditions, obey them, walk in them, and look to the result in faith and courage that God is faithful. If the Hebrews had listened to the two who believed in God, they would have saved themselves a lot of years and trouble. Let us learn from their lesson.

Ephesians 4:3-4 More than Representatives

Make every effort to keep the unity of the Spirit through the bond of peace. (NIV)

Colossians 3:14-15 And over all these virtues put on love, which binds them all together in perfect unity. (NIV)

More Than Representatives

Many people never will have a personal encounter with Jesus. The only way these people can see Jesus is when they see Him through a believer. Jesus dwells in us, the believers. We must remember we are possibly the only Jesus others might ever see. When they look at us, are they able to see the love and peace of Jesus? Since He is in us, are we allowing Him to show through our expression and speak through our words? We are more than His representatives. Since He dwells in us, we are Jesus to others. We need to connect closely and be real with others. What led me to Jesus was a smile on a lady when she looked at me (this is in one of my other devotions). We might never know the effect we have on someone else. Let's be sure the effect is a result of Jesus in us.

2 Corinthians 5:17 New Creation

Therefore, if anyone is in Christ, the new creation has come: The old has gone, the new is here! (NIV)

New Creation

We must ask if we believe this about ourselves. When we accept Jesus into our hearts, mind, and life, we become a new creation. We are now back in the image of God because Jesus, through His Holy Spirit, is now living in us. But so often we look at ourselves in the same way we were before Jesus entered us. We see ourselves as unrighteous sinners. We do this because we haven't renewed our minds. The only way to renew our minds is to become so very familiar with God's character that we know Him intimately. We do this by immersing our minds in the written words of God. Yes, once again I write about the importance of the Holy Bible. Without immersing our minds in those words, we can't renew our minds. Without renewed minds, we will continue to act out in our old ways. We will continue to side with Satan on how terrible we are. We will continue to think we have no authority against living in sin. Whenever we find our minds thinking wrong thoughts we need to immediately get into the word of God and bathe our minds in His character. God says our hands are Jesus' hands and our feet are Jesus' feet. Let us keep our minds renewed and make it so in the physical reality as well as the spiritual reality.

Matthew 19:18-19 First Four

"Which ones?" he inquired. Jesus replied, "'You shall not murder, you shall not commit adultery, you shall not steal, you shall not give false testimony, honor your father and mother,' and 'love your neighbor as yourself. (NIV)

First Four

Have you noticed Jesus didn't include the first four commandments? I believe that's because He knew mankind, in and of themselves, could not keep those four commandments. Therefore, Jesus had to come and die for our sins. This is also why the Holy Spirit has come to dwell in us. It is only through the power and guidance of the Holy Spirit that we can try to keep those four commandments. It is only through the blood of Jesus that we are forgiven when we slip in our efforts to keep those four commandments. The commandments Jesus quoted to that man are commandments we can choose to keep. They are within our power. Because of our sin of self-centeredness, the first four commandments are against the desires of our self-centered nature. These are the commandments that take dedication and love to and for God the Father, God the Son, and God the Holy Spirit. Let us continually ask for the infilling of the Holy Spirit to enable us to put God first in our minds, hearts, and lives making all his commandments the way of our daily living.

Luke 11:41a Changing Me

But now as for what is inside you (NIV)

Changing Me

I opened a cabinet and took out a seldom-used bowel. The outside was pretty and shiny. When I looked inside, I wanted to turn away. There were some old food bits and a dead bug. While the outside was pretty and inviting, the inside was the opposite. Jesus is concerned with what is on our insides. No matter how much we dress up outside, even when we plaster a certain expression on our faces, it's what is inside us that counts. We may fool ourselves into thinking we are tricking people into thinking we are better or nicer than we are, but eventually what is on the inside will come through. When we receive Jesus and His Holy Spirit in us, what is on the inside changes. However, if we don't discipline ourselves to renew our minds, we will continue to act like our insides are still the same old us. I know I would not be a very nice person if it weren't for the Holy Spirit inside me. My nature is very self-centered and critical. The Holy Spirit along with the renewing of my mind has slowly been changing me over the last several decades. If I were to get back with my college friends, they wouldn't know me. From glory-to-glory God's changing me from earthly things to the heavenly. If I am the same tomorrow as I am today, I'm not listening to the Holy Spirit. Let us all commit to continuing to move more and more into Christ each day which means less and less into ourselves.

John 10:27 Listening and Knowing

My sheep listen to my voice; I know them, and they follow me. (NIV)

Listening and Knowing

I was incredibly nervous when I first brought my first baby home. I was afraid to sleep because I thought I might not hear the baby when she cried. Gradually I learned my ears were always listening for my baby. I knew her cry so distinctly I could pick her cry out of the church nursery full of crying babies. As she grew older and more children arrived and grew, they didn't need to identify themselves on the phone. I knew by their distinctive voices who were talking with me. The same is true in listening and hearing the voice of God within us. As we learn how His voice sounds to us, as we train ourselves to continually listen for His voice, we learn to identify it. We learn through comparing the voice we hear with the words recorded in the Holy Bible, the written Word of God. Eventually, we find, that with practice in listening and following what the voice says, we can hear Him speaking to us through and in all situations. I recognize my children's voices regardless of what I'm doing when they speak. Let us be sure to develop the same ability with the One Who knows and loves us best.

Joshua 1:8-9 Strong and Courageous

Keep this Book of the Law always on your lips; meditate on it day and night, so that you may be careful to do everything written in it. Then you will be prosperous and successful. Have I not commanded you? Be strong and courageous. Do not be afraid; do not be discouraged, for the Lord your God will be with you wherever you go (NIV)

Strong and Courageous

There is a lot of fear today. Fear of home invasions, drive-by shootings, road rage, robbery, infectious diseases, terrorism, and on and on. Fear is an uneasy feeling. We may know what is making us fearful or we might suddenly be fearful without knowing what caused it. God does not want us living in fear. He has given us the spirit of power, love, and a sound mind. When we find fear entering, we need to focus on God. He may want us to leave a certain situation. He may want us to face a fearful situation head-on. Whatever way He wants us to walk, He has promised to be always with us through all things. Even when our situation is because of disobedience to God, He will see us through when we turn, listen, and choose to become obedient to His guidance. Difficult tasks take courage. Courage takes faith. Faith must be walked out in obedience. If you are facing a difficult circumstance now, get on your knees, open the Holy Bible, present it to God, and listen for His instructions. He is faithful and will never fail or leave us.

Psalms 133:1 Unity

How good and pleasant it is when God's people live together in unity! (NIV)

Unity

Last Sunday there was a different group leading the praise and worship. They were very loud, and the music was quite different. To me, it was not worship; it was noise. But as I prayed about it, God said He was pleased with it because for them it was worship from their hearts. Sometimes it is hard to be in unity when we are so very different from each other with our likes and dislikes. But the unity does not come from our likes and dislikes. Our unity comes from our being one in Christ Jesus and our desire to worship and obey Him. We can differ on how we do this, but our love for Him is shared as is our love for each other including our differences. Let us remember that we can disagree on how, but we are unified in why and Who.

Matthew 13:58 Miracles

And he did not do many miracles there because of their lack of faith. (NIV)

Miracles

Another way of writing this verse is "And He did not do many miracles there because of their unbelief." I just finished reading a Christian fiction novel where several times it said, "Miracles happen to those who believe." This is so true. Miracles surround us every day but, if we do not believe, we don't look for them and we miss them. Consider the creation around us. It is all a miracle. Consider how our bodies function. That is a miracle. Looking at these miracles and recognizing them for what they are and giving thanks to God for them enables us to receive and see even more miracles. When we live expecting them, we will receive them. But, with every promise of God, there is a condition. We must be walking in obedience to His word. Not only walking in obedience but releasing ourselves and our desires to be one in Him. The miracles we want to see and receive must agree with God. We do not get ourselves into debt through the accumulation of material things and then expect God to perform a miracle and make the debt disappear. We bear the consequences of our actions even though we have the forgiveness and love of God. Walking in obedience produces a joyful and abundant life in close fellowship with our God. Let us walk in loving obedience and keep our hearts and eyes open for the miracles God gives us every day.

John 14:6 Truth

Jesus answered, "I am the way and the truth and the life. No one comes to the Father except through me. (NIV)

Truth

Today many people define truth as whatever suits them and their desires and opinions. They easily become offended and often angry when others disagree with what they believe is true for themselves. Jesus said He is the Truth. That means everything He said is true. Anything that contradicts what He said is not true. It does not matter if it conflicts with our own opinions or desires. Truth is found in Jesus and His word. We are living in a society that wants nothing more than self-gratification. Many want it so much that they will even murder anyone who would stand in the way of what they want. These people walk with a heavy weight for the only way to freedom and an abundant life is living in the truth of Jesus. But those of us who do walk in the truth of Jesus must be sure to walk it in love for those who are living under the lie of what truth is. It is only through love that truth can prevail. Let's leave the judging to God, walk the truth in love, and let those who are deceived see the difference.

Mark 7:5 Law

So the Pharisees and teachers of the law asked Jesus, "Why don't your disciples live according to the tradition of the elders instead of eating their food with defiled hands?" (NIV)

Law

There is a substantial difference between law and tradition. God, through Moses, gave us ten laws. Moses added 613 to interpret the 10 laws God gave us. Mankind, mostly religious leaders added over 6000 laws of their own. These 6000+ are the traditions the Pharisees and teachers of the law were concerned about. They were in the practice of heaping burdens on others for their selfish gain and pride. Jesus came to fulfill the law of God. The law was we are dead because of sin. Jesus paid that price. He told us all the laws of God were summed up in the first 2 commandments. When we obey these 2 commandments, we are following all the laws God gave Moses, for those laws are to help us live in and through love.

Mark 12:29-31 "The most important one," answered Jesus, "is this: 'Hear, O Israel: The Lord our God, the Lord is One. Love the Lord your God with all your heart and with all your soul and with all your mind and with all your strength.' The second is this: 'Love your neighbor as yourself.' There is no commandment greater than these.

Let us live according to these two laws and only follow traditions that agree with them.

Psalms 43:4-5 Replace Discouragement

Then I will go to the altar of God, to God, my joy and my delight. I will praise you with the lyre, O God, my God. Why, my soul, are you downcast? Why so disturbed within me? Put your hope in God, for I will yet praise him, my Savior and my God (NIV)

Replace Discouragement

We all have times of discouragement, times when we are depressed and gloomy. That is the time to go into our prayer room and sing or speak praises to God. When we confess out loud with our mouths the glories of God, we also hear them with our ears. They penetrate deep into our inner being and change the focus of our minds. Before long we are lifted into His glory and our spirits are once again united with His. Our outlook has changed, and we are once again filled with unspeakable joy in our oneness with Jesus Christ our Savior, and God the Father through the enabling of the Holy Spirit. Our entire countenance changes along with the expression on our faces. Our problem is sometimes we choose to be discouraged. Maybe we want others to feel sorry for us or we feel sorry for ourselves. It's all a matter of choice. We can choose to remain in the dark pit of discouragement and gloom, or we can choose to praise God until the gloom and discouragement have been replaced with His unspeakable joy.

Matthew 3:13-15 Baptism

Then Jesus came from Galilee to the Jordan to be baptized by John. But John tried to deter him, saying, "I need to be baptized by you, and do you come to me?" Jesus replied, "Let it be so now; it is proper for us to do this to fulfill all righteousness." Then John consented (NIV)

Baptism

Why would Jesus submit to water baptism? Baptism is an external sign of dying to man's sinful nature and being risen to new life in Christ. Jesus was without sin and Jesus was and is already Christ, the Messiah. Why then did He want to be baptized? He said it was to fulfill all righteousness. But Jesus was already righteous. Jesus, through His baptism, was signifying His brotherhood with all mankind. He came to walk where we had to walk and showed us how to walk our walk in God's way. The baptism was the start of His ministry. Likewise, water baptism is the start of our walk in the righteousness of Jesus. As we read the scriptures and follow how Jesus walked on this earth, we can learn how we are to walk. The word "Christian" means little Christ. We are to be reflections of Christ. Let us be sure to know how Jesus walked on this earth and be good imitators of His walk.

Genesis 37:23-24 In the Pit

So when Joseph came to his brothers, they stripped him of his robe—the ornate robe he was wearing— and they took him and threw him into the cistern. The cistern was empty; there was no water in it (NIV)

In the Pit

To understand how God works with us we must understand why Joseph was thrown into a pit. He wasn't liked by his brothers. As we read about the early life of Joseph, we see he brags to his brothers about his dreams. He is also favored over his brothers by his father. Joseph made it worse by showing off the gift his father gave him and rubbing it into his brothers. Why is this important to us? We tend to blame other people when we face trials. We fail to ask God to show us what part we played in getting into situations. It's so much easier to blame others rather than take responsibility for our actions or inactions. The dream God gave Joseph would eventually be fulfilled but Joseph had to go through a lot of difficult circumstances to mold his character into what was necessary to serve God in the fulfillment of the dream. When we are down, we must get God's perspective on why we are down. We must be sure we are hearing God and not Satan. God will give us conviction, not condemnation. God never condemns us. He loves us and we stand forgiven. Condemnation comes from Satan. We must side with God, admit where we went wrong, and move on with the Holy Spirit as a righteous child of His through Jesus. Learn from our pits and move on with joy, thanksgiving, and faith in God's workings in and through us.

One more thing we must notice. The reason Reuben said to throw Joseph in the pit is so he could pull him out later and deliver him to his father. When we are in the pit, the Holy Spirit wants to get our attention, pull us out, and deliver us back to the Father. Pits are to get our attention back on God.

Luke 17:18 Giving Thanks

Has no one returned to give praise to God except this foreigner?" (NIV)

Giving Thanks

Worship is giving thanks to God. Today we tend to take things for granted. There is a lot of teaching today that we should always have anything we want if we ask God and believe in it. This attitude is why we live with disappointment. Ten lepers were healed. Nine of them were Jews, and one a gentile. It was the gentile who returned to give thanks to Jesus. There are 7 different Greek words for thanks. All of them denote thanking in open love. Our question is do we only worship God with thanksgiving when we get our way, or do we live in a state of thankfulness of worship to God in all circumstances? We might say the only reason that one man came back to thank Jesus was because he was healed. We have all been healed. We've been healed from sin which is a death sentence. We are healed to eternal life. What more do we need to constantly be joyfully giving thanks in worship to the God Who sent Jesus and healed us from that death sentence for sin?

Deuteronomy 31:6 Don't Fear

Be strong and courageous. Do not be afraid or terrified because of them, for the Lord your God goes with you; he will never leave you nor forsake you." (NIV)

Philippians 4:6-7 Do not be anxious about anything, but in every situation, by prayer and petition, with thanksgiving, present your requests to God. And the peace of God, which transcends all understanding, will guard your hearts and your minds in Christ Jesus (NIV)

Don't Fear

I tried to count the times God told us in His written word not to fear, not to be anxious, not to worry, not to be discouraged, and many other not-tos that have to do with fear. I lost count. Instead, He told us to be strong and courageous in our trust that He is true to His word. He has promised always to be with us regardless of the circumstances we must face in this sinful world. This doesn't mean we won't ever face dire circumstances. It does mean we need not fear the circumstances before they occur. We need only obey His word, worship Him, and trust Him. When we do find ourselves in dire circumstances, we can trust He will provide us with all we need to face them. It does no good to be anxious or afraid of what might be for then we don't live in the peace of the present. God told us that tomorrow will take care of itself. We are to live today in faith, thankfulness, and worship as we walk in fellowship with God, the Creator of all that was, is, or will ever be. Yes, there are some very evil things in our world that might affect us someday, but we can release those thoughts and allow God to keep His peace in our minds and our hearts. God is good all the time and all the time God is good.

John 3:10 The Entire Picture

"You are Israel's teacher," said Jesus, "and do you not understand these things?" (NIV)

The Entire Picture

I hope all readers have read the introduction to this book which states these devotions are just a jump start and looking up the scripture and reading the entire section is very important. I only clip in one or 2 verses to start you off.

We are looking at Nicodemus. He is a teacher and a Pharisee and yet he recognizes the teachings of Jesus are from God. He can't understand the teachings because he is bogged down with laws. He is accustomed to looking at individual statements rather than the whole picture. Without looking at the whole, the pieces don't make any sense. Before we condemn Nicodemus, we must look at ourselves. It doesn't help our understanding of the whole that the Bible is written in verses. We memorize verses but tend to forget how they fit into the entire picture. Without the entire picture, it is hard to understand. Nicodemus was looking at Jesus' statement of being born again from a worldly viewpoint. To understand he had to remember Genesis and how God breathed His Spirit, His image, into man and how man lost it through sin. It is this Spirit that must be reborn in us and that is only possible through Jesus by our accepting Him into our hearts, minds, and lives as more than our Savior. He must become the Lord (the leader, king, director, and instructor) of our lives. When we do that God breathes His Holy Spirit back into our lives and we are once again in the image of God. Let's be sure we read and meditate on entire sections of God's written word, not just take out a verse or 2 to prove a point we want to prove.

Proverbs 4:20-22 Health

My son, pay attention to what I say; turn your ear to my words. Do not let them out of your sight, keep them within your heart; for they are life to those who find them and health to one's whole body. (NIV)

Health

There is a lot of teaching going around that says just name it, believe it, and claim it. All promises in the Bible have a condition with them. Yes, we do live in a sinful world and are subject to diseases in this world, but God has given us instructions on how to stay in good health. If we smoke, we can expect heart disease or lung cancer. If we binge on a lot of sugar and gain a lot of extra weight, we can expect diabetes. Many diseases and sicknesses are attributed directly to our lack of discipline and eating correctly. God has given us freedom of choice. We can choose to maintain a healthy body for the temple of His Holy Spirit dwelling in us or we can forget wisdom and discipline and ignore the rules of good health. The choice is ours. When diseases of the sinful world assault us, we still have a choice to listen to the wisdom of the Holy Spirit for directions on receiving the miracle God has for us. Let us stop blaming other things or people and take responsibility for our health. Let us maintain healthy minds and bodies so the Holy Spirit has a healthy home within us and can flow unimpeded through us to this sinful world.

Psalms 119:37a Our Eyes

Turn my eyes away from worthless things;

Our Eyes

We are visual people. What we see goes into our mind and then our hearts tend to dwell on it. Because of this, it is important for us to not even look at what tempts us. If we have a problem with lust and sexual desires, we don't look at pornography. We don't even let our eyes look on a beautiful woman or handsome man. That way we won't lust. If we have a problem of consuming too many sweets, we don't go into a candy store or we don't look at the sweet section of a bakery or the dessert section of a menu. When we don't see it, we won't miss it. We are responsible for our actions. An alcoholic doesn't even go into a bar or that first drink will take over. Whatever our addiction is, we must choose to avoid being in the presence of that addiction. Eventually, with prayer and retraining of our desires, we might not be bothered with the old desire. Let us practice discretion and discipline in all we allow our eyes to see whether on television, movies, books, computers or just walking down a street. Let us keep our eyes on all that will feed us with the goodness of our God.

Matthew 3:9 As Abraham Did

Abraham is our father," they answered. "If you were Abraham's children," said Jesus, "then you would do what Abraham did. (NIV)

As Abraham Did

We must remember what Abraham did. He obeyed God. God told him to go to a place he didn't know, and he did. God told him he would wipe out Sodom and Gomorrah and he interceded for them. God promised him a son and he had one. God told him to sacrifice his son and he did so, though God stopped him just in time by providing another sacrifice. What do we put before God? What are we willing to sacrifice? God provided us with the perfect sacrifice, His Son. God wants us to put Him first in our hearts, minds, and lives. We must continually be on guard to put other people, things, or tasks before God. We must be like Abraham, doing what he did, putting God first, obeying God in all things, and interceding for others.

1 Corinthians 14:26-27 Fully Worship

What then shall we say, brothers and sisters? When you come together, each of you has a hymn, a word of instruction, a revelation, a tongue, or an interpretation. Everything must be done so that the church may be built up. (NIV)

Fully Worship

I love Sundays. That's when we have an opportunity to come together with other believers. How we do it has a lot to do with the size of the group we come together with. In a very large church, it is different than in a small one. It might be hard to feel a personal connection with others in a very large church. It might be hard to feel we, as individuals, really have a part in the coming together. But each person, regardless of how many are gathered, is a very important and integral part of the worship. We add our voice to the music and the songs of praise ascend to the ears of God. We pray, agreeing with the spoken prayers of the leaders and, our prayers throughout the service. So often the worship leaders present music we cannot participate in vocally. But we can participate in spirit, listening and agreeing and letting their songs of worship enter our spirits, joining them in spirit and worshiping God through our agreement in the spirit. When we gather, let us be fully present in our worship and praise of God. Let us prepare ahead of time and ask the Holy Spirit to guard our minds and keep us centered on God and why we are there. Let us fully worship in voice, heart, mind, and spirit along with our fellow believers.

1 Corinthians 2:14 Nouns

The unbeliever a does not receive the things of the Spirit of God, for they are foolishness to him. And he cannot understand them because they are spiritually discerned.

Nouns

Some people speak using very few nouns and many, many pronouns. They say things like "he said, they... " without ever using a noun to let you know who he, they, or that are. It makes it very hard to understand what they are saying. The Bible, God's written word, is like that. Unless we have received His Holy Spirit, we cannot understand what the written words mean. We can read the words; we can define the words, but we don't know what they are telling us. When we open the Bible, we need to pray and ask God to speak to us, give us understanding, and show us how to apply what we are reading to our lives right now. Because it is a Living Word the meanings have various depths, and the different depths will speak to us at different times in our lives. Our question is do we want to understand and apply what God has to say to us?

Exodus20:5 A Jealous God

You shall not bow down to them or worship them; for I, the LORD your God, am a jealous God (NIV)

A Jealous God

God says it like it is. He is jealous. He created us to have fellowship with Him He wants our first love and priority to be Him. He wants us to put Him first before all things and people. Where are our fellowship priorities? Who do we think about the most? Who do we talk to the most? Who do we love the most? I don't know anyone who shows with their priorities that they put God first in all things. We tend to rationalize that He is a forgiving God. He'll love us no matter what. Yes, He is forgiving, if we are covered in the blood of His Son, Jesus, and if we confess and repent. Yes, He is loving – more than we can ever conceive. He is also God, and He alone sets the ground rules. He said we must put Him first. We must love Him with ALL our heart, mind, soul, and strength. This shouldn't be hard for us, but it is. We are so distracted by things on this earth that are so very temporary. How I pray for God's Holy Spirit to help me keep my focus on God in and through all distractions. We do live in this world, and we have things we must do in this world but all that we do should and can be done to the glory of God – even something simple like taking out the garbage. I've mentioned this little book before, but it is worth mentioning again. It is "Practicing the Presence" by Brother Laurence. It is available as a free e-book. If you haven't already done so I recommend you download it and read it. May God help us all to really love Him and put Him first for His glory.

Ephesians 4:20-21 Changing Daily

That, however, is not the way of life you learned when you heard about Christ and were taught in him in accordance with the truth that is in Jesus (NIV)

Changing Daily

We must continually ask ourselves if we are different today from how we were yesterday. Old habits die hard. The person we were before we met Jesus tries to resurrect each day. We are to renew our minds daily. The way we respond or react to hurt is very different when we are in Christ than it was before. The things that make us angry and the way we respond to them should be changing. My dear friend told me (when she was 102) "Any day I don't learn something new about my Lord and Savior is a day wasted." This sentence has had a major impact on my life. How can we learn anything new if we don't get into the scriptures daily? How can we learn more about Jesus if we don't commune with Him daily? There is a song I sing a lot. "From glory to glory He's changing me...from earthly things to the heavenly." Let us commit to grow daily in our Lord. Let us allow Him to change us daily as we grow more and more in One in Him.

Genesis 5:22 Walk With God

After he became the father of Methuselah, Enoch walked faithfully with God 300 years and had other sons and daughters. (NIV)

Walk With God

When you leave this earth, how do you want people to remember you? I want them to remember me as someone who walked with God. Enoch walked with God. What does it mean to walk with God? To walk with God, we must completely trust Him, communicate with Him, and obey Him. Proverbs 3:5-6 says,

> "Trust in the Lord with all your heart and lean not on your own understanding; in all your ways submit to him, and he will make your paths straight (NIV)".

If we do this consistently, we are walking with God. It takes patience to learn to walk with God. It takes scripture study and meditation to learn to walk with God. But mostly it takes complete trust in what God says to us. Abraham trusted God enough to obey and offer his long-promised son as a sacrifice. He knew God would give him more descendants than he could count. I used to be like Abraham's wife, Sarah. I would pray for things and then I would see to it my prayers were answered in my way. This isn't trust. We must trust and follow what God says. Our biggest question is do we love God enough to want to walk with Him at all costs and through any circumstance? Each one of us must decide that for ourselves. What do you choose?

John 12:3 Giving Our Best

Then Mary took about a pint of pure nard, an expensive perfume; she poured it on Jesus' feet and wiped his feet with her hair. And the house was filled with the fragrance of the perfume. (NIV)

Giving Our Best

This pint of pure nard was worth a year's income on that day. Mary was giving her all to Jesus. This was an outward sign of love for her Savior. Mary didn't know she was preparing Jesus for burial. She only knew Jesus raised her brother from the dead and that He was the Messiah promised and sent by God the Father. She didn't understand all that the Messiah meant but she knew He loved them, and they loved Him. She worshiped Jesus with complete abandonment. I had a friend who learned from this lesson. A family in our church lost everything in a fire. We were all gathering household items to give them. My friend went through her linen closet looking for old sheets she no longer wanted. In the process, she had to move new sheets that hadn't even been opened. As she took out the old sheets, she heard the Holy Spirit say, "You keep your best for yourself and give me the discards?" She immediately put the old sheets away and gave the new, unused sheets. So often we are counting the cost of what we give like all of it belongs to us and we think we are doing great in sharing some of what we have with God. This is backward. All we have belongs to God and He allows us to share in what He has. As we see needs, let us give generously with love to God as we give to Him through others who are in need.

John 17:20 Jesus Prayed

My prayer is not for them alone. I pray also for those who will believe in me through their message,

Jesus Prayed

This is one of the most exciting verses in the Bible. Jesus is praying for you and me. It amazes me that, facing a most horrible time, Jesus took the time to pray for us. When I'm facing difficult trials (none anywhere as difficult as Jesus had to face), all I do is pray for myself. Praying for others is far from my mind. I know all of Jesus' prayers are answered exactly as He prayed them. That means His prayer for me is answered already in God's sight. I already believe in Him through the testimonies passed down through the ages. He continued to pray that we would be one in Him just as He and God are One. In God's eyes, that is already accomplished. In me, at this moment, it is still a work in progress, but I know it will come about because it was prayed for by Jesus and seen as accomplished by the Father. Thank You, Jesus, for thinking and praying about me in such a grievous time for you.

Hebrews 10:22-23 Draw Near (part 1)

Let us draw near to God with a sincere heart and with the full assurance that faith brings, having our hearts sprinkled to cleanse us from a guilty conscience and having our bodies washed with pure water. (NIV)

Draw Near (part 1)

First, let us look at "let us draw near to God." God is never away from us. He has even infused us with His Holy Spirit. He can't be much nearer to us than being in us. The problem is we tend to push away from God. Our minds and our hearts get distracted with the things of this world. We get busy and, if everything is going well, we push God to the back of our minds. We can only imagine how this must feel to God. He sent His only Son, His spoken Word through Him He created all things, to come apart from the Father and put on flesh and suffer for our sake. We must think about how we feel when the one we love pushes away from us. We must choose to draw near to God and stay nearby. We do this by immersing ourselves in His written word so it can always be in our minds. We do this by taking time multiple times of the day to talk to Him and listen to Him. Through doing these 2 things, we will gradually grow a strong desire to keep our minds and hearts on Him even as we do needed tasks in the world. He is always with us. Let us learn to always be with Him.

Hebrews 10:22-23 Draw Near (part 2)

Let us draw near to God with a sincere heart and with the full assurance that faith brings, having our hearts sprinkled to cleanse us from a guilty conscience and having our bodies washed with pure water (NIV)

Draw Near (part 2)

Draw near to God with full assurance. What do we need full assurance about? We need the assurance that God will allow sinners like us to draw near to Him. Jesus provided the way for us to draw near to the Father. The Holy Spirit within us confirms (assures us) that we can draw near to God. We must learn to turn our backs on the sins of our past (our separation from God) and, laying regrets and unforgiveness aside, move on with the freedom of being forgiven for all our sins and fully adopted into the family of God as joint heirs with His Son, Jesus. This gives us all the privileges and responsibilities that go with being part of the family. Guilt and regrets are gone as we stay near our Father and are replaced with joy in our cleansing with the purest water ever, the precious shed blood of Jesus. What joy it is to stay near to God.

James 4:6-10 Draw Near to God

"Draw near to God and He will draw near to you." (NIV)

Draw Near to God

That is an amazing promise! As we open ourselves up to the Lord, He opens to us. If we come to Him in submission, repentance, and brokenness, He rushes in with forgiveness, love, and faithfulness. There is no room for self-sufficiency or self-protection in this interaction. Only in the humility of helplessness will we discover the sufficiency of His presence.

At first glance, we may seem to be the ones who begin this open relationship, but it is God who has taken the initiative; we are merely responding to His overture (John 6:44). Many times, He uses situations and difficulties to get our attention and stimulate our thirst for Him. What appears to us to be a painful or desperate situation is His invitation to draw near. Even our greatest failures and sins can lead us to Christ, as we seek forgiveness from the Father. With an attitude of humble repentance, we can enter a more intimate relationship with God. However, if you and I continue living in rebellion and are unwilling to confess and repent, He will not open and reveal more of Himself to us. Sin always blocks our ability to know the Lord.

Have you let adversity or failure pull you away from God instead of toward Him? To put distance between you and Jesus, Satan will misuse the very situations that the Lord can utilize to draw you to Himself. Don't let the Enemy win the battle. "Resist the devil and he will flee from you" (James 4:7).

1 Corinthians 12:6 Differences

There are different kinds of working, but in all of them and in everyone it is the same God at work. (NIV)

Differences

Going to a different church or, for some of us, sitting in a different location in our church, can be quite unsettling and distracting for many people. We tend to be apprehensive and uncomfortable with new surroundings. We feel disoriented. Maybe the service is structured in a different way than we are accustomed to. Maybe the people around us sing differently or express their worship differently. We must admit we are more attuned to what or who is around us and what they are or aren't doing than we are to the reason we are there. We come together in a church building with other believers to unite our spirits in worship and praise of God. If some want to stand and raise their hands while others sit quietly it's fine. Back when I was a professional singer and in a large congregation, we were really into singing in worship. I heard the Lord ask, "Do you know who is making the most beautiful worship music?" In my pride, I was expecting Him to tell me. I was surprised when I heard Him point out the man next to me. This man was singing notes that didn't exist and, in a rhythm, totally unknown but, as I looked at him, I noticed he didn't notice anyone around him. He was immersed in worshiping God with his entire heart, mind, body, and spirit. Ouch. I accepted God's correction immediately and now, whatever church I may be in or whoever might be sitting (or standing) around me, I am there to worship God, not to pay attention to external differences. We are all there to bless and be blessed by God.

Matthew 24:8 The Season

All these are the beginning of birth pains. (NIV)

The Season

As you can probably guess from this scripture I live in southeast Texas with Harvey and all the rain. The disciples had asked Jesus how to know when He was coming back for His Bride (the church of believers). He said it would be just like in the days of Noah. We would all be going about our normal tasks. He said there would be earthquakes and wars and rumors of wars as we continued about our earthly business. The earth is in labor pains. The earth's normal weather system has been changing. Nations are continuing to rise against nations, not wanting peace but wanting to rule others. We believers must pay attention to the season. We don't know how long the season will last but we do know what we are to do. God wills that none be lost. We all know people who aren't believers. We must be in prayer for them. We must be sure we reflect God's light to them. We must talk to them. The harvest is ripe. Are we being harvesters for God?

Genesis 7:12-13 Noah

And rain fell on the earth forty days and forty nights. (NIV)

Noah

It's only the third day of rain from Harvey with a minimum of three more expected. I've been wondering how Noah and his family endured 40 days of the sound of rain yet even looking at water for another 130+. As I contemplated and read Noah's account, I saw God had provided him with a lot of animals to care for. But that wouldn't be enough to keep sanity through so very much. As I read more about Noah, I saw it was his complete trust and obedience to God that enabled him to stay at peace with the assurance all would be well for God was in control. Our attitude as we face trials is a choice. We can choose to fear, complain, be depressed, or choose to remember Who is in control. When we choose to look to God, trusting Him and obeying Him while giving Him praise and thanks, there is no room in our spirits for doom and gloom. Keeping the right attitude by choice brings emotions into order. Cabin fever (in my case) quickly vanishes, and the time of trial comes into line with the time of eternity. No matter what situation we find around us, we can take joy in the knowledge that God never leaves or forsakes us and will bring us to live with Him for all eternity.

Zephaniah 3:17 Rejoice Over Me

Jehovah thy God is in the midst of thee, a mighty one who will save; he will rejoice over thee with joy; he will rest in his love; he will joy over thee with singing.

Rejoice Over Me

This is God speaking. He says He will rejoice over us. Rejoicing over us brings Him joy; so much joy that He will sing. When I first read this verse, I couldn't believe that it was referring to me in any way. Who am I that God would rejoice over me? I look at myself and see a person who constantly stumbles into sin. If it is not with my mouth or actions it is in my mind; a critical thought about someone, a complaint about my road, and on and on. Then, as I read in the New Testament of God sending His Son, Jesus, to shed His blood for my sins – sins of omission as well as sins of action, as I read of His blood washing away my sins, I slowly come to understand how God, the Father, could rejoice over me. When He looks at me, He doesn't see my sins of action, thought, or omission. When He looks at me, He sees the blood of His beloved Son, Jesus Christ. This is how He can rejoice over me, to burst into joyous song. This is how He can rest in His love – love for His Son Who is seated at the Father's throne and who tells Him, "Look at her. She is your daughter because my spilled blood covers her.

Wow. That makes me want to rejoice and break out in song. If God can rest in His love, I can rest in His love through the knowledge that my sins are covered. I can rejoice that God the Father; the Creator is rejoicing over me with singing.

Luke 18:12 Twisting Scripture

I fast twice a week and give a tenth of all I get.' (NIV)

Twisting Scripture

There was an item on Facebook about tithing. The man said pastors are lying to us about tithing. He claims tithing is an Old Testament law and we are free from the Old Testament law. He claimed tithing is not in the New Testament. Then, why is it in Luke? Tithe means tenth. Jesus didn't say not to obey the law of tithing. He spoke often of giving. This man is confused because many pastors claim we should tithe. After all, if we do, we will get back that and more. That is a twisting of the promises in the Bible. True it says, "Give and it will be given unto you." This doesn't mean we give because we want to get it. We are to give out of love. God owns all that is in this world. That means He owns whatever we have. He allows us to be stewards of what He gives us, but He expects us to honor His word and give out of love and obedience. It is a joy to be allowed to use 90% of what God gives us (fewer offerings over the tithe He guides us to give). Tithing is a joy. I pray for that misguided man on Facebook and for those who believe his twisted interpretation of God's Word.

2 Corinthians 12:8-10 When God Says No

Three times I pleaded with the Lord to take it away from me. But he said to me, "My grace is sufficient for you, for my power is made perfect in weakness." Therefore, I will boast all the more gladly about my weaknesses, so that Christ's power may rest on me. That is why, for Christ's sake, I delight in weaknesses, in insults, in hardships, in persecutions, in difficulties. For when I am weak, then I am strong. (NIV)

When God Says No

Most of us pray for healing when we are sick or facing some challenge. Sometimes God says no to our prayers. There can be many reasons for His saying no. One of them is to show others how we, with God's help and grace, walk through those illnesses or challenges. We have a choice of a "woe is me" attitude. We can choose to complain and tell everyone how bad things are. We can choose to walk like Paul did through his infirmity. He continued to praise God and did all God enabled him to do without complaint but with contentment in the circumstance God allowed him to be and joy in the knowledge of his salvation through Jesus. Let us choose to walk with joy and thanksgiving through any situation God allows in our path.

Revelation 3:16 Religious or Related

So, because you are lukewarm—neither hot nor cold—I am about to spit you out of my mouth.

Matthew 7:22-23 Many will say to me on that day, 'Lord, Lord, did we not prophesy in your name and in your name drive out demons and in your name perform many miracles?' Then I will tell them plainly, 'I never knew you. Away from me, you evildoers!'

Matthew 24:4-14 Jesus answered: "Watch out that no one deceives you. For many will come in my name, claiming, 'I am the Messiah,' and will deceive many. You will hear of wars and rumors of wars but see to it that you are not alarmed. Such things must happen, but the end is still to come. Nation will rise against nation and kingdom against kingdom. There will be famines and earthquakes in various places. All these are the beginning of birth pains. "Then you will be handed over to be persecuted and put to death, and you will be hated by all nations because of me. At that time many will turn away from the faith and will betray and hate each other, and many false prophets will appear and deceive many people. Because of the increase of wickedness, the love of most will grow cold, but the one who stands firm to the end will be saved. And this gospel of the kingdom will be preached in the whole world as a testimony to all nations, and then the end will come.

Religious or Related

I was raised to go to church, to be religious, to be a "good" person. I tried to do all the church said to do. I served in the church. I volunteered in charity groups. I watched my language. Then, in 1974 I had a personal encounter with Jesus. I entered a relationship with Him. I am no longer religious. I no longer perform the "good deeds" religion says to perform. I do my best to follow the example of Jesus because I love Him. I pray and trust Him to answer rather than praying and then doing all I can to be sure I answer my prayers. So many people in the church are like I was. They are lukewarm. They do things in the name of Jesus, but they have no real relationship with Him. We need to take time to be sure we have a personal relationship with Him. Doing what He says to do in our strength without really knowing Him. I pray you take time to meditate in open honesty on the above verses and grow closer to a real relationship with Jesus every day. A day without learning something new about Jesus is a day wasted. Religion tries to reach up to God. Christians just need to take the hand of God (Jesus) reaching down to us.

Proverbs 1:8-9 Write What We Learn

Listen, my son, to your father's instruction, and do not forsake your mother's teaching. They are a garland to grace your head and a chain to adorn your neck. (NIV)

Write What We Learn

As I do my Bible study each day, I write notes under different verses and paragraphs much like a commentary. I do this not only for my benefit but also to hand it down to my children after I'm gone. Though my age is well into the senior category I still miss the wisdom of my parents. I know there are some real gems from them that I have forgotten. Many because, as a teenager or young adult we tend to have the misguided idea we know more than our parents. I have a wonderful relationship with my children, and they are with me. When I'm home with God, I want them to have something tangible they can read to remember the things I've taught them and the things I forgot to teach them. Seeing that you have a computer device and probably have at least one Bible translation on that device, I recommend trying this, if only for your benefit. Writing what we learn helps to impress it more securely on our minds and hearts. No matter how old we get, let us continue to pass the wisdom God imparts to us down to our children, not as hard rules, but as personal insights for them on our relationship and growth in God through His Son, Jesus.

Colossians 3:17 All Things

And whatever you do, whether in word or deed, do it all in the name of the Lord Jesus, giving thanks to God the Father through him. (NIV)

All Things

We naturally do things from a horizontal frame of mind. We do them in a worldly way. God wants us to do things vertically, His way. Our habits are horizontal, and habits are hard to break. It takes time to train ourselves to pause and ask God how He wants us to solve a problem, respond to a need, or even do a daily task. We can't just tack on the name of Jesus to things we do. Doing things in the name of Jesus means doing them like Jesus did and with His attitude of doing all things in a way that brings glory to the Father. We can give thanks as we do things that way because the Holy Spirit is in us enabling us to do them and enabling us to love and be thankful for our salvation and for a personal relationship with the Creator of all that was, is, or will ever be.

Proverbs 9:10 Fear is Knowledge

The fear of the Lord is the beginning of wisdom, and knowledge of the Holy One is understanding. (NIV)

Fear is Knowledge

This proverb is written as a corresponding or parallel couplet which means the two lines express the same thought with different words to aid in the understanding. This proverb defines what scripture means by the phrase "fear the Lord." We usually define fear as "to be afraid." We see, but in the second line of the couplet, the word fear is defined as knowledge. To fear the Lord means to know the Lord. We can only know Him through Jesus, His Son, and the Holy Spirit. Knowing God is the beginning of wisdom. When man ate from the Tree of Knowledge of good and evil, man separated himself from the knowledge and wisdom of God. We need not be afraid of God because He loves us. He loves us so much He put His only Son, Jesus, through a horrendous ordeal for our sake. We can choose to live without the knowledge of God and be without the peace, joy, and wisdom His knowledge brings or we can choose, through Jesus, to come into the knowledge of God and grow in understanding through His Holy Spirit.

2 Corinthians 5:17 Addictions

Therefore, if anyone is in Christ, the new creation has come: The old has gone, the new is here! (NIV)

Addictions

The moment we accept Jesus into our minds, hearts, and lives we become new creations of God. God brings into us His Holy Spirit. But through us, externally, it is a process to be revealed. We are full of old, sinful familiar, and comfortable habits. These habits don't automatically die. It takes time for us to listen to the Holy Spirit as He gently urges us to turn our backs on these old habits and allow the newness of His Holy Spirit to shine in and through us. These habits are often referred to as addictions. We tend to put restraints on what we call addictions thinking only of alcohol, gambling, etc. Any habit can be and most likely is an addiction. We must allow the Holy Spirit to reveal to us our addictions be it food, cigarettes, sex, money, power, or most anything under creation, and enable us to put the addiction in the right perspective (God's perspective). In all things and relationships, we are to put God first. The best instruction book for this process is the Holy Bible. There is a book I highly recommend helping in this process, "Goliath Must Fall" by Louie Giglio which is most helpful in identifying our addictions. We often don't recognize them in ourselves because they are so very comfortable. Once we do, it is important to stay away from all temptation until the Holy Spirit has made us strong. We are in a process of "from glory to glory He's changing me from earthly things to the heavenly." Let us continue moving on with God through Jesus and the power of His Holy Spirit.

Proverbs 3:11-12 Correction

My son, do not despise the Lord's discipline and do not resent his rebuke, because the Lord disciplines those he loves, as a father the son he delights in. (NIV)

Correction

I had a neighbor who would come down, sit at my kitchen table, and say, "God must love me today. He's chastising me." We tend to remain as little children. We don't like to be corrected or disciplined. When I was correcting my teenagers they would say, "Quit yelling at me." I wasn't yelling. I was speaking in a low, calm voice. But correction is heard as yelling. We need to understand correction, especially from the Holy Spirit, is an excellent form of love. God wants nothing but the best for us. He wants us to be and feel full of His love. He wants us to experience His joy. Things we are doing, saying, or thinking outside of love rob us of joy. Let us learn not to resent the correction of the Holy Spirit whether it comes straight from Him or through others. Let us be open to our misguided ways, even when our intentions were right. Let us learn to welcome the correcting love of God however, He chooses to make us aware of it.

Matthew 9:37-38 Harvest Now

Then he said to his disciples, "The harvest is plentiful, but the workers are few. Ask the Lord of the harvest, therefore, to send out workers into his harvest field." (NIV)

Harvest Now

We live in an exciting season. The earth is in labor pains with extreme weather conditions. There are wars and rumors of wars. Nations are rising against Christians. We don't know how long this season will last before Jesus comes back for His Bride. It could be a day or a hundred thousand years. God's days are different from ours. We do know God desires for not one person to be lost from Him. As trials continue to come, people become more aware they don't have control over their situations. They start searching to find peace. They begin to open. The harvest is right now. Our question is where are the harvesters? Every Christian is called to be a harvester. We must each ask ourselves if we are harvesting. Are we serious about harvesting? Do we care about the lost? If so, what are we doing about it? Let us get about the work God has for us to do. Let us lead others to the peace and love of God through Jesus Christ, His only Son, and the only entryway to the throne of God.

1 Samuel 17:40 Stone and Slingshot

And he took his staff in his hand and chose him five smooth stones out of the brook and put them in the shepherd's bag which he had, even in his wallet; and his sling was in his hand: and he drew near to the Philistine. (ESV)

Stone and Slingshot

He was just a small young boy sent on a simple errand. When David arrived to bring supplies and check on his older brothers, he could not understand why no one would answer Goliath's challenge. What was different about the boy, David? None of the men trained in warfare would face Goliath. David had a gift of faith. He knew he was God's chosen. David knew if he walked according to the will of God, God would protect him. He stepped out in faith and trust. David did not wear man's armor. He knew that armor was not made for him. He chose to wear God's armor of faith. He walked with calmness to face the giant. He calmly picked out some small stones. Then David declared God's power. I too, can be like David. Wherever, whenever, and however God would use me, I can walk in faith. He will equip me for the task at hand. My job is to be willing to obey. When I walk in obedience and faith, I can leave the results to God. Our question is not the size of the task at hand. God equips for every task regardless of size or difficulty. Am I willing to go, do, and speak what He bids? It only took a small stone and a slingshot in the hand of a boy to save a nation.

Haggai 1:5 Accidents

Now this is what the LORD Almighty says: "Give careful thought to your ways. (NIV)

Accidents

To get into our nearest town we must turn from a gravel road onto a highway where the cars are going 70 MPH or greater. Last week there were two major accidents just down the road from us. One of them left us sitting in stopped traffic for over an hour with frozen food in our car. These accidents were both caused by people not being careful. They were distracted when driving and though looking they did not see. We tend to go through our days like that many times. We don't see things God would show us and we don't hear things He would tell us. We are distracted by our thoughts and plans. We have determined our schedule for the day and don't want any interruptions. God tells us to give careful thought to our ways. He tells us to guard our hearts and minds. He tells us to keep our minds on Him. We learn to do this by practicing. Weightlifters don't start by lifting several hundred pounds. They start with small weights and gradually build up. They call this "working out." We are to "work out" God's instructions to us through study and meditation. We cannot expect to know what He wants if we don't learn to hear Him. Hearing God and living out His purpose in our lives takes practice and time. Let us not be discouraged as we learn to see and listen. With practice, we can become clearer in our vision and hearing. Our question is, who or what do we want to direct our lives? Our choices are our infallible shortsightedness or God Who is all knowledgeable and all-seeing.

Psalms 119:162 Found Treasure

I rejoice in your promise like one who finds great spoil. (NIV)

Found Treasure

If any of us were to walk down the road and find a couple of twenty-dollar bills, we would pick them up and tell almost all our friends of our find. If you are reading this, you have probably found something worth more than all the money in the world. You have found your relationship with God through His Son, Jesus Christ. This "find" is beyond value. Our question is are we as excited as we would be if we found those twenty-dollar bills? Have we told our friends of our "find?" If we found several thousand dollars, we would be telling everyone we meet. We have something worth far more than several thousand dollars. We have something that will take us into and through all eternity in the very real Presence of the God of all creation. Are we talking about it? There is more than enough to share. Sharing won't take any of our eternity away from us, but it will bring more people with us, and it will please the God Whose Presence we will be in forever. Let's just not think about this. Let's do this. Pass on God's plan for eternity in His Presence. It's available to all who will say yes to His Son, Jesus Christ.

Philippians 4:8 Think on These Things

Finally, brothers, whatever is true, whatever is noble, whatever is right, whatever is pure, whatever is lovely, whatever is admirable—if anything is excellent or praiseworthy—think about such things. (NIV)

Think on These Things

Paul tells us very plainly what we are to think about. When thinking about what is true (God loves us and has promised to meet all our needs), whatever is noble (God is true to His word), whatever is right (God is always right), whatever is pure (God is without sin), whatever is lovely (there is nothing lovelier than the love of God), whatever is admirable (the works of God are the most admirable) and what is excellent or praiseworthy (God is excellent and is worthy to be praised.). These are the things we are to allow our minds to dwell on. We have the power to choose what thoughts we will allow to stay in our minds and what thoughts we will push out. We can push out negative thoughts with praise to God. It is hard to praise and be negative at the same time. We can push out negative thoughts by thanking God for all He has already given us. Instead of looking at what we don't have or what we might not get let's look at what we do have and what God has already given us. He has given us forgiveness for our sins. He has given us eternal life. He has given us the gift of His Holy Spirit to guide us, comfort us, and intercede for us. What more can we ask for? Let us relax and trust God. God holds all our tomorrows in His hand.

Romans 15:4 The Holy Bible

For everything that was written in the past was written to teach us, so that through endurance and the encouragement of the Scriptures we might have hope. (NIV)

The Holy Bible

The Holy Bible, the written Word of God, amazes me. The components of it were written through different ages spanning hundreds of years. The writers were different people, living in different centuries, different cultures, different occupations, and different methods of thinking. Some were kings and some were lowly shepherds or fishermen. Some were poets and some were well-educated priests. Yet all is in symmetry and compiled together makes a whole. There are 66 books bound into the one Book we call The Holy Bible. This book has withstood the test of time and is the most unique of all books ever written. It is inspired and written by God's Holy Spirit and applies to every man in every walk of life in every century. It has been translated in a variety of languages and dialects yet remains steadfast. God speaks to man in man's language. It contains direct quotes from God as well as the experiences of those God has worked through in the past. It is fully inspired by the Spirit of God. No other book has ever or will ever move and direct people in the way this book has. Other books have been and will be inspiring in their way, but none can rival the collection of books we call "The Holy Bible." Yet, despite all this, it is amazing how many Christians treat this book as a decoration on a table. When used regularly and studied, it will provide answers and directions for every life at every time and in every situation. Give someone the gift of this glorious book.

Matthew 10:7-8 Preach

As you go, preach this message: 'The kingdom of heaven is near.' Heal the sick, raise the dead, cleanse those who have leprosy, drive out demons. Freely you have received, freely give (NIV)

Preach

Many Bible verses contain multiple instructions. Here Matthew first tells us we are to go preach. He isn't talking about giving a sermon. He is talking about declaring God's Word aloud to all who will listen. All believers are called to "preach." We are all to declare God's Word by sharing with others what God has done for and with us and by telling others about Jesus and sharing with them God's plan for their salvation. Sometimes it is hard to know how to start. When I don't know how to find an open door with someone I simply say, "God bless you." It's amazing how many doors open. Yes, occasionally someone might slam the door in my face but that is very seldom. Most want to hear why I said that. Let us remember we are to go forth and "preach."

Matthew 13:32 Small Becomes Big

Though it is the smallest of all your seeds, yet when it grows, it is the largest of garden plants and becomes a tree, so that the birds of the air come and perch in its branches." (NIV)

Small Becomes Big

From small to big is the cycle of life. We start as infants, small, and grow into bigger forms as adults. Faith also starts small and grows with use and proper nourishment (Bible study, prayer, meditation, and use.) Most everything starts with small. I know Jesus as my personal Lord and Savior because of a smile from a lady in church. A smile seemed like a small thing, yet it changed my life. I went from a church member and employee who knew the fact of Jesus being God's Son to a believer and follower because of that smile. We tend to look for God to use us for big things and we miss out on sowing small seeds that will become big. Our question for us today is are we willing to allow God to use us in the small, seemingly ordinary things and allow Him to determine the growth that will come forth? Maybe all He wants us to do this day is say thank you to someone who needs a kind word. Let us pay attention to the little and allow God to bring the growth.

Psalm 32:5 Sin

Then I acknowledged my sin to you and did not cover up my iniquity. said, "I will confess my transgressions to the LORD"— and you forgave the guilt of my sin. (NIV)

Sin

The word "sin" is in the Bible at least 420 times. We do not like to use the word "sin." We would rather say: made a mistake, messed up, goofed, erred, etc. Sin is anything that separates us from God's will for us. We say there are big sins and little sins, but sin is sin. We might disguise it or cover it up from others or ourselves, but we can never cover up or disguise sin from God. We live such a fast-paced life we fail many times to notice when we are separated from God. We do not notice when we no longer feel the amazing peace of God. There is no room in us for God's peace when we have unconfessed sin in us. I like to do what I call "spiritual breathing" every day. I exhale my sins by asking the Holy Spirit to reveal them to me and confessing them as sins to God then I inhale God's forgiveness and His peace. We have no room for air in our lungs if we are holding in old air. We must exhale the old to inhale the new. Our question is are we willing to admit to ourselves all things that are not in God's perfect will for us? God already knows. Nothing can separate us from His love, but sin does separate us from His peace.

Romans 8:27 Romans 8

And he who searches our hearts knows the mind of the Spirit, because the Spirit intercedes on behalf of the saints according to God's will. (NET)

Romans 8

This verse has had a new impact on me. God's word is the living word for many reasons. His word gives us life. His word also seems to grow as our understanding grows. I've known and experienced the Holy Spirit praying through and for me, but I've never thought how He would turn my prayers into perfection by God's will. All I need do is pray with limited understanding and I know that God's Holy Spirit in me will turn my words and thoughts into the words and thoughts that agree with God's perfect will for me and for those I am praying for. God loves us so very much. He provides for all our needs—even the words we need when we pray. Our question is are we willing to look to Him and allow Him to meet our every need? God will not force us. He reaches His hand out to us, and it is up to us to reach our hands to Him. He won't walk for us but will enable us to walk and will walk with us.

Isaiah 43:18 Rear View Mirror

Forget the former things; do not dwell on the past (NIV)

Rear View Mirror

Some of us live our lives looking into the rear-view mirror. Often, we say, "if only I had" or "if only I didn't." We seldom can do anything about what has already been. There are times we can make restitution for something in our past but mostly the past is finished. We cannot go back nor are we meant to go back. When we confess a sin to God, God forgets it. We are not to keep re-confessing the same sin. Lot's wife learned the hard way not to look back. The Hebrews wanted to go back shortly after Moses led them out of Egypt. The past is familiar. There is comfort in the familiar. When we keep looking in our rear-view mirror we are missing where we are in the present. When we miss the present, we miss out on what God has for us. Let us immerse ourselves in the here and now. God wants our attention now. He wants to use us now. If we are looking in the rear-view mirror, wishing for something that was or might have been we are not fully attuned to the present. Let us enjoy the now, thank and praise God for the now, and use the now to the fullest possible.

Matthew 6:34 Binoculars

Therefore, do not worry about tomorrow, for tomorrow will worry about itself. Each day has enough trouble of its own. (NIV)

Binoculars

In the previous devotion, we thought about the rear-view mirror – looking back behind us to what is already past. Many of us have even more trouble trying to live in the future. We cannot wait until something happens or something changes. Maybe it's because we are nervous, concerned, or afraid of what might be. We try to use binoculars to see what might be ahead for us. Jesus has a remarkably simple answer for that. He said not to worry about what is not yet. We have enough trouble living the day we are in without borrowing from a day that is yet to come. It's important to read the verses before this verse. Jesus is telling us how to live this way – without concern for the past in the rear-view mirror or the future in the binoculars. He tells us we are to seek His Kingdom and His righteousness. The word "seek" is in the present tense. This is what we are to be about – seeking Him in the here and now. We are not to wait until tomorrow to seek Him. We might not have a tomorrow. We are not to sit on the fact we sought Him yesterday. Yesterday is over. We are to actively seek Him today. This is a continual seeking. Our question is are we seeking Him each day we have? How do we seek our God? We seek Him through Bible study, meditation on His Word, and prayer – both active and listening prayer. Let us not get too concerned about what was or what might be and continually seek our God. That leads to a full and abundant life in the present.

Matthew 6:34 Worry

Therefore, do not worry about tomorrow, for tomorrow will worry about itself. Each day has enough trouble of its own. (NIV)

Worry

This is a command not to worry about tomorrow. It is not a suggestion. It starts with the word "therefore." Because of that Word, we must know what Jesus said preceding this command. In verse 33 He tells us to seek first – before all else – His Kingdom and His righteousness. He gives a promise to us if we seek His Kingdom and righteousness. He tells us all these things will be added or given to us. What things? All the things we need to live our lives. Since He promises to meet all our needs if we seek Him before all things what is stopping us? Do we believe in God? Do we believe He is true to His word to us? Belief and trust are choices. We can choose to trust, and we can choose not to trust. We can choose to be worried about things we cannot control (what happens next) or we can choose not to worry. We can choose to seek God above all things, or we can choose to seek worldly things. What we cannot do is blame anyone else for our choices. Whenever we start to feel anxious or worried about something we have a choice of where we will put our thoughts. Tomorrow we will look at that. Today we have a choice to make—trust what God says or not. What is your choice?

1 Corinthians 15:55 Watching Them Leave

"Where, O death, is your victory? Where, O death, is your sting?" (NIV)

Watching Them Leave

The hardest thing we can ever do is to watch a loved one slowly slip away from us. I have watched loved ones slowly slip away and watched Hospice patients slowly slip away. It is also hard watching a friend who is watching a loved one slip away. Even when we know they are headed to a far better place it is a difficult thing. It is not so much concern for the one slipping away but the loss of their companionship with us that makes it so difficult. When we are in this process quite often, we feel alone in our growing grief. God has been there. He watched as His Only Son, Jesus suffered a slow, painful death on the cross. He knew what the outcome would be, yet He was in pain watching. We sometimes feel God is not with us. We have prayed for healing for our loved one or friend. We tend to see healing only in our time and space. God's view of healing is sometimes quite different. There is nothing wrong with grieving over the temporary separation that is approaching if we do not allow ourselves to be swallowed up by it. How do we keep from being swallowed up? We allow our friends to stand by us. We allow ourselves tears of grief while at the same time praising and thanking God for His perfect wisdom and His continued presence and control of all around us. As a friend, we remember prayer is most important. Touch is also important. Words sometimes should not be said. Just knowing someone is there and cares about our feelings can bring about healing of growing grief. If you know someone facing this today, send them a note and say a prayer letting them know you are praying for them and are there for them.

Luke 9:51 Resolute

As the time approached for him to be taken up to heaven, Jesus resolutely set out for Jerusalem. (NIV)

Resolute

The word "resolute" means admirably purposeful, determined, and unwavering. Jesus knew what was facing Him in Jerusalem. He knew He would be rejected and betrayed by one of His disciples. He knew He would be beaten and crucified. He knew His Father would have to turn His face away as Jesus bore the sins of all mankind. Yet He purposefully set out for Jerusalem. He knew His purpose on this earth, and He purposefully and determinedly set out to accomplish it. God gave each of us a purpose on this earth. We are to learn of Him, worship and praise Him, and shed His Light to all those around us. Our question is how resolutely are we doing this? Most of us do not face physical abuse but only inconvenience to our selfish desires yet our resolve wavers. We are to resolve unwaveringly. We can only do this to the degree we allow the Holy Spirit to fill us and to flow through us. Today let us ask God to fill us deeper so that we may unwaveringly resolve to shed His Light to those around us.

Matthew 10:30 Little Things

And even the very hairs of your head are all numbered.
(The Holy Bible, New International Version

Little Things

We took a day off and went to a National Wildlife Preserve and a State Park to hike some trails. The scenery was beautiful, and I enjoyed taking a lot of pictures. I found myself very interested in taking photos of insects. I was especially drawn to a beautiful blue dragonfly. Most of the time we do not notice the little things. Often, we do not pray about what we consider to be a little thing. God does notice the trivial things. Jesus said He even knows exactly how many individual hairs are on our heads. If you can count your hairs, you might not consider it to be insignificant but most of us do not think about exactly how many we have. In taking photos of the dragonfly and a wasp on a dead log, I started thinking about how much I miss in not paying attention to the little things. We need to talk with God more often about more things – even what we consider to be insignificant. That is part of fellowship and fellowship is why God created us. Next time we are talking to God and ignoring something, let's talk to Him about it. It might be a simple thank You, God, for creating such a beautiful blue dragonfly. I did thank Him that one of the food sources of dragonflies is a mosquito. I also thank God for creating mosquitoes for food for beautiful, little dragonflies.

Psalms 119:7 Life as a Game

I will praise you with an upright heart as I learn your righteous laws. (NIV)

Life as a Game

Many think life is a game and treat it according. Life is not a game. Life on this earth is a training ground for eternal life in heaven in the very real Presence of God the Creator. Heaven is a real place, and we will have things to do in heaven. One of the most precious things we will be able to do is praise our God. We learn how to praise Him here in this life on earth. We practice in our times of devotion and meditation, and we practice when we gather together with some of His other children in collective worship services. We also train in various ministries and responsibilities according to the talents and gifts God gives us. We will be joyfully busy in heaven. But to get there we need a ticket. Our ticket is the blood of God's only Son, Jesus Christ. When we accept Him as our Savior and the director of our life we are washed in His blood and given His Holy Spirit, our ticket to heaven. Our question is do we have our ticket and are we actively training for our time in heaven or are we treating life here as a game? Let us choose to be diligent in our training.

1Corinthians 13:4-8 Keeping Score

Love is patient, love is kind. It does not envy, it does not boast, it is not proud. It is not rude, it is not self-seeking, it is not easily angered, it keeps no record of wrongs. Love does not delight in evil but rejoices with the truth. It always protects, always trusts, always hopes, always perseveres. Love never fails (NIV)

Keeping Score

Love keeps no account of wrongs. We are so good at keeping accounts. We use it as ammunition when we are arguing. We keep score. We want to be sure we hurt back the one who hurts us. God does not keep account of wrongs or sins after we confess. When He forgives, He strikes it from His book. He never brings it up to us again. He says it is as far as the east is from the west. The sins we do against God are much worse than anything that can be done against us. When we pray the prayer Jesus taught, the prayer we call "The Lord's Prayer," we ask God to forgive us in the same manner we forgive others. Our question is do we want God to keep score on us in the same way we keep score on others? Once again, as with all the aspects of love, the choice is ours to make.

Romans 8:17 Share in His Glory

Now if we are children, then we are heirs —heirs of God and co-heirs with Christ, if indeed we share in his sufferings in order that we may also share in his glory.

Share in His Glory

Wow! We may share in the glory of Christ. His glory is being in the presence of the Father. However, that promise is connected to a stipulation. We must also share in His sufferings. To share in someone's suffering we need to have an intimate relationship. We need to know them. Our question is, do we know Christ? Do we spend enough time with Him through prayer, meditation, and Bible study to know what sufferings He has? Every so often I am overwhelmed with the sorrow He must feel when He sees what people do to each other. Physical and emotional abuse is running wild in our society. We tend to compare ourselves with others and think we are not so bad. Jesus said if you even call someone "stupid" you are guilty of murder. To share in His sufferings, we must love all His creation. Next time we feel the need to criticize someone, we need to remember Jesus loves them as much as He loves us. It just might help us change the way we view others.

Exodus 3:1-22 Speaking Through Odd Circumstances

So Moses thought, "I will go over and see this strange sight—why the bush does not burn up." When the Lord saw that he had gone over to look, God called to him from within the bush, "Moses! Moses!"

Speaking Through Odd Circumstances

Can you remember a time when you were so engrossed in the details of your own life that you could not hear God at all? In times like those, we oftentimes cannot detect the Lord's whisper. So instead, He may shout through unusual circumstances.

Consider Moses in the third chapter of Exodus. Though well-educated and raised as a prince, he was exiled and humiliated in the wilderness. Life certainly was not turning out as he'd envisioned, and he was no doubt preoccupied with fear, disappointment, and pride. But God had big plans for Moses and needed to get his attention. So, the Lord arranged something that the shepherd just could not ignore: a bush that was on fire and yet was not being consumed. Even more startling, God spoke to Moses through the burning bush! Do you think that would have made you take notice?

Sometimes, this is exactly how God works. To speak to us, He must first get our undivided attention by doing something so unusual that we have no choice but to stop, look, and listen. There is no such thing as an accident for a child of God. Everything you see or hear is something that God allowed you to notice for a reason. We must learn how to perceive God in every circumstance, from the wild and unexpected to the simple and mundane. Whether our situation seems unbelievably good or unbearably bad, we are wise to step back and ask the Lord to help us view the matter from His perspective.

Ezekiel 34:26 Drought

And I will make them and the places round about my hill a blessing; and I will cause the shower to come down in its season; there shall be showers of blessing.

Drought

We lived in an area that was in drought. The water department came around to the houses to sell us shower heads which would conserve water. Oh, what a disappointing shower. It was more like a fine mist than a shower. God's blessings come in showers. His shower head is big, and the streams of blessings are great. The seasons come and go. When we are in the season of drought, we must be patient and learn the lessons of the season. Those seasons are always followed by God's showers of blessings.

Proverbs 3:5-6 Reasons to Trust

Trust in the Lord with all your heart and lean not on your own understanding; in all your ways submit to him, and he will make your paths straight.

Reasons to Trust

We often find it easy to trust the Lord when circumstances are pleasant. In challenging times, though, resting in Him can be challenging. Yet that is precisely what God told David to "Call upon Me in the day of trouble; I shall deliver you" (Psalm 50:15). Trusting the Lord is possible because of His love for us. In the Bible, we see this divine love demonstrated through the Father's character, the Savior's atoning death, and the believer's adoption as a child of God.

Another reason we can rely upon our heavenly Father is His infinite wisdom (Romans 11:33). He always knows what is best for us, and His judgments are perfect. We do not understand all that goes into God's plan—compared to the full, clear view He has of our lives, we see just a limited picture of reality. Therefore, what He chooses for us may not make sense at the time.

We can also depend upon the Lord because He is sovereign. In other words, whatever He—in His wisdom and love—chooses to do, He can accomplish. Nothing stands in the way of our God. He is in complete control of all things; even Satan must obtain His permission before acting (Job 1:9-12).

We understandably dislike adversity intensely and may feel tempted to ask, "Why, Lord?" Yet by recognizing that God acts in love, wisdom, and sovereignty, we can know that He's allowed the situation and has our long-term best in mind. So, we can replace "why?" with gratitude and trust.

Isaiah 41:9-13 Strength for the Fearful

I took you from the ends of the earth, from its farthest corners I called you. I said, 'You are my servant'; I have chosen you and have not rejected you. So do not fear, for I am with you; do not be dismayed, for I am your God. I will strengthen you and help you; I will uphold you with my righteous right hand.

Strength for the Fearful

When one of God's people is seeking an anchor in turbulent times, this is the right passage for the job. Here, Isaiah writes about the source of Christians' strength. In verse ten alone, the Lord promises strength, help, and protection. Moreover, He gives two commands: "Do not fear" and "Do not anxiously look about you." Among Satan's subtle and successful traps is the art of distraction. The Evil One knows that fear can choke faith. He works hard to make unsettling circumstances a person's sole focus. Once a believer's attention is diverted from God, natural human tendencies take over. In the absence of prayer and worship, anxiety and doubt grow unobstructed.

Staying focused on God can be hard. The flesh prefers to seek security by thinking through all possible angles: we tend to weigh what we think could happen against what "experts" say will happen, and then evaluate possible ways of preventing our worst fears from coming true. Instead of becoming more confident, we begin to realize how powerless we are. Thankfully, we serve an almighty God who says, "Surely I will help you" (v. 10). You can count on Him.

When we focus on our circumstances, we are choosing to feel anxiety and doubt. But these emotions do not belong in a believer's daily life. Instead, let's decide to trust in the promises God has given us. He's filled His Word with scriptural anchors to keep His children steady in the faith.

1 Kings 18:1-15 Travel Companions: Faith and Obedience

Elijah said, "As the Lord Almighty lives, whom I serve, I will surely present myself to Ahab today."

Travel Companions: Faith and Obedience

Faith and obedience are travel companions heading to the same "destination"—namely, to please and glorify the Lord. You cannot have one without the other. They grow simultaneously as they are practiced but will wither if neglected.

Elijah was a man with both qualities. He believed in God and consistently responded in obedience. When the Lord said to show himself to King Ahab, he did not permit fear to stop him. He had learned through experience that the Father was faithful and trustworthy.

Fear short-circuits faith when we begin to doubt that God's way is best. If we allow worry to gain a foothold in our minds, we will respond by refusing to do what the Lord says, which is disobedience. The result will be a change in our "travel plans"—by rejecting the way of faith and obedience, we are choosing the path of unbelief and sin.

Satan loves our fear and disobedience because they hinder the journey that God has designed for us. We cannot believe the Lord for great things in one area of our life if we are allowing sin in another. Self-examination is essential in the walk of faith. Where have you compromised by allowing sin a foothold? Are you resisting anything that God says in His Word?

Great faith begins with small steps. When you choose to follow God's Word, an ever-increasing cycle of faith and obedience will begin. Do not let fear or sin rob you of the great adventure He's planned for your life. Who has a better track record for choosing the right path—you or God? Believe Him!

1 Peter 2:2-3 Thirst for the Word

Like newborn babies, crave pure spiritual milk, so that by it you may grow up in your salvation, now that you have tasted that the Lord is good.

Thirst for the Word

Did you ever watch an infant take a feeding? Hungry little ones clutch the bottle, smack their lips, and make soft contented noises. They thoroughly enjoy their nourishment. But there comes a time when milk isn't enough to satiate a baby's appetite anymore. That is when a whole world of culinary possibilities opens.

Comparing new believers to babies, Peter said that they "long for the pure milk of the word" (v. 2). You would not feed a newborn steak and spinach, would you? Well, baby Christians must sip scriptural truths that they understand. Then, like a growing child, they shoot up as they feast on Bible passages, gradually taking in increasingly meatier principles and topics. Believers are not left alone to make sense of Scripture any more than babies and young children are expected to get their meals. The Holy Spirit, who indwells God's followers, illuminates the Word. That is, He makes the meaning clear to those who seek to understand. Moreover, according to Ephesians 4:11-16, God has given gifted Christians to the church to function as pastors and teachers. They are charged with equipping the saints for service (v. 12). These leaders instruct, clarify, and motivate people to grow in their faith and to fulfill the church's purpose of reaching the lost.

God's Word is a feast for our hearts, minds, and spirits. This is one banquet table where there is no such thing as taking too much. The advice many parents give their children at the dinner table applies to the Christian life as well: "Eat up! Scriptural food makes you grow strong."

1 Peter 1:3-9 The Source of Hope

Praise be to the God and Father of our Lord Jesus Christ! In his great mercy, He has given us new birth into a living hope through the resurrection of Jesus Christ from the dead, and into an inheritance that can never perish, spoil or fade. This inheritance is kept in heaven for you, who through faith are shielded by God's power until the coming of the salvation that is ready to be revealed in the last time.

The Source of Hope

Hope can be defined as the desire for something good and the expectation of receiving it. Jesus Christ is the only genuine source of hope. He alone knows what is best and has the sovereignty and power to secure its fulfillment. All other hopes are grounded on the shifting sands of circumstances beyond our control.

Each of us has expectations for the future, but these often pertain only to this earthly life. Christ promises us the "living hope" of an imperishable inheritance in heaven. Everyday desires will all fade away, but our home in heaven is eternal. This is our ultimate security and anchor when the storms of life are severe. But how do we endure times of trial right now? Heaven can seem so far away when pain is present and there is no relief in sight. Hope anticipates a change of circumstances for the better. And what about times when our situation is not improving—then, what is God doing that is "better"? Peter tells us He is refining our faith, which will result in praise and glory when Jesus returns. This is more valuable to us than gold or even relief from our distress. What a paradox! The difficulties which cause us to lose hope are the tools the Lord uses to increase our faith and hope in Him.

Christ promises us hope not only for eternity but also for this life. In those times that God does not deliver us from difficulty, we can be sure He is doing greater work within us. When we finally reach our eternal home, we will recognize the immeasurable value of the faith He produced in us as we kept our hope in Him.

Matthew 5:13-16 A City on a Hill

You are the light of the world. A town built on a hill cannot be hidden.

A City on a Hill

Reality television has become popular in recent years. On this type of show, the world is invited to watch as people go about their daily lives while participating in staged situations. While we may not run into as much drama or glamour, our lives are similar, in that people are observing what we do. Jesus likened believers' lives to a city on a hill, which cannot be hidden (Matthew 5:14). When others watch us, they ought to see reflections of Christ—which means we must let the Holy Spirit express His life through us.

First, we need to realize that God's goal is for us to become more like Him.

Second, we are to read Scripture daily, because we get to know the Father better through His Word, and then our lives will more clearly reflect Him to others.

Third, we should review how the Lord has worked in the past. Noting His faithfulness strengthens our trust and enables us to help others in similar situations.

The fourth step may seem unsettling, but it is wise advice: Be prepared and willing to suffer. God uses difficult times to draw His children close to Himself. So, if you are facing painful circumstances, know that He has allowed them for your growth, His glory, and encouragement to others. Recognizing this will help you surrender your will and desires to His plan. As you do, He will build a beautiful message into your life.

Think about both your public life and your private life. Are both glorifying to the Lord? Allow God's light to penetrate any "darkness" in your thoughts, words, or deeds. Then others may be drawn to the Father by what they observe in you (v. 16).

Genesis 39:21-40 A Faith-Filled Outlook

The Lord was with him; he showed him kindness and granted him favor in the eyes of the prison warden.

A Faith-Filled Outlook

If anyone had reason to be discouraged, Joseph did. His mother died when he was a boy. His brothers hated him, sold him into slavery, and convinced his father that he was dead. Joseph worked hard in Potiphar's household but ended up in prison because of false allegations. Yet he was not an angry person. The Hebrew slave maintained his faith-filled outlook because he consistently relied upon God, who remained with him and gave him success. Even in prison, Joseph was given responsibility over others (v. 21). Like that righteous young man, we might also be "held captive"—by unemployment, ill health, or a difficult relationship. In those hard places, we can nevertheless experience our Father's presence and thrive: His Holy Spirit will produce godly fruit in us when we depend upon Him (Galatians 5:22-23).

Regardless of his circumstances, Joseph refused to focus on himself. When two royal servants were jailed, he had compassion for them and gave them aid. In times of both blessing and crisis, we are to help others in whatever ways we can (2 Corinthians 1:3-4). And notice, too, how Joseph did not shrink back from speaking boldly about God to these men and Pharaoh. He told the Egyptian leader that the answer he sought would come from the Lord (Genesis 41:16).

Whether enslaved, imprisoned, or serving as Pharaoh's second-in-command, Joseph flourished. He endured much hardship but saw that the Lord had used it for good (Genesis 50:19-20). Because the Holy Spirit's presence is in us, we, too, can have a faith-filled perspective that glorifies God.

1 Peter 4:10-11 A Gift for Every Believer

Each of you should use whatever gift you have received to serve others, as faithful stewards of God's grace in its various forms.

A Gift for Every Believer

Even though the Bible clearly states that every believer receives a spiritual gift, some people nevertheless think they were overlooked. So, these people mosey through life refusing opportunities to serve. Other folks are so busy wishing they had a different ability that they do not use the one bestowed by the Holy Spirit. Both attitudes are sinful. God has a specific purpose and ministry for every Christian. Our spiritual gifts help us to fulfill His plan. We learn which one (or ones) we possess by getting involved in the life of the church. In other words, a believer will know his divinely appointed abilities when he begins to exercise them. God has a general purpose for handing out spiritual gifts. Christians exercise their specific skills for the common good (1 Corinthians 12:7). Everyone profits when believers do God's work through the power of the Holy Spirit. We are to use our gifts for equipping, edifying, and encouraging one another (Ephesians 4:11-13). To appreciate how this works, we may have to broaden our understanding of words like evangelist, prophet, and teacher. Biblically, these terms describe co-laborers who share Christ, spiritual mentors who explain biblical truths to new believers, friends who uplift the discouraged, and others doing similar work.

Every member of the Christian fellowship is important, and each one has a work to do. There are no excuses for bypassing God's will. Where He has gifted us and opened doors of opportunity for ministry, He also provides the strength and courage to exercise our abilities.

Judges 7:9-25 The Victory of Obedience

During that night the Lord said to Gideon, "Get up, go down against the camp, because I am going to give it into your hands. If you are afraid to attack, go down to the camp with your servant Purah and listen to what they are saying. Afterward, you will be encouraged to attack the camp." So he and Purah his servant went down to the outposts of the camp.

The Victory of Obedience

God orchestrated each element of His plan for Israel's success. However, if Gideon had disobeyed even one divine command, his army would have suffered instant defeat. Although the Lord's ways may seem risky or illogical, we can always trust His indisputable wisdom and rely on His mighty power.

God encourages the fainthearted. When the Lord commanded Gideon to attack the enemy, He also provided a way to relieve the leader's fears. By following God's directions, Gideon was led to the exact location where he would hear an encouraging message that caused him to bow in worship and arise with great faith. God removes the things we depend on. Gideon was marching to war with only 300 men armed with trumpets, pitchers, and torches. Their manpower seemed pitiful, and their weapons useless for battle. With weapons removed, they had to rely only upon the Lord.

God works in the other camp on our behalf. Everything is perfectly timed when God is in control—even the parts we cannot see. While Gideon was obeying each divine command, the Lord was working behind the scenes in the enemy camp to ensure victory for Israel. In the confusion and fear of darkness, their panic led to self-destruction.

The key to a victorious Christian life is obedience. The Lord will faithfully supply you with instructions for each step as you follow Him. His way may not be the easiest or the most comfortable, but it is always the best. As you rely on Him, He will lead you to victory.

Galatians 6:1-5 Bearing One Another's Burdens

Carry each other's burdens, and in this way, you will fulfill the law of Christ.

Bearing One Another's Burdens

If you are looking for a way to carry out Christ's command to love your neighbor, Paul has a suggestion: bear their burdens. At a point, everyone struggles under the weight of an oppressive situation. Believers must get under that load next to their brothers and sisters.

Jesus sets the pattern for burden-bearing. He calls to Himself all who are heavy-laden and gives them rest (Matthew 11:28-29). Since God predestines believers to conform to Christ's likeness, we must imitate His care and concern for those who suffer. Acts 4:32 shows that the early church followed His example. To lift the load of poverty, they pooled their resources so that no one was in need. Paul's letters make clear his concern for the physical and spiritual welfare of growing churches. He fasted and prayed for them and sent missionaries when he could. He felt it was his responsibility to strengthen them, even though he sustained a personal hardship—his thorn in the flesh (2 Corinthians 12:7).

A believer cannot wait until his life is clear of obstacles before reaching out to others, since that day may never come. Even though we have our own needs, we can do all things through Christ's strength—including sharing someone else's adversity (2 Corinthians 12:9). When you are willing to wade into someone else's troubles to help that person hold up under the weight, two things happen. First, he or she receives desperately needed blessings in the form of aid, support, and love. And second, you fulfill God's command to love a neighbor as yourself.

Psalm 139:14 Beautiful

I praise you because I am fearfully and wonderfully made;
your works are wonderful; I know that full well.

Beautiful

There is nothing more wonderful than to know Who created you, who allows you to take each breath and allows each beat of your heart. Yet even though we continually put other things first, He loves us enough to put part of Himself in our lowly, created form to show us it is possible to walk in our human existence and still be in communion with our Father, Creator. It is such a joy to know this. It is such a joy to seek communion with the Father that the Son, Jesus demonstrated. What a beautiful goal to seek. What a beautiful bridge across the chasm of sinful separation, the cross on which the Son was slain for our sins.

One night not too long ago I couldn't sleep. I started expressing my thanks to God for His love and expressed the love He has nurtured in me for Him. The feeling of love grew very intense. It was so beautiful and has stayed with me, though not as intense as that night. I now think of it as a taste of what it will be like in eternity in His presence. Thinking of that you cannot help but have a song in your heart and words of love and praise on your lips.

John 13:34-35 Communicating Through Our Life

"A new command I give you: Love one another. As I have loved you, so you must love one another. By this everyone will know that you are my disciples, if you love one another."

Communicating Through Our Life

Did you realize that everyone's life makes a statement? Perhaps you've never looked at your routine as anything more than merely traveling back and forth to work and accomplishing daily tasks. If so, you might wonder what message this could broadcast to the people around you.

The truth is that every one of us communicates to others through our character, actions, and words. The believer's life should be an expression of glory to God while conveying to onlookers the vital importance of divine truth. Wherever we are, Jesus' light should shine brightly through us so that He is evident in a dark world. And remember, the strength of our life message is directly related to the depth of our relationship with God.

Of course, this does not mean that our lives must be perfect. But our responses and actions should demonstrate that our heavenly Father is dependable, faithful, forgiving, and present. We are His ambassadors, representing the Savior to the people we encounter each day. Our lives are opportunities for others to see the Lord in action, as we serve others—or as we reveal peacefulness and trust, even during difficult times.

Coworkers, family, neighbors, and friends are all witnesses to our daily conduct and conversation. Every encounter we have is an opportunity to reflect Jesus into somebody's life. Ask the Lord to strengthen your faith and your walk so that those around you can't help but be drawn towards His light.

Colossians 1:1-9 Life-Changing Prayer

For this reason, since the day we heard about you, we have not stopped praying for you. We continually ask God to fill you with the knowledge of his will through all the wisdom and understanding that the Spirit gives.

Life-Changing Prayer

Today's passage includes a life-changing prayer, which was written by Paul in his letter to the believers at Colossae. What makes this prayer powerful is that every request agrees with God's will.

The first petition was for the Colossians to know the Lord's desires. To please our Father, we must comprehend what His plans are and then carry them out. This includes His general purposes for all His children—such as loving God and our neighbors (Luke 10:27)—as well as His specific plan for each of us (Ephesians 2:10).

Paul's second request was for God to give spiritual wisdom and understanding regarding such knowledge. He knew that to apply what we learn; we need the insight and clarity which comes only from the Holy Spirit (John 16:13). The result of these two petitions will be the ability to see from God's viewpoint. We'll perceive our choices and situations as they are, not just as they appear to be.

We could also make this request for those who do not trust in the Savior. Our Father offers salvation to all who believe in Christ. It is not His desire for any to perish (2 Peter 3:9). If unbelievers know God's will, their minds will be open to His offer of forgiveness, and they will accept the sacrifice Jesus made on their behalf.

Our heavenly Father has promised that those who pray in agreement with His purposes will receive what they ask. Therefore, it is important to start by discovering what His plans are. Try incorporating scriptural prayers—like the one from today's passage—into your conversations with the Lord.

Psalm 103 Created to Praise

Praise the Lord, all his works everywhere in his dominion.
Praise the Lord, my soul.

Created to Praise

Do you ever wonder why you exist? Day-to-day activities and worries pull in so many directions that most people seldom think about what the goal of life is. But our Creator made us with a purpose: to glorify Him (Isaiah 43:7).

In His Word, God is emphatic that we're to testify to His faithfulness and mighty works. Jesus considered this important as well—when teaching His disciples how to communicate with God, He began His well-known prayer with adoration (Matthew 6:9). Why, then, do we give so much attention to petitions but so little to praise? Perhaps some believers consider themselves too busy to spend "extra" prayer time praising the Lord. Others may feel awkward expressing their gratitude. Yet no excuses are acceptable. Psalm 103:2 warns us to remember God's benefits so we will humbly glorify Him. The Psalm also explains how to lift Him up with our words—specifically, we should praise God for His character and His work in

the past, present, and future (vv. 2-8, 19).

We can also exalt the Lord in other ways. The Old Testament's three primary words for "praise" refer to music, spoken words, and gestures like raising hands and dancing. But we can also glorify Him through our actions, thoughts, and creativity.

Praise may be something of a foreign concept to you. But it's the very purpose for which you were created. Notice how the Father is exalted in the Psalms. Then worship Him with praise as you spend time in His presence today.

Psalms 48:14 Another Decade

For this God is our God forever and ever; he will be our guide even to the end.

1 Corinthians1:8 He will keep you strong to the end, so that you will be blameless on the day of our Lord Jesus Christ (NIV)

Another Decade

Today I enter a new decade. Each year we walk on this earth brings us closer to the end of our walk here. I've searched the scriptures and can't find the word retirement in them. Retirement and "golden years" are terms made up in our modern culture. God designed us to follow His decrees and work to prepare the people on this earth for the coming of His Kingdom. Nowhere does it say to spend all of your later years traveling, playing games or sports, and generally just having fun. When we no longer find ourselves going to a job to earn income for our sustenance, we are blessed with more time for the blessing of serving our God more completely. In my younger years, I never thought God would enable me to preach His Word or write devotions every day. Though I still work for income I find more time to immerse myself in God. I still play golf and socialize but find my desire more and more in speaking forth His Word. He blessed me in the work of His service in my younger years and we are called to spread His Word all our years. As we look to years passing let us (regardless of what decade we are in) be sure to keep our priorities straight. Let us also practice being in the present and not always looking to the future. Our eternal life started the day we accepted Jesus into our lives. Let's not pass from one day to the next with regrets. Let us "stay strong to the end" in our love, devotion, and work God appointed us to do.

Hebrews 2:1 Be Careful

We must pay more careful attention, therefore, to what we have heard, so that we do not drift away. (NIV)

Be Careful

This is a very good caution. We tend to move ahead too fast and make decisions too fast without remembering what we've read in God's written Word or what He has gently spoken to our spirits. So often we miss the quiet, inner voice of God because we aren't careful to listen or to recognize Him. We live very distracted lives. We tend to think we are humans with little spiritual experience, but we are spiritual beings living a human experience. We are in the human experience only temporarily. Our spiritual being is from the time we accept Jesus Christ, God's only Son, into our hearts, mind, and lives through eternity which has no end. It would be so much better for us to be more careful to pay attention to what we hear in our spirits rather than what the temporal world is saying.

Genesis 1:1 Beginning

In the beginning God

John 1:1-2 In the beginning was the Word, and the Word was with God, and the Word was God. He was with God in the beginning (NIV)

Beginning

In the beginning. At the very start of anything God already was along with His Word, Jesus, His Son. All things every in existence or ever will be in existence have the base of their existence in God and His Word. God and His Word, Jesus, are the foundations for everything. This includes the lives of individuals like you and me. If our existence, our life, is to be on a firm foundation it must be on the foundation of God through His Son, Jesus. Everything we are, everything we do, and everything we think must be built on that foundation. When something is not on a foundation it will collapse. When we feel things collapsing around us, we must check to be sure we are still standing on the foundation of God and Jesus. When we stay on this foundation, we can be assured that all things in and around us will be for our good and for the glory of God. He alone holds the keys to life. He has given us the assurance of victory over death in this life through His Son, Jesus. Our question is are we making sure we are standing on His foundation – the only foundation that will last throughout all eternity?

Romans 8:28 Challenges

And we know that in all things God works for the good of those who love him, who have been called according to his purpose.

Challenges

Sometimes this verse is hard to believe. I have a friend going through a very tough time with a death in the family and sickness. My daughter has a friend whose house burned down. They lost everything. Most of them did not even get out with shoes. We all know people going through particularly challenging times. We have been there ourselves and you are there now. When things around us seem to be collapsing it is time to pray to God and tell Him all that concerns us, thank Him for hearing us, and thank Him for His provision, past, present, and future. Then we must choose to leave our worries with Him and trust He will show us the way through our challenge. Quite often His way involves other people whom He calls to reach out to us. It might be our time to be one of those who reach out to someone going through a challenge. What a privilege and blessing it is for God to allow us to be part of His love and provision for others. If you are in the midst of a challenge today, give it to God. If you aren't, tell God you're available and keep your eyes and your heart open to those around you.

Luke 12:3 From the Rooftops

What you have said in the dark will be heard in the daylight, and what you have whispered in the ear in the inner rooms will be proclaimed from the roofs. (NIV)

From the Rooftops

So many have been embarrassed or gotten in trouble for what they posted in their e-mail or some social media on the internet. They did not realize that what is on the internet can be seen by people other than the intended. Jesus said what we say, or whisper will be proclaimed from the roofs. We think it is safe to gossip about someone in confidence to another. What we say will come back to us. God hears our every word and thought. When we are talking to others, we must realize that God is also there. When we are thinking about what we will say or do God hears our thoughts. Paul gave us instructions when he wrote,

> "Finally, brothers, whatever is true, whatever is noble, whatever is right, whatever is pure, whatever is lovely, whatever is admirable—if anything is excellent or praiseworthy—think about such things. (NIV Philippians 4:8).

Bad thoughts will come to us. Critical thoughts about others will come to us. We are not responsible for those brief encounters but are responsible for what we do with them. Our question is will we remember God is always with us and quickly dismiss anything that doesn't line up with His Word?

Romans 2:11 Favoritism

For God does not show favoritism. (NIV)

Favoritism

God shows no favoritism. That is a hard concept for us. We continually show favoritism. We choose who we want to be with over others. We treat people differently according to how up high on our "favorite" thermometer they are. A teacher might say they have no favorite, but they do. It's hard to believe God loves each of us equally. It's hard to believe He chooses each of us for specific works. The works are as different as we are from each other, but no work is more precious to God than any other when it is His Holy Spirit Who works and moves through us. We see people like Billy Graham and say he must be extra special to God. God doesn't favor Billy Graham any more than He favors each of us. Our question is, will we choose to believe God loves each of us equally? He gave His only Son, Jesus, in the same proportion to each one of us. He gave His all. To say God does not love "me" as much as He loves "you" is a lie of Satan. Accept it today. You are incredibly special to God. You are as special to Him as anyone who ever walked or will work this earth. Nothing any of us can ever do will change God's love for us. He loves you as His child no matter what you say, do, or feel.

Hebrews 7:25 Faulty Equipment

Therefore, he is able to save completely those who come to God through him, because he always lives to intercede for them. (NIV)

Faulty Equipment

I have just finished programming my fourth Android phone. This one was ordered in less than 24 hours after my last replacement. Though it has been incredibly inconvenient and tried my patience and taken my time it reminds me how I am faulty equipment. Even though I am faulty, can rejoice because I have God's only Son, Jesus, constantly interceding for me. No matter how I might break down, sin, or miss program my life, He is standing the gap, and His Holy Spirit in me is gently steering me back into the best path God has chosen for me. This puts all of life's little irritants and inconveniences into proper perspective. Our question is where is our life, our eyes, our minds, and our hearts centered? Do we choose to look at the earthly things that will soon pass away and allow them to interfere with the peace that can only come from God, or do we choose to keep our focus on God and the preparation of His Kingdom coming on this earth?

Deuteronomy 6:9 Doorposts

Write them on the door frames of your houses and on your gates. (NIV)

Doorposts

Why did God want everyone to write His commandments on the door frames of the houses and the gates? When we leave our house, we walk out the door, turn around and lock it. When we turn around, we can see the door frame. When we go out of our yards we pass through our gates. God wants us to be reminded of His commands to us as we go out into the world. His commands are the basis on which we are made and are there for us to be able to have full fellowship with God. We are unable to do this in and of ourselves, so God the Father sent God the Son, Jesus, to show us how to do this. We still fail and God knew we would so Jesus, the Son, shed His blood on the cross in exchange for our blood. We still fail so God the Father and God the Son sent God the Holy Spirit to live in and through us to give us the power to remember, obey, and serve Him and have fellowship with Him. Yet we still fail. We fail because we don't write His words on the door frames of our houses and our gates. In the verse before He said to put them on our foreheads as well. We are to have His Word, Jesus, in the forefront of our minds and on all that enters us. We cannot enter a house without going through the door frame. Likewise, we should not let any thought enter us without first going through the door frame of the Holy Spirit. Our question today is are we staying connected with the Holy Spirit? Let's not start our day without asking God to bathe us afresh in His Holy Spirit to guide us throughout the day God entrusts to us.

Hebrews 7:25 God's Promise

Therefore, he is able to save completely those who come to God through him, because he always lives to intercede for them. (NIV)

God's Promise

I've heard others say, "I have done too many bad things for God to save me." At one time I thought this myself. Here we are told anyone and everyone who comes to God through His only Son, Jesus Christ, will be completely saved. Why is that? Jesus took our place on the cross and shed His blood for the forgiveness of our sins. Only He could do it as only He was without sin. Before He went to the cross, He knelt in the Garden of Gethsemane and prayed for us. It is my favorite prayer in the Bible because it is Jesus praying for me (and each one of us). "My prayer is not for them alone. I pray also for those who will believe in me through their message. (John 17:20) Take time to read all of John 1. When you come to the part that is quoted here substitute your name for the word "those." It's amazing what it does for you when you read the Bible like it was intended – a personal love letter and instructional letter to you specifically. If no other prayers were ever to be answered I know the prayer of Jesus is answered. That means if I allow God, through Jesus, to save me and to sanctify (make me holy as He is holy) He will do it. He will do it for you also if you ask. Our question is, have you asked? If so, walk in confidence God will do what He says. If you haven't asked yet I invite you to do so. All you need to do is talk to God saying you recognize you are a sinner, that you want Jesus into your heart, mind, and life as your lord and savior, and then thank Him. You will probably not feel much emotion at the time. Emotions come later by degrees. Emotions are not the sign. Faith, trust, and belief are the signs.

Ephesians 3:19 Ephesians 3

and thus to know the love of Christ that surpasses knowledge, so that you may be filled up to all the fullness of God.

Ephesians 3

There are several different Greek words for our one word "know." There is intellectual knowing. The acquaintance or friendship is knowing. There is the intimate marriage knowing. In this verse, Paul is talking about the intimate knowing. Satan knows Jesus as God's only Son, but it is not an intimate knowledge; only factual. To know the love of Christ that surpasses knowledge we must have an intimate relationship with Him. We must know Him on an intimate and deep level. It is only after we come to that level that we can be filled up with the fullness of God. Our question is, do we want to be intimate with God? To do that we must be real to ourselves and God. To be filled with the fullness of God we must be willing not to be full of ourselves. It isn't our nature to place anyone or anything ahead of ourselves. This is only possible through the power of God's Holy Spirit. Let us pray today for God to fill us with a burning desire to know Him intimately.

Isaiah 55:10-11 Not Return Void

As the rain and the snow come down from heaven, and do not return to it without watering the earth and making it bud and flourish, so that it yields seed for the Sower and bread for the eater, so is my word that goes out from my mouth: It will not return to me empty, but will accomplish what I desire and achieve the purpose for which I sent it (NIV)

Not Return Void

Many years ago, someone gave me a ride to a meeting. After picking me up they went and picked up someone I didn't know. On the way back after the meeting it was obvious this lady did not know Jesus. She also shared how her husband had glaucoma and could only see very large print. We had just purchased leftover large print New Testaments from a church that used them for a revival. I took one of these, signed "from Jesus with love" on the front cover, and left it on their doorstep. I thought nothing more about it and did not see that lady again. Several years later I heard a testimony on our local Christian radio. It was a man who shared how someone had left a large print New Testament on their doorstep and by reading it they both accepted Jesus as their Lord and Savior and opened a Christian bookstore. A few weeks later the lady came to my house and said she thought it might be me who left that New Testament at their door. She wanted me to know what happened to it. They gave it to another couple who accepted Jesus and passed it on to four other couples who each accepted Jesus. After that, they lost track of it. This goes to prove God's Word does not come back void. He will achieve His purpose with or without us. But when we allow ourselves to be part of His work, we receive a blessing. Our question is, will we be part of His work through passing on His Word, either written or oral? The choice is ours.

Romans 9:20 Willing Vessels

But who are you, O man, to talk back to God? "Shall what is formed say to him who formed it, 'Why did you make me like this?' (NIV)

Willing Vessels

People have told me they could never write a devotion or preach a sermon. I'm right in there with them. There is no way I can do either of those or anything else of value if God did not equip me. It is God Who made us and equips us. Apart from Him none of us can do anything of value. But each one of us can do anything God has called us to do. Many of us miss out because we look at our capabilities and perceived shortcomings rather than looking at God, His love, and His power. He shaped each one of us to be able to allow Him to flow through us in the way and the timing He wants. Who are we to say we can't when it is God Who calls? Our question is, are we willing to allow God to use us in any way and at any time He chooses? Let us be open and willing vessels.

John 1:12-13 Intimacy With Our Heavenly Father

Yet to all who did receive him, to those who believed in his name, he gave the right to become children of God. (NIV)

Intimacy With Our Heavenly Father

From the beginning, God intended to have an intimate, loving relationship with us. What evidence do we have that this is His desire? His Son. One reason Christ came to earth is for us to know and relate to God the Father. The Bible tells us that Jesus is His exact representation; His words and works were the same as God's (John 5:19; 12:50). Therefore, when we look at the Son, we see the character of our heavenly Father.

Invitation. Through the Scriptures, God invites us to join His family (John 3:16). He took care of all the arrangements; our part is to say yes.

Adoption. The closest tie we can have with one another is family. At salvation, the Lord adopts us into His own. This relationship with our heavenly Father lasts for eternity, providing us with support, encouragement, and love.

Friendship. By calling His disciples "friends" (John 15:15), Jesus revealed a new aspect to their relationship, which applied to His future followers as well. Christ is a forever friend, one who will never desert or turn away from us.

His Presence. From the moment of our salvation, the Holy Spirit indwells us. He is even closer to us than any earthly kin can be.

The Lord invites us to become family through faith in Christ. This is our highest calling—to believe in Him and live for Him all our days (John 20:31). Once we become God's children, His Spirit will work in us to make our family resemblance stronger and clearer in thought, word, and deed.

An Extra Word

God speaks to us through His written Word. He also speaks to us through His creation. I was sitting on the farm porch enjoying God's creation. The birds were singing, each with a unique song. The goat herd came through, grazing contentedly. Then, one of the goats decided leaves just out of reach seemed better than those easily reached and struggled to reach them. Other goats noticed what this goat was doing and decided they wanted those leaves. Before long, most of the goats were vying for the best position to reach those leaves. After a while, one by one, they each decided they could be contented with what God had provided for them at their reach. We are so much like those goats. We see someone with something and decide we must have it. Days like "Black Friday" shopping day in the U.S. are a prime example of that goat-like behavior. We forget God supplies all our needs. There's no need to fight for what He has provided for someone else or to ignore what He has for each of us as individuals. We are to be content in His provision in all situations. Some dogs start barking and one of the goats panics and runs. Before long the entire herd is following that panicked goat without knowing the situation. Sound familiar? Oh, to stay grounded in God's Word and in faith and trust in Him